Anton Bruckner

Constantin Floros

Anton Bruckner

The Man and the Work

2. revised edition

Translated by Ernest Bernhardt-Kabisch

Bibliographic Information published by the Deutsche Nationalbibliothek
The Deutsche Nationalbibliothek lists this publication in the Deutsche Nationalbibliografie; detailed bibliographic data is available in the internet at http://dnb.d-nb.de.

Cover Design: © Olaf Gloeckler, Atelier Platen, Friedberg
Cover Illustration: Anton Bruckner at age 39 Courtesy of
Direktion der Museen of the City of Vienna

In Deutsch erschienen unter dem Titel: *Anton Bruckner. Persönlichkeit und Werk*.
Europäische Verlagsanstalt, Hamburg 2004

ISBN 978-3-631-66203-8 (Print)
E-ISBN 978-3-653-05168-1 (E-Book)
DOI 10.3726/ 978-3-653-05168-1
© for the English edition: Peter Lang GmbH
Internationaler Verlag der Wissenschaften
Frankfurt am Main 2011
2. revised edition 2015
All rights reserved.
© for all other languages: Europäische Verlagsanstalt, Hamburg
PL Academic Research is an Imprint of Peter Lang GmbH.

Peter Lang – Frankfurt am Main · Bern · Bruxelles · New York ·
Oxford · Warszawa · Wien

All parts of this publication are protected by copyright. Any utilisation outside the strict limits of the copyright law, without the permission of the publisher, is forbidden and liable to prosecution. This applies in particular to reproductions, translations, microfilming, and storage and processing in electronic retrieval systems.

This publication has been peer reviewed.

www.peterlang.com

Table of Contents

Preface 1

Preface to the Second Edition 3

PART ONE
A Character Portrait 5

Who Was Bruckner? 7
Authoritarianism and Self-Assurance 13
The World as "Bad Lot" 16
Neurosis 19
Libido 22
Emotionality 24
The "Passionate Urge to Compose" 27
Securing an Income 30
Persecution Mania 32
Worries about the Success of the Work 40
Interest in the Exceptional 44
"Sympathy with Death" 46
Religiosity 50

Plates 53

PART TWO
Sacred Music 61

Personality and Oeuvre 63
Music as Religious Confession 64
A New, Dramatic Conception of the Mass 67
The Credo Settings 70
Religious Tone Symbolism 77
Jubilant and Devotional Music 84
"Let Me Not Be Confounded in Eternity" – The *Te Deum* 86
Music as Song of Praise 93

V

PART THREE
The Symphonies 97

The Fiction of "Absolute Music" 99
Originality and Modernity 100
Matters of Style 103
How Bruckner Came to the Symphony 106
Autobiographic Elements in the Second and Third Symphony ... 112
The Allegiance to Richard Wagner 118
The Triad of the Middle Symphonies 124
The Seventh – a Second "Wagner Symphony" 129
Secular and Religious 134
Imaginations – Bruckner's Associations in the Eighth 145
The Ninth – Bruckner's "Farewell to Life" 149
Reflections on the Bruckner Interpretation – Günter Wand,
Eugen Jochum and Sergiu Celibidache 161
The Progressive 168

Afterword 177

APPENDIX 181

Notes 183
Biographical Dates 215
Abbreviations 219
Works by Anton Bruckner 222
Selective Bibliography 226
Author's Papers 229
Photo Credits 231
Index of Names 232

Preface

Largely unrecognized and controversial during his lifetime, Anton Bruckner is regarded today as the greatest symphonic composer after Beethoven and Mahler. The originality, daring and monumentality of his music are universally acknowledged on all sides, and his impact, initially confined to the German-speaking world, has for some decades now begun to be global: today, Bruckner is recognized as a composer of symphonic as well as of sacred music in both the Anglo-Saxon and the Romance countries, even in Japan.

I have loved Bruckner's music ever since my youth: because of its modernity and sublimity, its intense expressiveness and the new "tone" it brought into the world, because of its "unspoiled forest darkness," as Adorno called it, because of its many contrasts and spacious effects, its intensifications and grandiose climaxes, but also because of its abysses and seeming ruptures. When, in 1951, I attended Hans Swarowsky's class at the Viennese Music Academy for the first time, he was in the process of going through the *Romantic* symphony. He pointed out the harmonic, metric and dynamic subtleties of the score and thought that Bruckner's real strength lay less in his art than in the "vis symphonica." I could not understand that at the time, and I still don't. For me, Bruckner was even then a magnificent symphonic composer, who had dared to advance to the very borders of atonality.

Already as a young instructor in the 'sixties in Hamburg, I gave lectures about his music, seeking to scrutinize it intensively in all its dimensions. In 1980, Breitkopf and Härtel published my book on Brahms and Bruckner, which was the first to shake the then still prevailing theses about these two composers. As a comrade in arms of Linz's Bruckner Institute, I have since then taken part in many symposia and given numerous talks about Bruckner in Austria, Germany, Great Britain and Japan.

This book, too, would hardly have been possible without the kindness of a number of institutions and individuals. Hofrat Dr. Günter Brosche and Hofrat Dr. Thomas Leibnitz (Music Collection of the Austrian National Library, Vienna), as well as Prof. Dr. Otto Biba (Society of the Friends of Music, Vienna) and the Director's Office of the Biblioteka Jagiellonska in Cracow allowed me to look at Bruckner autographs. In the rooms of the Commission for Music History of the Austrian Academy of Sciences in Vienna I could study microfiches of important sketches. During my frequent research stays in Vienna, I was able to discuss key research issues with the staff members of the Anton Bruckner Institute, Linz: Dr. Elisabeth Maier, Dr. Andrea Harrandt, Mrs. Renate Grasberger, Dr. Uwe Harten and Dr. Erich Partsch. On a number of psychiatric and theological questions I had the advice of Prof. Dr. Wolfgang Berner (Hamburg), Prof. Dr. Eugen Biser (Munich) and Prof. Dr. Tim Schramm (Hamburg). My son Marc-Aurel set the musical examples in computer print. Prof. Dr. Ernest Bernhardt-Kabisch (Indiana University) supplied the precise and sensitive translation into English; I also owe him a number of helpful comments and suggestions. Michael Bock, finally, provided crucial help in preparing the present text for printing.

My cordial thanks go to all of these individuals.

C.F., Hamburg, Summer 2010

Preface to the Second Edition

The present Bruckner monograph is one of a kind insofar as it combines biographic detail and psychological insights with analytical and hermeneutic scrutiny of the works for numerous fresh insights. The book, originally published in German in 2004, first appeared in English translation in 2010 at the Peter Lang International Publishing House and was competently and perceptively reviewed in the Bruckner Journal (Vol. XV, November 2011) by Professor Crawford Howie. Since it received wide attention, it now appears in a second edition.

Years ago I published another book about Brahms and Bruckner (Wiesbaden: Breitkopf & Härtel), which likewise caused a stir. I am delighted that it will soon also appear in English with Peter Lang under the title Brahms and Bruckner as Artistic Antipodes.

Studies in Musical Semantics. It centers on the polarities between the two composers, on the early Brahms, and on Bruckner's pecular relation to program music, and does not overlap in any way with the present Bruckner study.

C.F., Hamburg, Summer 2014

PART ONE

A Character Portrait

Who Was Bruckner?

Many noted artists have had, and have, to tolerate seeing their image change radically in the course of time, perhaps enriched by additional traits but often also misrepresented. Anton Bruckner is an extreme instance: his image has been distorted like virtually no other, so as to become all but unrecognizable. During his lifetime, his eccentric way of dressing and even more eccentric manners gave many people the impression of a maverick and oddball, a "character.". No less a person than Gustav Mahler coined the aperçu: "Bruckner, a simpleton – half genius, half imbecile."[1] The saying about Bruckner's supposed simple-mindedness went around.

Biography in the 19th century had a more than ordinary tendency to idealize and heroize eminent personalities. In contrast to Beethoven, Bruckner is not well suited to being represented as a hero. It was perhaps for this reason that his earliest biographers stylized him as an unrecognized genius, and several sought in his religiosity a key to a deeper understanding of his personality. Ernst Decsey apostrophized him as "God's musician" – the catchy phrase became a favorite topos of Bruckner reception.[2] In the 1920's, he was frequently labeled a "mystic" or a "metaphysician."

Only the last twenty-five years have succeeded in doing away with many of the prejudices about the artist and the man. It could above all be shown that the supposedly so unworldly artist was a man who thought realistically and did things in a purposeful way; Manfred Wagner even called him a "social climber,"[3] who ascended the rungs of the career ladder quite single-mindedly. His rise in society was in fact hardly less phenomenal than that of his far more successful "rival" Johannes Brahms. His path led him from rural Windhaag at the Bohemian border, where he worked as an assistant teacher, through the office of organist at the cathedral chapter of St. Florian and organist at the Linz cathedral, to Vienna, where he served as court organist and professor at the conservatory and eventually received an honorary doctorate from Vienna's university.

It has to be said for the more recent Bruckner biographies that they put many things in the proper perspective. At times, however, they went too far in their endeavor to de-idealize and de-mythologize the common image of the man by designing a counter-image that dwelt with great glee on Bruckner's supposed "character flaws" and negative aspects, It became fashionable to speak of his "careerism," his "avarice" and "miserliness," of his "infantile traits" and his "pathologically peculiar behavior."

Who, then, was Bruckner in reality? Was he a career-obsessed oaf? It must be the aim of all personality research to understand human beings in their contradictoriness. (The heart and soul of hermeneutics, according to Hans-Georg Gadamer, is the supposition that the other fellow could be in he right.) If one speaks of Bruckner's stinginess or greed for money, one has to ask where that came from. Again, regardless of whether one characterizes the relationship of the press to Bruckner as one of opposition or even of enmity, the fact is that his fear of the attacks of the Viennese press in general, and of the powerful high priest of music, Eduard Hanslick, in particular, at times took on the semblance of a persecution complex.

In what follows I shall try to get to the core of Bruckner's personality, to uncover how he dealt with life's borderline situations, what impelled him, and how he coped with the existential questions that plagued him.[4]

I rely hereby primarily on his letters, which tell us much about important events in his life as well as about his thinking and feeling.[5] Often awkward in expression, at times also seemingly fragmentary, they have throughout the character of factual and succinct communication. One will look in vain for discussions of philosophical, literary or aesthetic questions. Therein they differ fundamentally from the letters of a Richard Wagner, Franz Liszt, Johannes Brahms or Gustav Mahler.

Of great value are also Bruckner's entries in his calendars, of which no fewer than 22 have been preserved. Bruckner was in the habit of entering appointments, dates, the names of his numerous private pupils and of young ladies whom he adored, as well as countless addresses, his honorariums, living and household expenditures and, not least, his prayer lists, into his pocket calendars. The generally meager notes extend from references to his migraine attacks and his manicures and pedicures to drafts of letters and analytical observations about Mozart's Requiem, Beethoven's Third and Ninth Symphonies and Bruckner's own *Romantic Symphony*. Elisabeth Maier, who deserves much credit for having edited and annotated these private records in years of intensive labor, is surely right in saying that they open an access to Bruckner's "hidden personality."[6]

A third essential source of information, finally, is the so-called memoir literature. Bruckner encountered many people in the course of his life, of whom not a few, including many of his pupils, were fond of remembering him. Representations of his life are commonly embellished with a plethora of stories and anecdotes, whose authenticity is not always confirmed. Manfred Werner has therefore emphatically warned of the "peril" of the anecdote and urged to utilize only authentically documented sources.[7] Caution is certainly advised, but the value of the memoir literature as such should not be underestimated, though the mass of information it conveys must of course be tested as to its truth content. If an anecdote is transmitted independently by more than one author, its veracity may be presumed.

In September of 1977, the noted psychiatrist Erwin Ringel gave a lecture in Linz under the title "Psychogramm für Anton Bruckner" that caused a considerable stir. He shocked the public with the thesis that Bruckner was psychically ill, that he suffered from a neurosis without knowing it. Ringel pointed to several symptoms that seemed to support his diagnosis: for one thing, that Bruckner was an "immensely insecure individual," the "very opposite of self-confident"; and, for another, that his relations to other people were unquestionable "disordered": that here one could observe a direct connection between feelings of inferiority and authoritarianism. Another grave neurotic symptom, Ringel said, was the fact that as a result of unresolved early childhood conflicts, Bruckner had remained an "infantile" person. For this reason, many people had felt the urge "to look after and support him, but then also to keep him under their tutelage."[8]

Ringel was fully conscious of the controversial nature of his arguments, and tried to qualify them by citing the aperçu of the Swiss psychoanalyst Wilhelm Stekel, according to which "every artist is a neurotic – but not every neurotic is an artist." He might have referred to the more impressive insights of American psychologists like Abraham Maslow, according to whom only one percent of humanity is psychically entirely healthy: artists of the rank of a Richard Wagner, Lord Byron or Vincent van Gogh had been "sick geniuses." According to Maslow, only individuals capable of self-realization were psychically "healthy."[9]

The questions we must ask most urgently are: on what is Ringel's Bruckner pathology based, and how can an authentic psychograph about a dead artist be constructed? In his study of Leonardo da Vinci, Sigmund Freud has demonstrated the limits of what psychoanalysis is capable of doing in biography.

"The materials available to a psychoanalytical investigation," he says there, "are the data of a person's biography, the accidents of events and environmental influences, on the one hand, and the recorded reactions of the individual, on the other."[10] Applied to the case of Bruckner, this means that the psychiatrist can embark on a psychoanalytical study only once the historian has completed his work, that is, when all the data capable of revealing anything about the personality have been collected, sorted, and critically examined and evaluated. That includes not only the documentary but also the anecdotal tradition, whose relevance, for all the justified reservations, should not be underestimated. Now it must be said about Ringel that he could not have had knowledge of this often very important material, since a portrait of Bruckner "in selected recollections and anecdotes" appeared only in 1991.[11] To all appearances he relied on the slender monograph of Karl Grebe, and thus it can be said that his psychoanalytical profile lacks the proper prerequisites at least in part. We shall cite two examples.

Ringel thought he could diagnose a "profoundly reduced feeling of self-worth" in Bruckner. He could not deny that Bruckner's life showed some signs of self-confidence, but these, he thought, were very rare. In general, the case of Bruckner seemed to Ringel a notable demonstration of the thesis of Alfred Adler that "the insecure person also tends at times toward an overcompensation of his defect." Now it is noteworthy that authenticated reports of several of Bruckner's pupils and confidants do not at all agree with this depiction. Everything points instead to Bruckner having had a strong self-assurance. He did feel misunderstood, however. It pained him that his works were largely denied recognition. Thus his pupil Franz Marschner reports: "His bearing seemed imposing to me at the time, suggesting great self-confidence and a touch of greatness." And then again: "The strong sense of self that understandably filled him often gave way to fits of depression and doubt, whether his opponents might not partly be right after all. But then he consoled himself again: 'Even though I cannot compare myself to Schubert and such masters, I do know that I am Somebody and my things are of consequence.'"[12] Franz Schalk spoke in similar terms about his one-time teacher: "The consciousness of his own greatness could then at times flash from him like lightning and was mesmerizing to the young people. For moments he would feel victorious, only then to be all the more bitter about the indifference, and even disparagement, he met with from the chieftains of the day."[13]

Bruckner had not only a strong self-assurance but beyond that a pronounced sense of mission. The more closely one studies his biography, the clearer it becomes that the composer's work was paramount to him: he subjected his entire life's planning to it. What Adorno said of his teacher Alban Berg can be asserted equally about Bruckner: that he subordinated his "empirical being" to the primacy of production.[14]

Bruckner is probably the only major composer of the 19th century who seemed like a fool to many of his contemporaries. Not only his appearance but his entire manner conveyed that impression to many. His Upper Austrian dialect, his odd manners and the obsequiousness of his bearing were bound to puzzle a cosmopolitan town like Vienna. The way in which the one-time village schoolmaster, church and cathedral organist conducted himself struck many as altogether strange.

Even more extreme than the peculiarity of his exterior was the foreignness of his nature. His personality stood in crass contrast to his time, and Franz Schalk was right when he spoke of the gulf that separated his revered teacher from his environment. "It was a time of moral and spiritual liberalism, when intellectualism and calculation choked off every other human impulse and threatened to usurp the rule of the world, into which he suddenly intruded with his symphonies and his medieval and cloistral notions about humanity and human existence."[15] Johannes-Leopold Mayer came to a similar conclusion a few years ago, when, arguing altogether sociologically, he called Bruckner's music an "offense to society" and Bruckner himself an "anti-citizen": "Bruckner never sided with power. He collided as much with the ossified structures of the clerical-patriarchal society of his Austrian homeland as he did with the egoistical, arrogant megalomania of Liberalism."[16]

Indispensable as such sociological reflections are to the discussion of the problems at issue, the most revealing insights are derived from an intensive study of Bruckner's personality. Rudolf Louis wrote about him that he lived in an entirely different world, one "completely alien to us"[17] – a remarkable statement, which one begins to understand all the better the more one immerses oneself in Bruckner's spiritual world and above all in his religiosity.

Bruckner was so well read in the Bible as to match professional theologians in learnedness. He also took great interest in Christological treatises like David Friedrich Strauß's then highly controversial *Life of Jesus*.[18] In contrast to Hugo Wolf, Gustav Mahler and many of his own culture-hungry pupils, however, he took no interest in European literature or philosophy. The fierce discussions about Arthur Schopenhauer and Friedrich Nietzsche left him cold.[19] Several of his pupils concluded from this that he had "hardly any intellectual needs"[20] – an altogether misleading assertion that has been peddled time and again and been confused with "lack of intelligence."

Important in this connection is the nuanced and detailed report of the medical man Dr. Alexander Fraenkel, who for many years regularly associated with Bruckner in the restaurant Riedhof in Vienna's Josefstadt. Fraenkel observed that Bruckner had a rather modest general education but emphasized his receptivity "for all branches of knowledge," his ability to widen his intellectual horizon and the adaptability of his intellect, and attested to his more than ordinary intelligence: "Although the sum of the knowledge he carried with him had no exceptional weight, his intelligence far exceeded an average endowment."[21]

His intelligence and rich imagination, as well as his ability to transmute poetic images into musical ones, can be inferred from the relation between word and tone in his vocal works – a highly revealing area of research that to date has been very little explored. Bruckner had a way of musically interpreting the texts of his spiritual and secular works in very subtle ways, not least by an expert use of the leitmotif technique.

Theodor W. Adorno summed up his view of the relation between Mahler and Bruckner in the sentence: "Regardless of the advantage that Bruckner's unspoiled forest darkness seems to have over Mahler's fracturedness – the latter is superior to the clumpy in Bruckner, that somewhat obstinate static quality that has no firmer foundation than the fact that Nietzsche had not yet been bruited about in St. Florian."[22] If one leaves the value judgments here out of account, the sentence gets at one thing correctly: that Bruckner remained untouched by the shock that Nietzsche's "transvaluation of all values" caused everywhere. The affirmative intention and the power of his often jubilant works are due not least to the firmness of his religious faith – a firmness that Gustav Mahler sometimes lacked. Adorno's saying that Mahler was a poor yes-man[23] could be applied inversely to Bruckner: that he was a good yes-man.

Even during his lifetime, numerous anecdotes about Bruckner's drolleries went round. One of the oddest was recorded by his authorized biographer August Göllerich. As a young assistant teacher Bruckner is supposed to have terrified the dignitaries and ordinary citizens of Windhaag by decorating crayfish, which he had caught, with small burning candles and letting them crawl around the churchyard in the dark of the night (Göllerich did not say what if anything came of this "prank").[24] Hans Commenda, who commented on this story, saw it as Bruckner's capital revenge against his narrow-minded Windhaag environment.[25] For some time, the anecdote was occasionally viewed as a peculiar case of cruelty to animals, until the folklorist Leopold Kretzenbacher proved in two penetrating studies that this odd story has been known as a comic motive in popular European literature since the Trecento and ever since the 16th century was used in polemical religious writings as a dig against clerical-popular beliefs about poor or lost souls.[26] Kretzenbacher argued that the story was pinned on Bruckner, as it did not at all fit the image of the extremely devout person that he was. One has to consider, however, that Bruckner was 17 and 18 years old when he served as assistant teacher in Windhaag between October 1841 and January 1843, and that, as Göllerich writes, he quite loved playing practical jokes. Everything, including the wide-spread belief in lost souls in the 19th century, suggests that Göllerich did not just dream up the story.

Authoritarianism and Self-Assurance

In his late years, Bruckner was repeatedly a guest at Klosterneuburg, a chapter of the Augustine canons. There he associated with the subsequent abbot Josef Kluger, to whom we owe an informative characterization of the aged master. Kluger writes: "It remains an unsolved enigma in Bruckner's character: his profound humility (I choose this word advisedly) side by side with his proud self-consciousness. Indeed, these two sides of his character sometimes were so immediately juxtaposed that they were thereby inevitably made to appear all the more outsized and thus caused many people not to know what to make of Bruckner and to be to apt to mistake the one for simple-mindedness and the other for conceit."[1]

Like so many other contradictions, this one, too, can be resolved when one visualizes Bruckner's youth, education and socialization. The world in which he grew up was dominated by the cathedral chapter of St. Florian, the cultural, intellectual, and religious center of the entire region. The village of Ansfelden in Upper Austria, where Bruckner was born on September 4, 1824, is only a few kilometers from St. Florian, and its parish was subject to the chapter. Since both his father and his grandfather were teachers, his life's career seemed predetermined, and even as a boy he looked forward to a pedagogical vocation. Upon the early death of his father in 1837, the financially strapped mother was able to place the thirteen-year-old at St. Florian as a choirboy. Having attended the teachers' seminary in Linz, the so-called *Präparandie*, in 1840, he worked for some years as a teacher's assistant in Windhaag and in Kronstorf. In 1845 he was hired as an assistant teacher in St. Florian and already after three years was appointed provisional chapter organist; another three years later he was promoted to the post of the regular chapter organist. The many years he spent at St. Florian (he stayed there until 1855) stamped him for life. He was deeply impressed by the Baroque splendor of the monastery, its spacious grounds, and the magnificence of the liturgy with its rich musical embellishments.

Authority at the time meant the decisive influence of a person or institution. It brooked no dissent and took subservience, submissiveness, subjection for granted. In the long years the young Bruckner spent at St. Florian, he came face to face with authority so defined, learned by personal experience what it meant to be dependent on the prelate, the head village teacher and the parish priest. Nothing is more telling in this respect than an episode related by August Göllerich. Although promoted to chapter organist, Bruckner was apparently not very happy at St. Florian in the long run and secretly applied for the post of cathedral organist in Olmütz. When the prelate learned of this, he ordered him, quasi as a penance, to help him take off his shoe and warned him never to try anything similar again.[2]

Against this background, the markedly obsequious tone Bruckner adopted in many of his letters becomes more understandable. Readers who, ignorant of the immediate circumstances of the time, object to Bruckner's tone of voice when they read an early letter of his to the Viennese court conductor Ignaz Assmayr or the dedications of the Third Symphony to Maestro Richard Wagner, the Seventh to Ludwig II., or the Eighth to the Emperor Francis Joseph I., should also consider that such a submissive posture vis-á-vis a potentate was still quite customary in the 19th century. Bruckner can in this respect be compared neither with Ludwig van Beethoven, nor with Richard Wagner, nor with Johannes Brahms, who associated with the nobility at eye level.

To persons who were well-disposed toward him and whom he deeply respected he often responded with a humility he otherwise reserved for high church dignitaries. His limitless veneration for Richard Wagner acquired the character of a religious adoration in later years. When he visited Wagner in Bayreuth in 1882 and the latter assured him that he would perform all of his works, he fell on his knees, kissed his hand and said: "Oh maestro, I worship you"; whereupon the Wagner, realizing the awkwardness of the situation, replied: "Take it easy – Bruckner – good night!"[3] Similar incidents are recorded by Bruckner's Linz patrons Moritz and Betty von Mayfeld. At a performance of the F Minor Mass in the Viennese court chapel, Bruckner is said to have rushed toward his friend as soon as he spotted him, in order to embrace him and to kiss his hand. And when he once played four-handed piano with Betty von Mayfeld and they reached a particularly powerful passage, he supposedly fell at the feet of his partner and, spreading his arms, called out: "Madam [literally "Gracious Lady"], you are my goddess!"[4]

Among those of Bruckner's character traits that impressed Mahler most deeply, Mahler's confidante Natalie Bauer-Lechner underscored his "unbelievable modesty and heart-felt humility." Thus Mahler related how, when he visited him, the old man would accompany him at parting all the way down from the third floor in order to honor him as his guest.[5]

From childhood on, Bruckner was used to showing obeisance to persons of rank. Whether obeisance always entailed respect was another matter. There is no doubt that he respected dignitaries of the church, such as the Augustinian canons with whom he lived at St. Florian. With the art-loving bishop of Linz, Franz Joseph Rudigier, and the dean of the Linz cathedral – two clerics who supported him – he enjoyed a personal relationship. In the arts he revered above all musicians who held an attraction for him and who spoke up for his work. This is true above all of Richard Wagner and of four conductors who sympathized with Wagner's art: Arthur Nikisch, Hermann Levy, Hans Richter and Felix Mottl. Oddly enough Bruckner called all four of them his "guardians" – Hermann Levy he even referred to as his "artistic father." Seen in this light, consciousness of authority by no means excluded the proud sense of self and of mission that also filled him. From his time in Linz on, at the latest, Bruckner was guided by the firm conviction that he had a mission to fulfill on earth.

Humility as a mental attitude is mainly rooted in religion. But it can also be applied to the musical sphere. Thus numerous chorales in Bruckner's symphonies, constructed in strict periodic form and *piano* in their dynamics, strike one as clear expressions of humility. Others, on the contrary, which rejoice *fortissimo* in the brasses, convey in music a sense of glory – a gesture that one may well relate to both Bruckner's self-assurance and his religious conviction.

The World as "Bad Lot"

> "I am often very sad and discontented here. False world – miserable lot."
>
> Bruckner to Rudolf Weinwurn

It is a truism that many creative people pay a high price for their work of creation. Many artists, for example, could and would not bind themselves to a woman, so as to be able to concentrate entirely on their work. Thus Johannes Brahms, like Beethoven and Schubert, remained a lifelong bachelor. All three, however, surrounded themselves with friends so as to avoid becoming isolated. The case of Anton Bruckner is well-nigh unique in this respect. For although friends and acquaintances (and in later years numerous pupils) played a role in his life, he was basically so alone that his pupil Franz Schalk rightly said of him: "He went through life as a solitary."[1]

Bruckner himself laments his loneliness in some of his letters, talks about melancholy, and hints that a tormenting feeling of desolation at times overcame him. In the first half of 1852, he seems not to have liked being at St. Florian. On March 19, he wrote to his boyhood friend Josef Seiberl: "I always sit miserable and forsaken and altogether melancholy in my little chamber"[2] – a lament that was to become the leitmotif of his life. Some four months later, on July 30, 1852, he revealed his feelings to the Viennese court conductor Ignaz Assmayr: "I have no one here to whom I could open my heart, am also in many respects unappreciated, which often is secretly very hard on me. Our chapter treats music and hence also musicians with utter indifference – oh, if only I could soon speak to you in person again! I know your excellent heart – what a consolation! I can never be cheerful here and must not give the least indication of having any plans."[3] He was evidently thinking of leaving the chapter at this time and seeking his fortune elsewhere, and hoped for Assmayr's protection.

It took several years before he was able to realize this secret plan and leave the monastery. On December 8, 1855, at last, he was appointed organist at the Linz cathedral after an audition and moved to Upper Austria's state capital. During the first years of his stay there, his frail psychic health seems to have stabilized. After successfully completing an intense course of studies in music theory under Simon Sechter, Ignaz Dorn and Otto Kitzler, a period of creative work set in during which the first fully achieved works came into being: the three great orchestral masses in D minor, E minor and F minor and the first Symphony. No later than early 1864, however, there appeared the first symptoms of a severe distress, which, in the spring of 1867, grew into a serious mental disorder. We can gather something about Bruckner's state of mind from his letters to Rudolf Weinwurm, his closest friend at the time. On February 25, 1867, he confessed to him that life in Linz was "insipid" to him – "always alone – with nothing to cheer one up."[4] On March 1, he wrote to him that he was "very often very sullen and sad,"[5] and on October 10, that "for some time already" he was suffering "from melancholy again."[6] Weinwurm was in a similar frame of mind and thus full of understanding. "Besides, you are only melancholy – I am gradually turning into a misanthrope," he replied to him on October 12. This remark in turn prompted Bruckner to pour out his heart to Weinwurm and to vent his displeasure about the "false world," the "dear human race," whom he thought he had come to know as a "miserable lot." On October 18, 1864, he thought the time had come to make his views more emphatically known to his friend and wrote him: "What I meant by melancholy – I did not express myself well – is for the most part only animosity toward humanity, whose kindness, sincerity and loyalty I, too, certainly have often had to feel bitterly enough and still have to feel."[7]

Bruckner led a settled life in Linz. His sister Maria Anna, whom he called Nani, kept house for him, his office as cathedral organist was respected, and he enjoyed the well-wishing of the bishop Franz Joseph Rudigier, who fully appreciated his art. What was it, one must ask, that prompted such misanthropic invectives and crass formulations as the world being a "miserable lot"? How can such embitterment be explained?

In spite of everything, Bruckner evidently did not feel sufficiently appreciated. Tensions between him and musicians troubled him. In a letter of January 27, 1866, to Weinwurm, he complained about the "countless" enemies "whom I have in Linz" and feared that he had become the victim of calumnies. But more than anything he suffered from the repeated rejections he experienced from very young women. A girl whom he had presented with Schubert's "Serenade" refused to accept the gift, although she had given him cause to hope. "You see," he wrote to Weinwurm on January 29, 1865, "I have no luck here even with the most modest claims. The whole world vexes me – there remains only art and a few valued friends, among whom you always rank at the top."[8] In the same letter he confesses openly that composing was his sole consolation over the adversities of existence. Thus he wrote with reference to his work on the C minor symphony (WAB 101): "Enemy of the world and of mankind that I am, I seek some relief in it from the nice treatment in Linz."[9]

Bruckner's prevalent state of mind during these years, in which the Mass in D minor, the first Symphony and the Mass in E minor were composed, was clearly depressive. Loneliness and desolation tormented him. Time and again he pleaded with Weinwurm, who served as chorus master at the Vienna Choral Society, to come visit him in Linz. His emotional strain became so intense that in May of 1867 he fell seriously ill. He suffered a nervous breakdown and had to undergo treatment at the cold water sanatorium in Bad Kreuzen. On June 19, 1867, he enumerated the symptoms of his illness to Weinwurm: "Complete dilapidation and desolation – being totally unnerved and overwrought."[10] A Linz physician emphasized the gravity of his illness to him and prognosticated "madness as a possible consequence."[11]

Bruckner remained at the cold water mental hospital for a total of three months, until August 8. His state of health improved rapidly, so that he was able to begin work on the F minor mass. Nevertheless he was not spared several relapses. He considered leaving Linz and accepting Johann Herbeck's offer to become court organist and professor at the conservatory in Vienna, but was at first unable to make a decision. Then, when he noticed Herbeck's reserve, he deeply regretted not having accepted instantly and wrote to Weinwurm: "I feel insanely unhappy about it, can't eat or sleep, feel as though I have to crawl down." And he added: "You can have no idea of my agonies and my ghastly sadness; I only wish that you yourself may be all the merrier."[12] These expressions suggest a renewed attack of depression. His despair grew so acute that he even thought of suicide. Luckily Herbeck kept him from that with a sensitive letter and the resolute challenge not to go "from the world" but "into the world."[13]

On June 6, 1868, Bruckner exchanged his post as cathedral organist in Limz for an appointment as professor for organ and harmony at the Conservatory of the Friends of Music in Vienna. At first, however, he was not at all happy. Time and again he regretted that he had given up the position in Linz. It appears that in the Danube metropolis he felt even more lonely than in the provincial capital, His natural disposition, his vulnerability, the constant rejections from the young women whom he adored, the derision he sensed, the consciousness of living in an entirely different world, the idea that he was not accepted and not recognized – all that drove him into even deeper isolation. Occasional successes and a growing reputation did not change anything about his embitterment and resignation. "Everything is all right by me in this world already, and I am becoming altogether indifferent to that noble human race," he wrote on February 25, 1885, to his first "apostle," the Leipzig conductor Arthur Nikisch.[14] And in his lecture course at the University of Vienna, he greeted the young listeners who revered and were loyal to him with the words: "I have nothing left in this world but you, my dear academic citizens, and my composing."[15]

Neurosis

On July 21, 1867, in a long letter, Bruckner told his friend Weinwurm at length about the treatment he had to undergo in Bad Kreuzen. He described in detail the events of each day, the medical applications, the dietary plan, the social life at the institution ("I prefer peace and quiet"), the expenses and the length of the medical treatment (between six weeks and six months), and remarked: "The length of the treatment differs greatly with *Nerviosen*"[1] Judging from that, the doctors had evidently diagnosed his ailment as a "neurosis." What sort of neurosis was it?

Until his sixtieth year, Bruckner was generally completely fit and hardy. "The teeming abundance of vital energies that sound from his works with such irresistible, elementary power," as Rudolf Louis put it, "also pervaded his physical constitution."[2] His immense industry and downright pedantic conscientiousness impelled him to a maximum of achievement but also to overwork. There may be a connection between this and that state of being "totally unnerved and overwrought" of which he speaks in the letter of July 18, 1867, to Weinwurm. In all likelihood, the doctors, upon releasing him from the sanatorium, had advised him to take it easy, warning him of undue excitement and overwork, since in the letters of the time after his release he speaks repeatedly of his strained "nerves." [3] He thought a great deal about his illness, which he regarded as sent him by God. Thus on June 23, 1872, he wrote from Vienna to the cathedral dean Schiedmayr: "Where on this earth will I find a man who, ever since it has pleased the most High to deprive me of my complete nervous health (probably in order to humble me), has shown greater sympathy than your Grace?"[4]

Irritability – that is, excitability and touchiness – is a psychic condition that is observable in many people of genius. Extreme affects, enormous sensibility, ready emotional excitement and rapid mood swings characterize Bruckner as well as Richard Wagner or Gustav Mahler.[5] Otto Kitzler, who in February of 1863 conducted the Linz premiere of Wagner's *Tannhäuser* and gave Bruckner lessons in instrumentation, records that he found him at the time in a state of "musical excitement" that he never again had occasion to observe in him later on.[6] And on July 12, 1890, Bruckner was given leave from the Conservatory of the Society of the Friends of Music after the physician Gustav Riehl had diagnosed a "high degree of nervosity" in him in March.[7]

Besides the extreme excitability, the neurosis also manifested itself in a control compulsion and a pronounced scrupulosity. The treatment at the cold water institution at Bad Kreuzen had become necessary because he thought he had to count the leaves on the trees, the stars, the grains of sand, the beads on a dress, or had to bail out the Danube.[8] Bohemian musicians who played for the patients at the resort drove him to flight: he was found in the deepest, as yet not passable part of the "Wolf Ravine" and had to be hauled up with ladders and ropes.[9]

He felt compelled to exert control over things. Thus he would repeatedly return to his apartment to check if everything was still the way he had left it. After the death of his sister Maria Anna, he bitterly reproached himself for having let her move to Vienna with him.[10] His friends regarded him as scrupulous. On August 6, 1868, his former teacher Ignaz Dorn wrote to him: "Incidentally, don't saddle yourself with any new scruples."[11] There is some reason to trace not only the metrical digits that are so typical of his scores, but also a number of other traits, such as his regular notations about migraine attacks and manicures and pedicures in his pocket calendars, to control compulsion.

According to the findings of modern psychiatry, compulsive individuals suffer oppressively. They are plagued by obsessive ideas, images and impulses, against which they have no defenses. The idées fixes trigger feeling of anxiety and guilt and are commonly accompanied by massive self-reproaches. Many such patients brood perpetually about whether they have completed a given work properly or not. The psychiatrist Gerhard Nissen put it like this: "The pedantic observance of compulsive rituals, hour-long compulsive washing and showering, the endless repetition of movements and touching, of oaths, vows and supposedly neutralizing 'counter-ideas' serve as escapes from the accompanying anxiety. Compulsions in this respect can be understood as attempts to displace the anxiety, to bind it and to package it into 'smaller parcels'."[12] One must ask whether Bruckner's constant wrestling with "improvements" in his symphonies – in other words, the much-discussed problem of "versions" – is not also connected with his compulsive ailment.

He could easily be made uncertain, quickly lost his composure, was often upset and desperate. Yet all this is accompanied by an astonishing creative energy. Although he hardly received any outside encouragement during the first sixteen, seventeen years of his time in Vienna, and in spite of numerous severe failures and the negative attitude of Vienna's influential critical establishment, he kept on composing. A striking example is the genesis of the Eighth Symphony. He had sketched the symphony during a euphoric phase in 1884/1885 and developed it during 1886/1887. On September 4, 1887, he reported the completion of the work to his supporter Hermann Levi and on September 19 sent him the score in the hope that Levi would perform the oeuvre in Munich. Levi could not find his way through the gigantic score. Already on September 30, he requested Joseph Schalk in writing to break it to Bruckner that he, Levi, lacked the courage to perform the work. Levi's critique profoundly shook Bruckner and brought on a severe nervous crisis.[13] He was deeply unhappy and inconsolable, though Schalk was convinced that, given Bruckner's "colossal natural energy in both a physical and a moral respect," the adverse situation would soon go away.[14]

Is there a connection between Bruckner's neurosis and his music? Erwin Ringel answered in the affirmative and interpreted Bruckner's oeuvre as a "grandiose attempt to overcome the existential constraints under which he suffered so much." He went one step farther in maintaining that Bruckner's method of working was undoubtedly shaped by "symptoms of neurotic compulsion." It may make sense, however, to put the question differently. It makes sense that Bruckner's sensibility, his affective life, should also precipitate itself in his music. His "overexcitement" – what is called "exaltation" – certainly finds expression there. Even in his lifetime, some critics had sensed and criticized the "ecstatic" element in his music. Thus Hanslick, Bruckner's notorious opponent, writes about the Seventh Symphony: "One of Germany's most respected musicians describes Bruckner's symphony, in a letter to me, as the ghastly dream of an orchestral composer *overstrained* by twenty *Tristan* rehearsals. That seems concise and fitting to me."[15] And about the Eighth he said: "Characteristic also of Bruckner's C minor symphony is the abrupt juxtaposition of dry, contrapuntal book-learning and *measureless exaltation.* Thus buffeted between intoxication and dreariness, we attain to no firm impression, no artistic satisfaction."[16] I leave it open whether Hanslick knew anything concrete about Bruckner's neurosis.

Libido

> "He loved again and again, but always only at a distance and discreetly."
>
> *Josef Kluger about Bruckner*

Bruckner dreamed all his life about having a wife – it was tragic for him personally that his wish could never be fulfilled. His estate includes numerous pictures of very young and very beautiful girls. Some contemporaries made fun of his way of courting. He was easily enflamed, fell readily in love, always with young women, and after a brief acquaintance would make them offers of marriage, which were regularly refused.

It is rightly presumed that he was sexually abstinent all his life. He told the Hamburg music critic Wilhelm Zinne, who visited him in Vienna in 1892, that he had never in his life had a "relationship,"[1] and in later year he confessed to his housekeeper, Kathi Kachelmeyr, that only once in his life, when he was young, he had kissed a girl – and repented of it as a "sin."[2] This becomes more understandable when one considers his strict religious upbringing, which permitted sexuality only in marriage. To be sure the self-imposed abstinence was hard on him. Anecdotes lead to the conclusion that he was not without sexual urges.[3]

His correspondence with his friend Weinwurm during his time in Linz included also matters of the heart. As a cathedral organist, he wanted to live a settled life and get married. Perhaps for this reason, though also to seek refuge from his melancholy, he eagerly attended dances, and he asked his sixteen-year-old piano pupil Emma Thaner, to whom the piano piece "Quiet Reflection on an Autumn Evening" (WAB 123) is dedicated, to teach him to dance.[4] On October 30, 1858, at the age of 34, he wrote to Weinwurm: "I also have a lot to do, am quite well, only once again a little in love."[5] Several years later, on January 29, 1865, he complained to him with great bitterness that the "foster daughter of a pure house" had to his great disappointment turned him down. In August of 1866, he was deeply hurt again by the refusal of Josefine Lang, the beautiful and graceful Linz butcher's daughter, who was 22 at the time. Bruckner had proposed to her in a letter and asked her either to accept or to refuse him but not to put him off, "since with me it is already high time."[6] But Josefine refused his proposal, saying that she greatly respected him but that her affection for him was not strong enough.[7] Josefine's letter is said to have evoked a fit of rage in him. It is therefore all the more surprising that two months later he was thinking about marriage again. The chosen one this time was Henriette Reiter, an eighteen-year-old Viennese girl, whom he greatly fancied. He asked Weinwurm to find out about the financial situation of the family, since he was thinking of an appropriate dowry. The 3000 florins she had at her disposal appeared to him "somewhat too little," especially "if the girl is used to a noble life."[8]

In 1874, Bruckner was hard at work on his Fourth Symphony, the so-called *Romantic*. When Otto Kitzler visited him in Vienna at one time and, looking at the "genial chaos" in his apartment, asked him why he did not get married so as to attain a regular domestic situation, Bruckner answered him: "My dear friend, I have no time: I have to write my Fourth."[9] It may be that after so many disappointments, Bruckner at times resigned himself. But one should by no means conclude that he did not really want to get married in order to devote himself exclusively to his creative work. As late as November 6, 1885, the sixty-two-year- old wrote to his Linz supporter Moritz von Mayfeld: "As far as marriage is concerned, I have no bride to date; if I could only find a dear, suitable flame! Not that I do not have many female friends: lately the fair ladies very much pursue me, thinking they have to act idealistically! It is awful not to feel well! Quite forsaken!"[10]

Even in old age Bruckner felt drawn to good-looking women. Many stories made the rounds in Vienna about his innocuous flirts with young singers and pretty waitresses.[11] It weighed upon him that he had found no partner for life. Thus he remarked to Wilhelm Zinne in the summer of 1892: "I have also always been so full of ideals, that's why I got nowhere – I didn't even manage to get a wife."[12] Surprisingly, in 1894, at the age of seventy, he got engaged to Ida Buhz, a young Berlin chambermaid, but he dissolved the engagement again, because Ida did not want to convert to the Catholic faith.

To all appearances he always resigned himself relatively quickly when his proposals were refused, and tried again and again. For this reason some of his friends thought that he had not been all that serious about it all and imputed a lack of genuine passion to him – Karl Waldeck, for example, his successor as cathedral organist in Linz, maintained that "with him everything was only straw fire."[13] Josef , the cathedral conductor of Pressburg (Bratislava), too, teased him in a letter of 1890 that his worship of a lady had become extinguished as quickly as a "straw fire."[14]

Nevertheless some of the refusals told on him. He seems to have been deeply in love with Josefine Lang. When he visited her in Neufelden in 1890 after the death of her husband, a merchant, and met her nineteen-year-old daughter Karoline, who resembled her strikingly, he was so moved that he thought he found a "dear substitute" in the young woman.[15]

It appears, then, that he clung all his life to an illusion, the dream of finding a young, charming and beautiful partner, a "dear flame," who would inspire him in his creative work. And honestly: does this life-long penchant for young women not remind, for example, of the old Goethe, who in 1822, at the age of 73, fell in love with the very young Ulrike von Levetzow?

Emotionality

> I thank you from my heart for your love of me and beg of you most fervently to preserve it.
> *Bruckner to Rudolf Weinwurn*

Bruckner's music speaks to countless people everywhere in the world, by its sublimity and monumentality but also by its emotional depth. Can one say something more precise about the affective side of his personality? To learn something about that, one should above all study his letters. Though they strike one at times as conventional, even formulaic,[1] they often also permit deep insights into his inner make-up.

On November 11, 1869, Bruckner's fervently loved mother, Theresia, died, not yet sixty, at Ebelsberg near Linz. Still on the same day, Bruckner communicated the sad event to his sister Rosalie Hueber in Vöcklabruck in the following words: "Dear Salie! I am sorry to have to tell you that the issue has come to an unexpected end. Today (November 11) at 4 a.m., our dear mother passed to the better beyond. The funeral is on Tuesday [November 13], early in the morning, where I hope to see you. Maybe the brother-in-law will come as well."[2] The laconic message gives no hint of Bruckner's grief: it is understandable only in view of the hurry Bruckner was in to inform the sister instantly so as to make it possible for her to arrive in time for the burial.

A little less than ten years later, on January 16, 1870, Bruckner's favorite sister Maria Anna died at the age of only 35 in Vienna, where she had kept house for him. Bruckner notified Rosalie again in similarly terse language and nearly identical formulation: "Dear sister! Today, Sunday, at 3 p.m., our dear sister Nani was called by God to the better beyond. Sisters of mercy ministered to her to the end. Pray for her. The funeral is on Tuesday."[3] How profoundly he was in fact affected by the death of his favorite sister he revealed only a week later in a letter to the Linz cathedral dean Johann Baptist Schiedermayr, where he writes that he was bitterly reproaching himself for having made her "do all the housework": "If I had had any idea of this, I would not at any price have let the unforgettable girl move to Vienna with me at all but would rather have stayed in Linz myself. Your Grace, who knows my nerves, can easily judge what I suffered now. Oh, if I could only get away from Vienna for a while!"[4]

More than anything he loved his mother. He once told Carl Hruby that the only great love of his life had been that for his mother.[5] After her death on November 11, 1860, he had a photograph made of the deceased and for the rest of his life kept it in his room, covered by a green curtain. It is said that especially in times of crisis he often prayed in front of it. How much he loved his mother also appears indirectly from accounts of his pupil August Stradal, according to which he was deeply moved by the passage in Wagner's *Siegfried* (second act) where Siegfried is thinking about his mother, and that he loved to improvise about this theme on the organ.[6]

How great his capacity for love was is evident not least from the story of his many years of friendship with Rudolf Weinwurm. He met Weinwurm, who worked as choral director and composer in Vienna, in September of 1856, and until his move to Vienna in 1868, he was in close personal and epistolary contact with him. The numerous letters he wrote to Weinwurm are among the most personal ones he ever penned. For many years, Weinwurm was Bruckner's only confidant and personal point of reference. He regarded him as his "only true friend," to whom he could reveal his innermost thoughts and pour out his heart. "I would love to speak to you in person once," he wrote on February 25, 1864, "for you are indispensable to me – I have only one friend – and that is you."[7] Brucker repeatedly confessed to be yearning for his friend, to be "attachéd" to him and to love him. Thus we read in a letter of June 6, 1859: "I am already greatly looking forward to seeing you again, since I have no such friend here. It was only at my departure on the steamer that I realized how much I love you."[8] He greatly esteemed Weinwurm's "noble heart" and was ecstatic when he learned that Weinwurm returned his amicable feelings. When he was at Bad Kreuzen, his friend sought to console him in a letter, which unfortunately has been lost. Deeply thankful and moved, Bruckner replied on July 15, 1867: If it can be a balm of life for any man to have a true friend, I in my situation surely gain a thousand-fold from it! I will always be thankful to Divine

Providence for this happiness and this mercy."[9] And in a letter of January 7, 1868: "I wish you a very happy New Year and entreat you for your lifelong love and friendship. If I could only spend my later years close to you!"[10] His wish soon came true. How this intimate friendship developed after Bruckner's move to Vienna, however, is very difficult to say, as Andrea Harrandt has rightly remarked.[11] But we know that Weinwurm did not stop to support Bruckner and that he performed several of his choral works in Vienna.

The attentive reader of the 45 letters Bruckner wrote to Weinwurm during his time in Linz will notice especially their intimate and tender mode of expression. Later on, Bruckner would use a similarly warm tone in his letters to his favorite pupils Josef and Franz Schalk, who tirelessly and entirely unselfishly intervened in his behalf.[12] On August 10, 1883, he wrote to Josef: "I am so touched that even far away you think of me with equal fondness!"[13] And in a letter to Franz Schalk, on New Year's of 1887, we read: "Since your departure I am a hermit again as before!"[14]

One will not find similar emotional outpourings in letters that the amorous young Bruckner addressed to young women: "decency" forbade it. In the letter to Josefine Lang cited before, he merely says he was certain that his "quiet but steady waiting for you" was known to her.[15] In later years he was less reserved in this respect. In 1885, at the age of 61, he had fallen in love with the then twenty-year-old Marie Demar, had sent her a picture of himself with an inscription and asked for one of her in return.[16] On May 11, 1885, he thanked her for the "gorgeous picture" and indirectly confessed his love to her: "Those innocent beautiful eyes! How often they console me! This relic will be precious and priceless to me to the end of my life. And what joy it is to look at it frequently! etc. I also beg for your cherished friendship, dearest Miss! May I never be deprived of it! You can be assured of mine to all eternity."[17] In language, Bruckner could express his feelings for the most part only discreetly. How hard it was for him to leave his beloved activity as organist at the old cathedral in Linz one can tell from one touching detail. Some time ago a penciled inscription in his hand was discovered in a hidden spot on the cathedral's organ console, reading "Farewell."[18] This brief good-bye reveals more than even his letters about his feelings. It is in his stirring music, however, that Bruckner's emotionality finds its transcendent expression.

The "Passionate Urge to Compose"

Compared with the careers of other leading composers of the 19th century, Bruckner's course of development seems in several respects unusual, Until his 31st year he essentially worked in the teaching profession, being active as "school assistant" and then as "junior teacher" in Windhaag, in Kronstorf and in the parish of St. Florian. Late in 1849, he was additionally hired as "provisional" chapter organist, but he seems not to have found that activity entirely satisfactory, since on July 25, 1853, he applied for a post as clerk at the district court of St. Florian.[1]

Alongside his pedagogical occupation he eagerly pursued the musical studies begun in youth, in order to perfect his abilities and his knowledge of organ-playing and music theory. He took lessons from his cousin Johann Baptist Weiß in Hörsching, Johann August Dürrnberger in Linz and above all Leopold von Zenetti in Enns.[2] Instruction in organ he received once again from Anton Kattinger in St. Florian, who upon his leaving gave him a splendid reference. During his many years at St. Florian, Bruckner had ample opportunity to acquaint himself with sacred music from the late Renaissance through the Romantic period. His own early work is both voluminous and varied and is revealing for his later oeuvre. Chief creations in the years between 1843 and 1855 include a Requiem in D minor (WAB 39) on the death of one of his supporters, the court scribe Franz Sailer, and a Missa Solemnis in B flat minor (WAB 29), composed in 1854 for the solemn investiture of the newly elected prelate Friedrich Mayer, who was well-disposed toward Bruckner.

In 1855, Bruckner was appointed cathedral organist in Linz. The work in this new, respected office brought him satisfaction, at least at first. But his music-theoretical expertise still did not measure up to his expectations. He therefore established contact with Simon Sechter, the renowned professor for music theory in Vienna, with whom for the next six years he studied the subjects of harmony, counterpoint, canon and fugue with such zeal that Sechter felt compelled to admonish him to look after his health. Much later, Bruckner once told his pupil Dr. Franz Marschner that for seven years he studied counterpoint for seven hours daily, at least during the "vacation months," under Sechter's direct supervision.[3] Upon the completion of his studies in November of 1861, he voluntarily underwent the notorious and notoriously strict examination at the Conservatory of the Friends of Music in Vienna, which he passed with flying colors. Johann Herbeck, who was a member of the examination commission, remarked afterwards: "He should have been examining us!"

From Sechter, Bruckner learned to master the strict compositional (contrapuntal) technique in all its nuances. Even so, he sensed that his musical education was rather one-sided. Until 1861, he had not come in contact with the really "new music" of his time, the music of Wagner, Berlioz and Liszt. When Otto Kitzler, a excellent musician who was open to the New Music, came to Linz in 1861, where he worked at the municipal theater, first as a cellist and eventually as conductor, Bruckner was able to obtain him as a teacher for the theory of musical form, instrumentation and composition.

Bruckner distinguished himself by his high sense of responsibility, exceptional conscientiousness and enormous self-discipline. One can but marvel at the intensity with which he pursued his studies, his perseverance and staying power. His study plan was both methodical and long-range. At the latest since the beginning of his activities as cathedral organist, he appears to have regarded composition as one of the chief goals of his life. Significantly enough, however, he was able to suppress his desire to compose during the long years of study with Simon Sechter. On November 10, 1861, he told the board of directors of the Viennese Conservatory that he wished to devote himself to free composition only after having taken the examination.[4] He postponed the fulfillment of that wish once more when he took up his studies with Kitzler in December of 1861. The compositions he produced for Kitzler he regarded as "homework," as studies for later works. Thus he wrote to Rudolf Weinwurm on September 7, 1862: "Only I can't set out with any compositions, because I still have to study. We are already doing instrumentation and then the symphony, which, as you know, is also merely sonata form. [...] Later, next year, I'll surely be busy composing. Right now it's just mostly homework. I'll be done in 3-4 months." This was the moment when Bruckner felt ready for church music. "Should a mass be required," he informed Weinwurm in the same letter, "I would of course have to interrupt my studies."[5]

The studies with Kitzler have a special importance for his compositional development. He got to know the score of Wagner's *Tannhäuser* and, on February 12, 1863, witnessed the Linz premiere of the work. It made such a lasting impression on him that it is no exaggeration to say that this Wagner experience set off a new and in fact the decisive creative impulse in him. He discovered himself and began to develop his own style but also became a Wagnerian, who all his life remained loyal to the then notorious as well as noted Bayreuth master. Substantial impulses also came to him from he works of Berlioz and Liszt, to whom Ignaz Dorn, a likewise modern-thinking Linz musician, had drawn his attention.

In September of 1864 he completed the D minor Mass, which he personally conducted on November 20, 1864, in the old Linz cathedral, and which on December 18th of the same year was performed as a *concert spirituel* in Linz's Redoubt Hall with considerable success: the press was full of praise for the work. At this point at the latest, his resolve to make composing the "chief task" of his life was probably confirmed. Since he was greatly taxed by his many professional obligations, he had little time left for composing, which required sustained concentration and was a also considerable strain on his "nerves," Time and again he was compelled to address petitions for salary increments, stipends and financial support to various recipients. On December 2, 1867, he asked the episcopacy in Linz for a "raise or an annual personal salary supplement."[6] In a letter to the minister for education, Lord Karl von Stremayr, dated January 27, 1873, he spoke of his "urge to compose," which for many years had filled him "passionately," described his professional situation – "my lessons, 30-40 per week, take up so much of my time and energy that my creative activity has flagged considerably" – and asked for a "subvention."[7] On November 9, 1873, he even turned to the Austrian parliament (*Reichstag*) through one of its representatives with the request for a "life-long annuity anchored in the budget,"[8] and on April 18, 1874, he petitioned the education minister to create a "permanent position" in music theory at the University of Vienna for him.[9] Nearly all of these requests remained initially without success.

Securing an Income

> Busily piling up debts, eventually to enjoy the fruits of my busyness in debtors' prison and there to sing of the folly of my move to Vienna may be my ultimate destiny."
>
> *Bruckner to Moritz von Mayfeld*

When Bruckner died on October 11, 1896, in his last apartment in the upper Belvedere, the news spread like a wildfire, and according to his last physician, Dr. Richard Heller, both authorized and unauthorized persons descended like vultures on his estate.[1] The worth of that was estimated by the executor, Dr. Theodor Reisch, as amounting to 20,000 florins, including ca. 14,000 in ready cash.[2] His estate was thus a respectable one – Bruckner died by no means as a pauper. Nevertheless he continued to give private lessons to individual pupils even in his last years.[3] The question is: was he dependent on the honoraria for these private lessons, or were those persons right who imputed "greed" and "avarice" to him?

One should recall that Bruckner had grown up in very strait financial circumstances and often suffered bitter penury. As a mere youth he was forced not only to assist with the teaching in the village school but also to "play dance music on his violin all night" at the pub for pay for the peasants of Windhaag.[4] It is thus understandable that peace of mind and mental equilibrium should all his life have depended on his sense of economic security. He lived thriftily and even as a young man thought about making provisions for his old age. Already in 1841, when he had barely been approved as teaching assistant, he concluded an old-age pension insurance contract.[5] Later, during his years in Linz, he paid high premiums to a pension and life insurance company.[6] And when, in the summer of 1868, he finally decided, after prolonged doubts and scruples, to resign from his post as cathedral organist in Linz in order to accept a professorship at the Conservatory of the Friends of Music in Vienna in the fall, he requested the Linz diocese, as early as July 24, 1868, to hold his organist post "graciously in reserve for a few years," as the granting of this request would "redound to his consolation and inordinate reassurance."[7] Bishop Rudigier, who was well-disposed toward him, saw to it that his request was granted.

Bruckner would soon rue the removal to Vienna, as the hopes he had attached to his new field of activity were fulfilled either not at all or only hesitantly. Though appointed, on September 4, 1868, as the "prospective" court organist at the court chapel, the post was at first an unpaid honorary one. His initial financial situation in Vienna was meager, his income from the Conservatory small. He had financial worries, was forced to run up debts and give private lessons to survive. All of his endeavors to find a patron ended in failure,[8] and his attempt to obtain a salaried teaching appointment at the University of Vienna met with unyielding resistance from Eduard Hanslick.[9] Bruckner poured out his distress to his Linz supporter Moritz von Mayfeld. On January 12, 1875, he wrote: "I have only the Conservatory, which it is impossible to live on. Had to take out another loan in September [1874] if I did not want to starve (500 fl). Nobody helps me. Stremair [the Minister of Education Stremayr] makes promises – and does nothing. Luckily some foreigners have arrived, who are taking lessons from me – otherwise I would have to go begging."[10] Another letter to von Mayfeld of February 13, 1875, includes the sentence quoted as the chapter motto. Here it says: "1000 fl. annually have been taken from me, and no substitute – and no stipend, etc. either – given this year. I can't have my 4th Symphony copied."[11]

Bruckner's workload of doing his job and giving lessons was considerable. For the decade from 1870 to 1880, an average of 30-40 weekly hours can be estimated.[12] It is all the more remarkable that, given this burden, he had the energy, in a burst of creativity, to compose no fewer than five symphonies (the Second through the Sixth) and the String Quintet. His complaints about the lack of time for composing were justified. His enormously fruitful productivity sprang from an inner urge; from outside he received no encouragement whatever.

His financial situation improved at the end of 1880, when the Ministry of Culture converted his honorary teaching appointment at the University of Vienna to a salaried one.[13] Even so he wrote as late as September 19, 1885, in a letter to the Berlin critic Wilhelm Tappert, that he had to "slave away so much at schoolmastering to be able to subsist" that he had no time or "yet much too little time" left "for composing."[14] He made similar remarks even four years later (on August 28, 1889) on the occasion of an excellent organ concert at St. Florian.[15] Under the circumstances he must have been very happy upon receiving word that the parliament of Upper Austria had voted on October 30, 1890, to grant him an "honorary gift" of 400 florins annually in recognition of his work as "musician to the fatherland."[16]

Speaking of his need for security, Bruckner, like virtually no other composer of the 19th century, had a passion for examinations and reports. He loved to take exams voluntarily and collected points accordingly. Whenever he had taken an exam, after resigning from a post, concluding a course of studies or finishing an individual course, he always asked superiors, teachers, pastors or noted artists to issue a report to him. The number of his accumulated credits is high.[17] Simon Sechter alone wrote five evaluations on him. People have condescendingly spoken of Bruckner's "report-card tick." In reality it was that, as an autodidact, Bruckner needed testimonials for his inner reassurance and as proof of his competence.[18]

Persecution Mania

"You have no idea how especially a class of musicians now persecutes me."

Bruckner to Moritz von Mayfeld

"Lies – insinuation – division are the weapons of my enemies."

Bruckner to August Göllerich

On September 23, 1886, Bruckner was received by the Emperor Francis Joseph I. in the Hofburg. He wanted to thank His Majesty for having been decorated with the Franz-Joseph order. When the emperor asked him if there was any wish he could fulfill, Bruckner supplicated that he would "most graciously" forbid Eduard Hanslick to write nasty things about him in the *Neue Freie Presse*. This anecdote is usually told as an example of Bruckner's helplessness and unworldliness. [1]

No attentive reader of Bruckner's letters will be able to overlook how often the words "enemy/enemies" and "persecution" recur in them. Evidently he felt time and again hounded. According to Carl Hruby, he once remarked to his students at the University of Vienna: "When I'm gone someday, tell the world how much I suffered and how I was persecuted."[2] Did he really have that many enemies, and was he in truth persecuted, or did competitors balloon into enemies in his imagination? Was he possibly paranoid, or did his complaints about supposed persecutors only serve to solicit pity, as has likewise been surmised? Questions like that can be answered only case by case.

On January 27, 1866, Bruckner told Rudolf Weinwurm how painful it had been to him when his confidant Alois Weinwurm had broken off their friendship – a circumstance Bruckner blamed on the influence of his "enemies," "whom I have in great numbers in Linz."[3] Who these "enemies" were he does not say in so many words. But one should probably look for them in the vicinity of the singing circle *Frohsinn* ("Mirth"), which Bruckner had joined as an active member in March of 1856, where from September 7, 1860, he functioned as first chorus master, and from which he resigned a year later. In the same letter he tells Weinwurm that he had been urged to apply again for the re-advertised position, but that he had no success – "which is only natural with such opponents."[4]

In an attempt to improve his finances, Bruckner, who from the start had not been happy in Vienna, accepted an offer in October of 1870 to give piano lessons at the teacher seminary of St. Anna. Slightly less than a year later, he was made the target of an anonymous denunciation there, which resulted in his dismissal. As the Linz newspaper *Tages-Post* reported on October 12, 1871, he supposedly had had paid "court to his female pupils" and treated some preferentially.[5] Prompted by this supposed affair, the Viennese satirical magazine *Die Bombe* published an article, in the form of a fictive letter by a Viennese prostitute to her girlfriend, that parodies Bruckner's supposed amorous piano lessons.

The director of the institution rehabilitated him in a letter to the *Tages-Post*, in which he emphasized Bruckner's "strictly moral deportment."[6] Yet Bruckner was so deeply hurt by this affair that from then on he refused to teach the female classes. In letters to Karl Waldeck and Moritz von Mayfeld, he spoke about "villainies" that "make one's life miserable,"[7] imputed a malicious intention to his "enemies" of wanting to deprive him of his livelihood,[8] and once again lamented his ever having entered "this land of intrigues and persecutions."[9] "The month of October," he wrote to Moritz von Mayfeld, "has done infinite damage to my nerves. I have lost every last interest and pleasure in Vienna. One has to attend to so many issues that there is no time left for art."[10]

To all appearances, Bruckner never felt really comfortable in the Danube metropolis, the city where, after all, he spent 28 years of his life. Again and again he regretted ever having moved there and yearned back to Linz and his position as cathedral organist. In January of 1875, his dissatisfaction reached a climax. In a letter to Moritz von Mayfeld, he bitterly complained about the way he was being treated at the Conservatory. "Never in my life would I have let myself be carted to Vienna if I had had an inkling of that. It would be easy for my enemies to push me out of the Conservatory. I am surprised that hasn't happened yet. Students at the University, faculty at the

Conservatory, even the servants there are appalled by the conduct toward me. My life has lost all interest and enjoyment – in vain and for nothing. Would I could go back to my old post!"[11] Again and again he thought about emigrating abroad, if it were possible to obtain a position there.

Bruckner's complaints were not unfounded. In the Conservatory, he had to bear the petty chicaneries of his colleague Leopold Alexander Zellner, who, for instance, had the lights turned off while Bruckner was still teaching. Zellner, who for a while had taught harmony and organ-building at the Conservatory, was the general secretary of the Society of the Friends of Music and as such Bruckner's superior. Without much talent as a composer, he envied Bruckner his musical gifts. How hostile and primitive he could be, we learn from a remark made to Bruckner after the fiasco of the Third Symphony's premiere in December of 1877: "You can wipe your ... with your symphonies. You are better off earning your keep making piano reductions. That is smarter and brings in some money!"[12] ." Poor Bruckner just cringed – perhaps because he was afraid of losing his position.

But he suffered most from the attacks of those segments of the Viennese press that vehemently opposed him as a composer. His relation to Eduard Hanslick, the powerful "high priest of music," has been repeatedly described from a variety of angles. But it appears as if the psychological implications of the antagonism have not hitherto been examined sufficiently. Bruckner formulated his own view of the matter most comprehensively in May of 1884, in a letter to the critic Anton Vergeiner, who planned to publish an article about him and had interviewed him in that connection. Bruckner wrote to him:

Hanslick was, except for Herbeck, my highest and greatest supporter. What he wrote about me until 1874 (when I was promoted to the university as lecturer) will hardly ever happen again; even as composer and conductor he treated me with great distinction. And please do not in any way criticize Hanslick on my account, for his wrath is terrible, and he is capable of destroying me. You cannot fight him. One can approach him only in supplication. I myself can't even do that, since he always has himself denied to me.[13]

Bruckner had gotten to know Hanslick at the latest during his time in Linz. In September of 1863, he met him in Munich and conversed at length with him. On January 21, 1865, he asked Rudolf Weinwurm, who was working as chorus master at the University in Vienna, to send Hanslick the score of his D-minor Mass. Early in 1865, the festival of the choral union took place in Linz, during which Bruckner's *Germanenzug* ("The Germanic Migration"), after a poem by August Silberstein, was successfully premiered. On this occasion, Hanslick presented Bruckner with a signed photograph. In the spring of 1866, he encouraged Bruckner to give an organ recital in Vienna in the fall. In June of 1872, Bruckner's Mass in F minor was performed in the Augustine church in Vienna. In an unsigned notice in the *Neue Freie Presse*, which Bruckner ascribed to Hanslick,[14] the writer praised the composition and recommended that the mass be presented in a regular concert performance.[15] Still quite positive, but now noticeably distanced was Hanslick's review of the premiere of the Second Symphony in October of 1873 in Vienna. He mentioned the "very solemn, pathos-laden character" of the work and the "numerous beautiful, meaningful details," but objected that "the total impression [was] spoiled by the insatiable rhetoric and the excessively broad, at times hopelessly disjointed musical form.[16]

From all this it seems probable that for a while Hanslick had some sympathy for Bruckner. That changed radically when Bruckner, in a lengthy letter of April 18, 1874, applied to the Ministry for Culture and Instruction for a "permanent appointment (with a salary and eligibility for a pension)" as an instructor in music theory at the university. Hanslick, who held a chair for the history and aesthetics of music at the Vienna University, was asked for his opinion. In a famous report, he requested that Bruckner's application be turned down. In it he reproached Bruckner with having unwarrantedly asked for a "chair," charged him with "lacking any and all scholarly training," and found fault with his having failed to submit any attests as to his "teaching activities."[17] Thereupon the minister urged Bruckner to make clear in a supplementary appeal that he was not asking for a professorship but for a simple "teaching post." This time Hanslick complained about the lack of proof that Bruckner had achieved any "fruitful results anywhere" as a composition teacher.[18] Thereupon Bruckner, in a third petition, presented suitable evaluations and compositions to the Dean of the Philosophic Faculty, but this time, too, Hanslick refused to yield. It was only after a member of the Reichstag for Upper Austria had intervened that Bruckner submitted a fourth petition, this time for a lectureship in harmony and counterpoint and Hanslick's ferocious resistance could finally be broken. By decree of the ministry, Bruckner was appointed on November 8, 1875, as an unsalaried lecturer. He was undoubtedly right when, on October 1, 1876, he wrote to the Berlin critic Wilhelm Tappert: "Because of my activity at the university as an unpaid lecturer for harmony and counterpoint, Dr. Hanslick has become my bitter enemy."[19]

It has been asserted that Hanslick's objections to Bruckner's appointment were purely factual – a contention only superficially correct. Letters of Rudolf Weinwurm's make it quite clear that Hanslick did not shy away from using dishonest means to prevent Bruckner's being hired by the university.[20] Evidently his one-time friendship with Bruckner at some point turned into opposition and spiteful enmity. It is likely that he simply could not get over his ultimate defeat in the long struggle against Bruckner's lectureship. To make matters worse, Bruckner, who, ever since his studies with Otto Kitzler, was a confirmed Wagnerian, had visited Wagner in Bayreuth in September of 1873 and subsequently dedicated his Third Symphony "in profoundest veneration." On October 15, 1874, he joined Vienna's Academic Richard-Wagner-Association and thereafter missed no opportunity to profess his adherence to the "New German" camp. In two of his petitions of 1874, he referred expressly to the goodwill of Wagner and Liszt and to the honor of Wagner's having accepted his dedication of the Third Symphony. All of this Hanslick, who had become Wagner's relentless adversary, and who zealously championed his friend Brahms, must have regarded as a provocation.

Ever since the events surrounding the lectureship Bruckner felt persecuted by Brahms, Hanslick and the critics close to them. Thus he wrote to Moritz von Mayfeld on January 12, 11875: "Brahms [at that time director of the Choral Group of the Society of the Friends of Music] seems to have suppressed my C minor Symphony No. 2 in Leipzig. Richter [Hans Richter] is said to have remarked he would like to perform the D minor Symphony in Pest some time. What Hanslick has done to me can be read in the old Press of December 25."[21] A longish article had indeed appeared in the *Presse* of December 25, 1874, under the title "The Thorough-Bass in the Philosophic Professorial Collegium" about the rejection of Bruckner's petition. The anonymous author, who seems to have been very well informed, clearly sides with the "well-known accomplished organ virtuoso Pruckner" and criticizes Hanslick's position, whom he does not identify by name.[22]

Between 1864 and 1884, Bruckner produced an astonishing oeuvre – alongside his time-consuming teaching and his service at the Court Chapel – including six gigantic symphonies, the String Quintet and the sublime *Te Deum*. Yet until 1884, few of his works were premiered in Vienna. The premiere of the Third Symphony on December 16, 1877, was a spectacular flop: after every movement, members of the audience left the concert hall in droves. The Fourth was received positively in 1881, but the Fifth was never performed in Vienna during Bruckner's life, and of the Sixth only the middle movements were played in 1883. Bruckner ascribed the fact that he was performed so little to Eduard Hanslick and the campaign that a portion of the Viennese press had started against him. He was convinced that the Brahms biographer Max Kalbeck (*Presse*) and the music critic Gustav Dömpke (*Allgemeine Zeitung*) were "forced" at Hanslick's "command" to write negatively about his music, and that some conductors, like the generally well-disposed Hans Richter, refused to perform his music out of fear of Hanslick. Thus a letter to Rudolf Krzyzanowski of May 5, 1884, states: "Here in Vienna nothing has been performed except the String Quintet by the Academic Choral Society. Hans Richter does not perform anything either here or there! He blows Hanslick's horn!"[23] And in a letter to Josef Sittart of March 24, 1886, we read: "But now your Highness must know that Hanslick (*Neue Freie Presse*) has been my enemy ever since 1874, because I accepted the lectureship at the University and he did not want to have any music theory there; so the old Presse and the *Allgemeine* have to write hostilely about me, too. That's already three – same with *Extrablatt* and *Sonntagsblatt* – makes five hostiles."[24]

Today one can only be shocked and amazed to read the critiques of Bruckner's oeuvre that Hanslick, Kalbeck and Dömpke penned, and that not only because they do not take him seriously as a composer but above all because they go out of their way to make him look ridiculous. They take it upon themselves to judge and condemn not only the music but the man. Their tone is almost uniformly arrogant, spiteful and sneering, designed only to entertain their readers at his expense. While Kalbeck once called Bruckner a "Romeling,"[25] Dömpke spoke of the "abnormalities of a sexagenarian" and went so far in tastelessness as to say that "Bruckner composes like a drunkard."[26] No critic today would dare to write in similar terms about a contemporary composer. The Bruckner pupil Friedrich Klose surely hit the nail on the head when he remarked that there was method to this kind of "reportage": the aim was to prevent Bruckner from being performed at all.[27]

The proverb "Nemo propheta in patria" seems to prove true again in Bruckner's case: the decisive turn in the reception of his music came from outside. It was reserved for his Seventh Symphony to bring about the breakthrough for his so long ignored, misunderstood and often derided oeuvre. It was the first work of Bruckner's that really earned great successes and thereby paved the way to the concert halls for the other symphonies as well. Shortly after its path-breaking Munich performance under Hermann Levi's baton on March 10, 1885, the Seventh began a triumphant advance through the world's major metropolises.

The news of the great success of this performance quickly reached Vienna and did not fail to have an effect there. Hans Richter, the conductor of the Philharmonic Concerts, conveyed his readiness to Bruckner to perform one of his works and expressed interest specifically in the Seventh. By now, however, Bruckner's fear of Hanslick was so extreme that he did not want to grant Richter's wish under any circumstances. He revealed his reason in a letter to Levi of September 7, 1885: "Herr Richter told me yesterday he wants to perform the *Te Deum,* – he won't get the seventh! Hanslick!!! – I told Herr Richter, if he ever wants to perform a symphony, let it be one of the ones that Hanslick has already ruined anyway; let him demolish that even more."[28] And on October 13, he asked the Committee of the Vienna Philharmonics in writing to refrain from any performance of the Seventh for the time being, "for reasons that stem solely from the sad local situation in regard to the leading critical establishment, which could only get in the way of my still recent successes in Germany."[29] The letter is surely one of the most distressing documents in music history.

As was to be expected, Bruckner yielded to the pressure of Richter and the Philharmonics, and the Seventh was performed, in one of the Philharmonic Concerts, on March 21, 1886, to great success (one has to say: surprisingly). As Bruckner reported to his "artistic father" Herman Levi on March 25: "No balking and begging helped: on the 21st the 7th Symphony was performed by the Philharmonics. Richter took great pains. The reception was an indescribable jubilation. Already after the first movement, 5 or 6 frenzied calls for the composer, and so it continued, after the Finale endless tumultuous enthusiasm and curtain calls, laurel wreath from the Wagner Society and festive banquet." And in a postscript, he added: "The five hostile papers will at Hanslick's request take perfect care of the success's annihilation."[30] He was right in his apprehension: Hanslick's, Kalbeck's and Dömpke's critiques this time, too, were devastating. Hanslick wrote in the *Neue Freie Presse* for March 30, 1886: "Bruckner has become army command and the 'second Beethoven', an article of faith with the Wagner sect. I confess openly that I could hardly do justice to Bruckner's symphony, it seems so unnatural, pretentious, morbid and pernicious to me."[31]

Bruckner's fear of Hanslick was also justified because the *Freie Neue Presse* – the organ in which the latter published – was the leading newspaper within the variegated Viennese press landscape. One consolation for him was that several of the Viennese music critics – Theodor Helm, Ludwig Speidel, Gustav Schönaich – had recognized his genius and the importance of his creations and spoke up for him wherever they could. But their positive reports about his successes appeared in papers (*Morgenpost, Vaterland, Deutsche Zeitung, Fremdenblatt, Tagblatt* et al.) that could hardly compete with the *Neue Freie Presse* in terms of circulation.[32]

Bruckner's hope that the triumphant performance of the Seventh in Vienna would soon bring about a positive change in his situation was not fulfilled at first. On June 16, 1886, he told the Hamburg critic Wilhelm Zinne: "About Hanslick and sadly also Brahms I have been told such hurtful stories that I'd rather not say anything, but my heart is full of grief!!!"[33] And he added: "Hanslick dictates to two other critics to run me down; they even try by any means to turn Hans Richter, who is enthusiastic about me, against me, knowing Richter's fear of the press." And a few months later, on November 16, 1886, he wrote to Hermann Levi: "Things are back as they were in Vienna. (Schönaich, too, is said to have broken away from me again.) Without Hanslick, Vienna is lost!"[34]

The reality, however, is that the successful performance of the Seventh in March of 1886 had a significant impact on Vienna. Bruckner was gradually able to prevail. On November 7, 1891, the University of Vienna, in a festive session, bestowed the title of an honorary doctorate on him, and the premiere of the Eighth Symphony under Hans Richter on December 18, 1892, was a triumphant success for him. People began to see through the backgrounds of the polemic against Bruckner. Around 1895, Otto Böhler produced two colored pen-and-ink drawings, which, taking off from one of the *Struwwelpeter* stories, show Bruckner marching out in front with an open umbrella (or parasol), followed by the mocking "ink boys" Eduard Hanslick, Max Kalbeck and Richard Heuberger. The texts in the caption translate roughly thus: "A composer in a jolly fling Went walking on Vienna's Ring; But since 'twas Austria that bred him, The critics there were slow to get him." And : "The maestro walks in sunshine clear, The ink-boys bringing up the rear."[35]

Worries about the Success of the Work

> Would you, like the Messrs. Levi and Nikisch, put your entire artistic self to work for your old one-time teacher, who has always loved you, and rehearse and perform this Adagio with the tubas and the funeral music for the blessed maestro as if it were your own work? If you can develop enthusiasm for that, you are, as a famous conductor, the right artist!"
>
> *Bruckner to Felix Mottl*

On April 15, 1886, the choral circle *Frohsinn*, where Bruckner had already twice been chorus master, celebrated the 41st anniversary of its founding with a concert, in which, under the direction of Wilhelm Floderer, Bruckner's *Germanenzug, Um Mitternacht* ("At Midnight"), the *Te Deum* and the Adagio from the Third Symphony were performed, the choral piece *Um Mitternacht* (WAB 90) having its premiere. At the end of the concert, Bruckner expressed his thanks in an extended address, which deserves special attention. He said in part:

It is true that I lived through difficult years, it is true that even in Vienna, our imperial capital, natives generally have to take a backseat; it is also true that ill-will and everything one does not want conspired there to make my life miserable. Luckily there were only three such elements that opposed me by name. That also was the reason why nothing was performed for such a long time and I had to float in the dark for so long. It was in the year 1882 at the first performance of *Parsifal*, that our blessed, unforgettable maestro Wagner took me by the hand and said: 'Depend on it, I shall perform your works, I myself.' Well, now that the dear maestro has been called away, it seems as though he had, in the goodness of his heart, appointed guardians for me: my first guardian was Herr Nikisch in Leipzig, the second one the conductor Hermann Levi in Munich. With every bit of energy, they have done everything possible to perform my works, and the success was quite extraordinary, as is not often the case. Well, that has given me enormous strength. I have had already two guardians by now. Then Herr Hans Richter appeared in Vienna as my third, and then also a *Kapellmeister* in Karlsruhe [the reference is to Felix Mottl].[1]

The four conductors, whom Bruckner so strangely calls his "guardians" here, tirelessly stood up for his works and brought about their breakthrough. As early as 1873, Arthur Nikisch (1855-1922) had been part of the premiere, under Buckner's direction, of the Second Symphony as a violinist, and confessed later that his enthusiasm for Bruckner's symphonic work had been awakened already at that time.[2] At the urging of Joseph Schalk, he performed the Seventh Symphony on December 30, 1884, in Leipzig at the municipal theater, where he was engaged as first *kapellmeister*. That drew the attention of the Wagner conductor Hermann Levi (1839-1900) to the Seventh Symphony, and he performed it to great success on March 10, 1885, in Munich. From then on Levi became Bruckner's chief "champion." It was owing to him, among other things, that Ludwig II. accepted the dedication of the Seventh, and that Bruckner was awarded the Franz-Josef-Order in Vienna. It was also Levi who authored the recommendation for Bruckner's honorary doctorate at the University of Vienna.[3]

Hans Richter (1843-1916), who had already served as Richard Wagner's assistant in Tribschen, conducted the Philharmonic Concerts in Vienna from 1875-1882 and from 1883-1898. He championed both Bruckner and Brahms (which offended Bruckner) and conducted several of Bruckner's symphonies in Vienna, mostly with great success: on February 20, 1881, the Fourth, on March 21, 1886, the Seventh, on December 21, 1890, the reworked Third, on December 13, 1891, the "Viennese" version of the First, on December 18, 1892, the second version of the Eighth and on November 25, 1894, the Second. After hearing the First Symphony on the piano in 1889, he is said to have "tearfully smothered [Bruckner] with kisses" and "prophesied immortality" to him.[4]

Felix Mottl (1856-1911), finally, the youngest of the "guardians," had studied music theory under Bruckner at the Conservatory of the Society of the Friends of Music in Vienna. From 1881 to 1903, he worked at the court theater in Karlsruhe as *kapellmeister* and later as general music director. On December 10, 1881, he conducted the Fourth Symphony there, with moderate success. However, the performance of the Adagio from the Seventh on May 30, 1885, in Karlsruhe was a great success, which contributed significantly to Bruckner's breakthrough.[5]

Hermann Levi was in some sense Bruckner's protector. In letters, Bruckner several times addressed him as his "artistic father,"[6] – a strange formulation, which Ingrid Fuchs interpreted to mean not in relation to himself but to "his children," as he sometimes called his symphonies.[7] There are, however, some other aspects to this. Already in 1868, Bruckner had called the Viennese court conductor Johann Herbeck, whose protégé he then was, his "second father," and he repeatedly referred to himself as "unrecognized" and "forsaken." He felt in many ways in need of protection, unable, by his own strength, to assert his work, which meant so much to him, against the opposition of his powerful "enemies." He therefore needed "guardians," trustees, agents, executors, brilliant and famous conductors, who took charge of his symphonies and were able also to carry them through. Incidentally, the passage from one of his letters to Felix Mottl prefixed as motto to this chapter make clear that he demanded the utmost from his "guardians"/interpreters, namely total commitment, enthusiasm for his work, identification with him and meticulous rehearsing.

A letter of Bruckner's to Arthur Nikisch is very telling in this connection. On July 7, 1885, he wrote: "Illustrious great supporter and friend! You were my first *apostle*, who with brilliant art and fullest power and dignity proclaimed my hitherto unheard word in Germany. It will be to your everlasting renown that you let your great high genius shine for me, the unrecognized and forsaken. For that, thanks be to you in all eternity, from me as well as from my true friends."[8]

A strong, unshakable self-awareness speaks from these sentences with their religious vocabulary. When the Saxon painter Fritz Uhde, who was working on a Last Supper in 1885, met Bruckner in Munich, he supposedly asked the latter's friend Carl Almeroth to prevail upon Bruckner to sit for the head of one of the apostles. Bruckner resolutely refused, pointing out that he was not worthy of being in the company of the apostles.[9]

It is often said that Bruckner was difficult, overly sensitive, even mimosa-like, and that he could be altogether unjust at times. These and similar assertions sound "objective," but they often mislead, because they leave crucial psychological factors out of account.

One can say without exaggeration that since his time in Linz at the latest, composing had become the sole content of Bruckner's life. It was only natural, then, that he wanted to be performed. But until his sixtieth year, his works were seldom, if at all, performed. So one can understand that the worry about the realization of his work, which he himself regarded as original and significant, would become a principal motive of his life. Since he received nothing but bad critiques from the leading Viennese press, it meant much to him for at least the few papers that were well-disposed toward him to publish reports about successful performances in Vienna or abroad.

For a long time, his symphonies were regarded not only as overly long but also as difficult to play. Some of his pupils therefore did their best to present the works to the public in the form of piano reductions, in the context of the concerts of Vienna's Academic Wagner Society. On December

22, 1884, his favorite pupils Ferdinand Löwe and Joseph Schalk performed the opening movement of the Fourth and the Scherzo of the First Symphony on two pianos in Bösendorfer Hall. Already on the 26th of December, Bruckner wrote to Schalk: "Dr. Helm has written nothing at all about the concert at Bösendorfer's. Since this has been the biggest success I have had in Vienna, I would like to ask you to see to it that something gets reported about it in the *Deutsche Zeitung.*"[10] He had overlooked that fact that Dr. Helm, one of his champions, had reviewed the concert already on December 24. Less than half a year later, on June 19, 1885, he turned to Helm directly with the request to report in the *Deutsche Zeitung* about the successful performance of the Adagio from the Seventh in May of 1885 in Karlsruhe under Mottl.

The story of the publication of Bruckner's scores is a chapter all its own. Until 1885, he lamented repeatedly in his letters that he was unable to find a publisher and that only a few of his works had ever appeared in print[11] – complaints that were not always justified.[12] For of the altogether 131 complete works listed in the index of his works, at least 30, nearly one fourth, that is, were printed during his lifetime. The story of the publications, however, was erratic in its course. After the two early printings from the time in Linz, those of the *Germanenzug* (WAB 70) and the hymn *In St. Angelum custodem* (WAB 18), no other work of his appeared in print for ten long years. In 1878, the Third Symphony (WAB 103) came out at the instigation of Theodor Rättig, and only during the years between 1884 and 1894, after Bruckner's fame had begun to spread, twenty-seven additional works appeared. He received virtually no honoraria for the printing of his works. On the contrary, Friedrich Eckstein, the Schalk brothers and Hermann Levi, who tirelessly promoted the printing of the works, were forced to raise money, and the *Te Deum* was published by Theodor Rättig only after Friedrich Eckstein had assumed the printing costs himself. On November 5, 1884, Bruckner wrote to Anton Vergeiner: "As long as the Doorman [the reference is to Hanslick] does not repeal the banishment, all is lost! A heavy but a certain fate! Whereas recommended persons have received 30,000 marks and more for a symphony, a non-recommended one is unable to submit a symphony to the printer even for nothing."[13] That was not without justice. Johannes Brahms, for example, who had acquired renown early on, received opulent honoraria from his publisher. The reason why Bruckner did not see to the printing of his works in person but left that up to his friends and pupils was perhaps that he knew his own clumsiness in dealing with publishers.

To Johannes Brahms, we know, the honors with which he was showered did not mean much. It was different with Bruckner, who in his later years deliberately strove for honors and loved to receive them. He was, among other things, honorary citizen of the towns of Ansfelden and Linz, honorary member of the choral group *Frohsinn* and the Salzburg Mozarteum, and bearer of the Franz-Josef-Order[14] His delight in distinctions of this kind must be seen as a compensation for the bitterness of the non-recognition he had met with for such a long time.

More than anything else, Bruckner envied his rival Brahms the latter's doctoral title.[15] He had himself tried, unsuccessfully, to obtain an honorary degree from Cambridge University. With the same goal in mind, he signed, three years later, a petition written by a certain Dr. Vincent, which was initially addressed to the president of the University of Pennsylvania and subsequently had a label reading "Cincinnati" glued over it. It has not been ascertained to date whether the petition was actually sent to the American university, or whether Bruckner was taken in by a swindler.[16] It was in any case not until November of 1891, that his long-held wish came true, when the University of Vienna made him an honorary doctor and thereby, as he said in his grateful acceptance speech, gave him the "greatest joy of his life."[17]

Interest in the Extraordinary

> "It remains a psychological enigma, how this gentlest and most peaceable of men – and one no longer all that young, either – at the moment of composing turns into an anarchist, who mercilessly sacrifices everything one would call logic and clarity of development, unity of form and tonality"
>
> *Eduard Hanslick about Bruckner*

Unlike some of his chief contemporaries – Richard Wagner, Franz Liszt, Johannes Brahms, Gustav Mahler, Hugo Wolf – Bruckner was interested neither in literature nor in the theater or the philosophical debates of his time. Of the three-and-a-half years he spent with Bruckner as his pupil, Friedrich Klose could remember Bruckner having read only three books and a brochure (though those repeatedly), namely a work about the Mexican war, an account of a "North Pole Expedition on the Ship Tegetthoff," a small, illustrated volume of biographies of Haydn, Mozart and Beethoven, and a "little tract" about the "miracle-working Virgin of Lourdes." From this Klose concluded that Bruckner had virtually no intellectual "needs."[1]

How ever one may think about that, the fact is that Bruckner took a lively interest in persons in extreme situations as well as in extraordinary things generally. Thus he followed the Austrian North Pole expedition on the *Tegetthoff* during the years 1872 to 1874 with the keenest interest. His pocket calendar contains the note: "8000 miles from the nearest human beings – Tegetthoff."[2]

He loved the sight of the Alps, their height and monumentality. To view Mont Blanc, Europe's highest peak, and the Swiss organs, he took a trip to Switzerland that took him to Zurich, Geneva, Lausanne, Fribourg, Berne and Lucerne. On September 2, he was able to marvel at the panorama of the Mont Blanc massif from "La Flechère." His entries in his pocket calendar document how receptive he was to the sublime in Nature. He enthused about the "gorgeous sunsets" and the "magnificent Bernese Alps" and analyzed his impressions this way: "Behind lower or lopsided peaks one looks at others in the distance; the more distant, and likewise the more lopsided, those others, the better."[3]

He was also interested in pathological and medical cases. In Vienna he liked to go to the restaurant "Riedhof," where medical regulars met for their "doctors' *stammtisch.*" There he associated above all with Dr. Alexander Fraenkel, who after Bruckner's death wrote a detailed report about him, and another physician, Dr. Gustav Riehl. According to Fraenkel, Bruckner regularly listened to the medical conversations with the closest attention, and with a touching concern for the people whose diseased conditions were being discussed, and displayed, moreover, the utmost receptivity for all he branches of science.[4]

Bruckner's interest in the extraordinary was not limited to scientific discoveries and existential borderline situations, but also extended to the vast field of compositional science. It is generally known with what rigor, discipline and conscientiousness he had pursued his studies in music theory. As a teacher, too, he placed a high value on the exact observance of the rules. As his pupil Franz Marschner recorded: "He worked very slowly, both for himself and with us, because most thoroughly. Often we managed to produce only a few lines. 'You gentlemen are working much too fast,' he once said; 'I work very slowly, much more slowly, but I also think about everything that needs to be considered."[5] Yet he drew a sharp line between the thorough mastery of the technical craft of composition and free creativity. His pupil Felix Mottl recorded the following statement in his diary: "While in school, you may not use any forbidden harmonic sequence, but everything must be strictly by the rule. Once you are out of school, if you then bring me a strict and regular work like that, I will throw you out the door."[6] And Ernst Schwanzara, one of his students at the University of Vienna, noted down the dictum that the craftsman-like mastery of the theory could be learned, but that composing required the "divine inspiration" one could not get from instruction.[7] Against this background it becomes clearer why Bruckner committed himself to Wagner and the New Germans, why he enthused about the new, unprecedented, and why he himself became such a bold innovator. For all its polemical acuity, the critical remark by Eduard Hanslick cited at the outset of the chapter contains a grain of truth: the shy Bruckner could at the moment of composing indeed morph into an "anarchist."

"Sympathy with Death"

> "Like a necromancer, he feels drawn by signs and relics of death."
>
> *Oskar Loerke about Bruckner*

In his 1911 essay about Palestrina, Thomas Mann tells about a conversation he had with the *Palestrina* poet Hans Pfitzner. Pfitzner compared his "musical legend" with Richard Wagner's *Meistersinger*, saying: "The difference is most obvious in the respective final scenes. At the end of *Die Meistersinger*, a brightly lit stage, public rejoicing, engagement, all in grand style; in my work, Palestrina, likewise celebrated, but alone, in the twilight of his room under the portrait of the deceased, fantasizing at his organ. *Die Meistersinger* are the apotheosis of the new, praise of the future and of life; in the *Palestrina* everything inclines toward the past, it is dominated by *sympathy with death*." The loaded phrase *sympathy with death* 'moved Thomas Mann deeply, because he had used it himself as a thematic-structural element in a "small" novel he had started to write prior to the War.[1]

Even during his childhood Bruckner had been confronted repeatedly with dying and death, so that one can readily speak of traumatic repercussions. Of his ten siblings, only four survived their childhood: his sisters Rosalia, married Hueber, and Josefa, married Wagenbrenner, his brother Ignaz, and his beloved sister Maria Anna, called "Nani," who remained single, kept house for him and died at the age of 35 of consumption. Another death that greatly upset him was that of his confirmation godfather, friend and teacher Johann Baptist Weiß, who at the age of barely 37 committed suicide in the cemetery of his native village of Hörsching.

All his life Bruckner had a considerable penchant for dead bodies and funeral processions, skulls and exhumations, jury trials and sensational happenings generally. Some commentators have accordingly spoken of "abnormal" traits in his personality and of "necrophiliac tendencies." The term necrophilia, however, is inappropriate here, as, strictly speaking, it signifies a perverse sexual desire for corpses. Bruckner's case is different.

Among the things that interested him vividly was the life and fate of Maximilian, the hapless emperor of Mexico and younger brother of the Emperor Francis Joseph. Dissatisfied with his work in Linz and his life in Austria generally, he played for a while with the idea of emigrating to Mexico or to Russia. He is even said to have received an offer to come to the court of Maximilian in Mexico as court organist.[2] On June 19, 1867, Maximilian was shot by rebels in Querétaro. The execution caused a great stir in Europe; no less an artist than Edouard Manet eternalized the scene in an impressive large-scale painting. The body of Maximilian was transported to Vienna and was to be buried on January 18, 1868, in the Capuchin crypt in Vienna. Two days before, Bruckner wrote to his friend Rudolf Weinwurm in the greatest agitation: "My present request and pestering concerns my highest interest. Even during my illness, this was the only thing that was close to my heart: it was Mexico, Maximilian. I want at all cost to see the body of Maximilian. Be so good, Weinwurm, as to send a completely reliable person to the *Burg*, preferably: have him ask at the office of the chief master of the imperial household, if the body of Maximilian will lie in state visibly, that is, in an open coffin or at least under glass, or if only the closed casket will be on view. Then be so kind as to tell me telegraphically, so that I don't arrive too late. I beg you most urgently to do this. I will refund your expenses with thanks."[3] It is not known whether Bruckner followed through on his intention to travel to Vienna: the passionate tone in which he conveyed his request suggests that he did.

What sets one to thinking are the reports about his conduct at the exhumations of the remains of Franz Schubert and Ludwig van Beethoven in the cemetery of Währing, a suburb of Vienna. After the exhumation of Schubert's corpse on September 12, 1888, measurements and photographs of the master's skull were taken in the presence of a small gathering of fans. Buckner is said to have asked for permission to touch the skull.[4]

The incident was repeated three years later during the exhumation of the remains of Beethoven. Accompanied by his pupil Carl Hruby, Bruckner rode to the Währing cemetery, where a commission of physicians measured and examined the skeleton scientifically. Although the physicians had expressly forbidden it, he supposedly took Beethoven's skull in his hands with the deepest emotion and whispered: "You *will* let me touch you, dear Beethoven, won't you?"[5]

Beethoven was for Bruckner the "incarnation of everything great and sublime in music." Carl Hruby reports: "He wove the hallowed name into all the contingencies of his own life and in critical moments would often ask how Beethoven might have acted in the same situation."[6] He undoubtedly identified in some manner both with Schubert and with Beethoven, so that his touching of their skulls could be seen as a symbolic enactment of this identification.

Strangely enough, Bruckner also exhibited a special interest in the procedures at jury trials and reports about executions, as is told by his pupil August Stradal: "Bruckner devoured these reports with a nervous hunger, and the special edition often did not suffice him: I sometimes had to bring him a dozen newspapers in which some exciting affair was described. Naturally all these papers said pretty much the same thing, but Bruckner painstakingly read every single report about a case that interested him from beginning to end." He had been immeasurably agitated after having attended the trial of a notorious murderer of women. He stayed awake all night prior to the execution to pray for the murderer. The main-spring for this conduct Stradal thought to find in Bruckner's "love of mankind."[7] "Together with his own suffering," his biographers August Göllerich and Max Auer write, "his sympathy for the sufferings of others likewise rose to the highest degree of compassion, something that in turn was an effluence of his genuinely religious cast of mind."[8]

Most illuminating in this connection is the report of a visit by the fifty-year-old to the castle Altpernstein near Kirchhof on the river Krems. After having dwelt in prayer in the castle chapel, he insisted on also seeing the torture chamber and the dungeons. "Suddenly," it is reported, "a nervous twitching ran through his body and, explaining that he had to experience the torments of the solitude, eternal darkness and musty smell of decay at close quarters, he actually crawled back through the small gap into the lightless rock cellarage, had every light be extinguished and even had himself locked up for a while." He remained in the death cell for five whole minutes. Then, with a solemn *resurrexit* (he is risen) he reemerged to the light."[9]

Bruckner is buried in the crypt at St. Florian, directly beneath "his" organ. The free-standing sarcophagus is located across from a niche filled with hundreds or thousands of skulls. He had determined his place of rest in his last will of November 10, 1893: "I wish for my earthly remains to be interred in a metal coffin, to be placed freely, without being lowered, in the crypt beneath the church of the regulated Lateran chapter of the canons of St. Florian, specifically beneath the great organ, and have already secured the consent of the Reverend Lord Prelate during my lifetime." He made two other provisions. The body was to be "injected" (i.e., embalmed) by Professor Richard Paltauf, with whom he had already come to an understanding. Furthermore, the transport and interment of his body was to be "First Class."[10] Bruckner thus wished to be embalmed, and his metal casket was not to be buried beneath the floor. In all probability these provisions are connected with his religious beliefs.

He was by no means unreflective but thought a great deal about death and an afterlife. In a now lost pocket calendar he wrote down a sentence of the anatomist Josef Hyrtl from the latter's 1864 inaugural address as president of the University of Vienna. It reads: "Is the soul the product of the brain's working according to irrefutable organic laws, or is this brain, on the contrary, merely one of the conditions, through which the commerce of an immaterial soul with the world is mediated in space?"[11]

Bruckner had an enormous power of empathy and a considerable gift for identification. He could imagine himself in the psychic condition of people in desperate straits and was burningly interested in existential questions: the borderline situations of life, the torments of solitude and the reality of death. His religious preoccupation with the doctrine of salvation certainly had much to do with this.

Religiosity

> Bruckner was a believer without compare. He believed with an intensity and power that bordered on the miraculous.
>
> *Franz Schalk*

The more carefully one compares the reports that tell us anything about Bruckner's renowned religiosity, the more clearly a many-facetted picture emerges. His pupil Friedrich Klose made some remarkable statements about the matter that seem altogether credible. He writes: "Bruckner was a strictly believing Catholic; what bound him to the cult of his church was not some aesthetic or poetic inclination, but solely the unshakable faith in it, in the omnipotence, wisdom and goodness of his God and the promise of a better beyond." Klose rightly doubts whether Bruckner would have "borne the cross of his existence," as he puts it, as victoriously as he did "if his unshakable faith in a divine providence and justice had not been his firm support."[1] In a letter to his protector Johann Herbeck, Bruckner himself speaks of his "trust in God."[2]

Friedrich Blume aptly remarked about Bruckner's religiosity: "There is no other composer in the 19th century who was rooted so firmly in a lived, heart-deep devoutness, to whom prayer, confession, sacrament and profession were vital elements to such a high degree."[3] It is well known that Bruckner fulfilled his religious duties with extreme conscientiousness. He regularly went to confession –even in his daily life fathers confessor seem to have played a role – he adhered strictly to the fasting rules, and when he felt physically weak, he would always ask for dispensation.[4] That perpetual prayer and spiritual exercises were part of his daily life even in his time in Vienna seemed to many people irreconcilable with the conception they had of an artist. It was this devoutness Johannes Brahms had in mind when he made the much-quoted remark that Bruckner was a poor, crazy man whom the priests of St. Florian had on their conscience. During his final years, as Joseph Schalk and Hugo Wolf agreed, his religiosity increased to a religious mania.

Leopold Nowak called Bruckner a "ceaseless prayer".[5] His prayer notations in his pocket calendars confirm that. From February 1882 to the day of his death on October 11, 1896, he kept a record of his daily prayers. The lists of prayers in his pocket calendars consist of letters and vertical and horizontal lines. Thus the initials R, V, A, S stand for *Rosary, Lord's Prayer (Vaterunser), Hail Mary (Ave Maria)* and *Salve Regina.*[6] The lines evidently signify the number of repetitions of the individual prayers. Other codes like D and Gl have not to date been unlocked. For these prayer lists Bruckner did not use the current calendars but wrote them mostly into an older one – which gives one the impression that he wanted to conceal his innermost being from the public and even from his own pupils, who had access to his apartment.[7] His habit of scrupulously noting down the number of his prayers apparently dates back to his time at St. Florian. Lay brothers in the Augustinian monasteries were obligated by the Lateran Congregation to recite numerous *Paternoster*s and *Ave Maria*s in lieu of observing the regular canonical hours.[8]

As several witnesses have testified, Bruckner had religious visions. According to August Göllerich, he was always deeply moved by the miracle of the Nativity.[9] To his pupil Friedrich Eckstein he occasionally spoke of the shudders evoked in him by the Good Friday liturgy and of the mystery of the night from Maundy Thursday to Good Friday, whereby his facial features supposedly took on a totally changed expression of fear and aching rapture.[10] The authenticity of this report is confirmed by an entry in the autograph of the Mass in E minor, composed in 1866 for the dedication of the votive chapel in the Linz cathedral. When he went over the work ten years later to check its periodic proportions, he noticed that the seven measures (mm. 106-112) before Christ's words in the Gloria formed an irregular period. He tried to correct that but could not succeed. He finally left the passage unchanged but noted with an N.B.: "Mystery (unexpectedly after the 7th measure of the period)."[11] He evidently wanted to say that the mystery of "Jesus Christ" occurred as a "surprise." With Arthur Nikisch, too, he once spoke in Bad Ischl of his religious visions, from which he derived the conception of many of his most splendorous passages in his symphonies.[12] Bruckner felt a profound compassion for suffering humanity – he appears at times even to have identified with the Passion of Christ. When his illness took a turn for the worse in 1892, he is said to have prayed in prostration before the unveiled crucifix on Good Friday: "Lord, you have suffered more than anyone, you understand also my suffering, let it come to you!"[13]

It is said of Ludwig van Beethoven that he greatly esteemed Immanuel Kant and repeatedly studied the latter's *Natural History and Theory of the Heavens* of 1755. The famous utterance in the *Conversation Booklets*, "The moral law within us and the starry heavens above," refers explicitly to Kant.[14] It is not known whether Bruckner had ever heard of Kant. But the starry heavens moved him to reflections as well. As his secretary Anton Meißner reports, he once looked up to the starry sky on the way home and found it incomprehensible how there could be people "who did not love their creator and did not want to believe in him."[15] Generally it seems to have been a puzzle to him that there were intelligent and educated people who did not believe in anything.[16]

Obstinate as he was with regard to atheists, he could be very tolerant toward people of other faiths. His Jewish students he respectfully called "the Israelite gentlemen" ("die Herren Israeliten"). Once when he entered the classroom of a course on the theory of harmony and noticed a new student with black curly hair, he walked up to him and said almost piteously: "Dear child, do you really not believe that the Messiah has already come to earth?"[17] He refused to accept confessional differences between Christians. His pupils and friends included many Protestants, whom he esteemed for their "exceptional intelligence" but also for their energy and industry, though he supposedly did say to Anton Meixner once: "Ya know, Anton, we are two fiery natures and Catholics. Brahms is for cold natures and Protestants!"[18]

Religion and Christianity were topics Bruckner judged more frankly and dispassionately than one would have expected, given his ingrained piety.[19] Having once been asked whether he really believed in the life after death, the possibility of rewards and punishments in the next world and the miraculous efficacy of prayer, he is said to have answered: "I'll tell you what: if the story is true, all the better for me; if it's not true, prayer can't do me any harm either."[20]

The problem of death was one of the themes that Bruckner thought about all his life. The deaths of his mother and of his beloved sister Maria Anna he commented in his letters with the Christian formulation, "Recall to the better world." But he also knew about, and feared, the possibility of what the devout call the "eternal darkness" and placed all his hopes in God' mercy and in the affirmation in the concluding line of the *Te Deum* about the *Nichtzuschandenwerden in Ewigkeit* – the *not being confounded in eternity*.

Anton Bruckner at age 39 (1863)

The sister Maria Anna "Nani" (1836-1870)

The birth house in Ansfelden near Linz

The brother Ignaz (1833-1913)  *The sister Rosalia (1829-1898)*

The Bruckner Organ in the Old Cathedral in Linz

Rudolf Weinwurm (1835-1911) Bruckner's closest friend ever since his years as organist in Linz

Felix Mottl (1856-1911), Bruckner disciple, who later championed his works

Eduard Hanslick (1825-1904), early admirer and later arch-enemy of Bruckner, Vienna's leading music critic

The brothers Joseph and Franz Schalk. Both belonged to Bruckner's circle of disciples and promoted his work. Franz (1857-1911) was regarded as the Bruckner conductor par excellence in the early 20th century. Josef (1863-1931) championed Bruckner especially with the Viennese public.

Josefine Lang (1844-1930), the daughter of a butcher in Linz. She rejected Bruckner's suit and married an estate owner.

Minna Reischl. Bruckner met the merchant's daughter in 1895, when he was 71.
Her parents prevented a marriage Minna also did not want.

Anton Bruckner at the age of 70 (1894)

PART TWO

Sacred Music

Personality and Oeuvre

> "I read his human significance in his work, at the risk of underestimating the artistic worth."
>
> *Karl Amadeus Hartmann about Bruckner*

One of the key issues in the psychology of creativity concerns the secret of artistic inspiration, the question as to the sources and resources from which artists draw. According to an early theory, artistic inspiration comes from on high, as a gift of the Muses or a divine revelation. This notion, which originated in antiquity, runs through European intellectual history like a red thread, a nexus, as it were, connecting the religious belief of a Hildegard von Bingen with the aesthetic views of a Johannes Brahms. It survives in the 20th century as the secular variant according to which the artist does not belong to himself but is guided by the instinct of the production. Thus Arnold Schönberg, during his final years, felt himself to be a mouthpiece of divine power. Karlheinz Stockhausen regarded himself as an emissary conveying messages whose meaning he did not know. In similar terms, Theodor W. Adorno thought that composers like Gustav Mahler and Alban Berg made themselves the "instrument," the "subordinate executor" for the production of significant works of art.

According to a very different view, one often associated with Johann Wolfgang von Goethe, the artist creates from his "inner experience." Many composers, including Richard Wagner, Gustav Mahler, Béla Bartók, Arnold Schönberg or Alban Berg, were firmly convinced that there was a close relation between art and life, and that experience was the indispensable prerequisite, a *conditio sine qua non*, of artistic creation. Thus Mahler confessed on frequent occasions that his music was "lived," that many of his symphonies were autobiographical in conception. Richard Strauss created autobiographical tone poems like *Ein Heldenleben* (op. 40) and *Sinfonia domestica* (op. 53), and many of the personal problems that beset Richard Wagner found artistic expression in his music dramas. The autobiographic dimension of *Tristan und Isolde* is unmistakable, the fatal triangle between Tristan, Isolde and King Marke paralleling Wagner's relationship with Mathilde Wesendonck, the wife of his friend and supporter Otto Wesendonck.

The difficulties Bruckner's contemporaries had with the man and his music are due in part to the fact that he did not fit the common cliché of the artist. Many felt that there was a glaring discrepancy between his "odd"-

seeming personality and the grandeur of his music. As late as 1924, Oskar Lang, who counted Bruckner among the great "metaphysicians" of German music, spoke of his "strange double existence," where an "exceptionally genial endowment" was confined solely to the "unconscious creative activity" as such but genius hardly entered into the "subjective-personal" sphere.[1]

For a long time it was a matter of controversy whether the Romantic doctrine of the unity of the life and work of prominent artists also applied to Bruckner. Thus Rudolf Louis stated emphatically in the preface to the first edition of his monograph of 1905: "There is hardly any other musician of the modern age in whom the artist is so closely and indissolubly linked to the man, where the work of art is as faithful and honest a mirror image of its creator's human individuality as is the case with Bruckner."[2] By contrast, the anthroposophist Erich Schwebsch seems to have been the first to maintain that the composer Bruckner's "external biography" was altogether superfluous for the interpretation of his music. "The outward life," Schwebsch thought, "therefore also plays in fact no significant role in the genesis of his works."[3]

It can be shown that this view is altogether beside the mark.

Music as Religious Confession

> "Music can never, and in no combination it enters into, cease to be the highest, most redemptive of all the arts."
> *Richard Wagner*

The meaning of life has always been a chief conundrum of philosophy, especially of the Philosophy of Life and Existentialism. Countless thinkers, writers and artists have pondered it time and again. Two diametrically opposed philosophical outlooks, which one can label by the catchwords Idealism and Philosophy of the Absurd respectively, suggest very different answers to this question. The representatives of the former answer the question, whether life has any meaning, in the affirmative, setting out from the assumption of a comprehensive world order and a firmly established system of values. Mystics, as well as thinkers like Blaise Pascal, Søren Kierkegaard or Gabriel Marcel, find their answer to the problem of existence in religious faith. The adherents of the opposite outlook, on the other hand, deny that existence has any absolute meaning and confess themselves atheists. Their motto is: there is no God, no transcendence, no afterlife, no tomorrow, no scale of values, no hope and also no consolation. According to Albert Camus, the myth of Sisyphus centers in the fundamental decision "whether life is worth it or not." "There is," Camus says, "only one really serious philosophical problem: that of suicide."[1]

Sigmund Freud regarded religion as an illusion, but he was willing to think about the source of religiosity. He was prompted to do so by his friend Romain Rolland, who traced religiosity back to an "oceanic" feeling – "a special feeling, which never left him personally, which he found confirmed by many others, and which he could assume to exist in millions of human beings." Rolland called this feeling the sense of "eternity," a feeling of something limitless, unbounded, in short, "oceanic."[2]

If one accepts this view, one would be inclined to see in music a medium uniquely adapted to giving commensurate expression to such an "oceanic" feeling. No wonder, then, that especially the Romantics kept referring to the close relation between music and religion. For Wilhelm Heinrich Wackenroder, music was the "holy art,"[3] for Ludwig Tieck, "the ultimate secret of faith, the mystique, the completely revealed religion";[4] and E. T. A. Hoffmann had no doubt that by its "innermost, unique nature," music was nothing other than a "religious cult," wherefore he thought he found its origin solely in religion.[5] In a letter to an unknown addressee, Franz Liszt wrote on May 20, 1865, that music was in its essence religious and, like the human soul, *naturaliter* Christian.[6] Today, no one will deny that music has a special affinity to the cultic,[7] albeit not exclusively to that but also to such other areas as magic, the arcane and the erotic.

It is justly said of some books that they changed the world. The *Confessions* of St. Augustine is surely one of them. Written abut 400 C. E., it astonishes even today by its modernity. In thirteen books, Augustine delineates his road from being a passionate pagan to becoming a devout Christian and expatiates in meditations and reflections about existential and philosophical questions, the problem of time and, above all, his personal relation to God. The *Confessions* impress not so much by their theological knowledge as by their religious subjectivism, and anticipate by centuries the so-called confessional literature – a genre that became regularly established only in the 18th century, when multitudes of writers, from Jean-Jacques Rousseau to Marcel Proust, Thomas Mann or Norman Mailer, began to try their hand at the genre of the literary confession.

The notion that art is confession or profession took possession of music as well. Sacred music is often religious confession. Ever since the 19th century, countless composers have declared their allegiance to religious, philosophical, social and humanitarian ideas in their musical works. Almost the entirety of Richard Wagner's music dramas can be viewed against this background. A work like Gustav Mahler's Resurrection Symphony proclaims the composer's belief in immortality,[8] and Anton Bruckner, too, conceived of his productions as "professions." He let himself be guided by the conviction that the "good Lord" had destined him for art[9] and regarded his compositional talent as God-given – as his repeatedly confirmed allusions to the Parable of the Talents plainly import. Thus it becomes understandable that the feeling of responsibility for his creative work determined his entire life. According to Josef Kluger, his compositional work was borne by his "sense of responsibility to God."[10]

Bruckner's oeuvre repeatedly takes on traits of a religious dialogue: he evidently conversed with the Being that was the highest spiritual authority for him. And it is a part of this nexus that he had a recurrent need to give thanks for the surmounting of critical situations. In May of 1885, he told the conductor Hermann Levi that he had dedicated the *Te Deum* to God "as a thanksgiving for the many afflictions overcome in Vienna."[11] It is therefore only logical that the letters O.A.M.D.G. should be emblazoned on the title page of this important work, the abbreviation of the famous device of the Jesuit order, *Omnia ad majorem Dei gloriam*, "All to the greater glory of God" – a formula one also encounters in other works of Bruckner's.[12] The formula strongly reminds of the device *Soli Deo Gloria* at the end of many of Johann Sebastian Bach's scores.

The *Te Deum* is by no means Bruckner's only confessional work. His desire to give thanks for his recovery from his grave illness in 1867 motivated the repeat performance of his F minor Mass in Linz on January 6, 1868.[13] And by including quotations from the "Benedictus" and the "Kyrie" of this Mass in his Second Symphony, he wanted, much later, to give thanks for the rescue from a "spiritual death."[14] Johann Wolfgang von Goethe stated that all of his works were merely "fragments of a great confession":[15] it is no exaggeration to say that this characterization also, and more literally, fits the work of Anton Bruckner.

A New, Dramatic Conception of the Mass

> "Bruckner's church music, too, is an honest and faithful image of his personality."
>
> *Rudolf Louis*

Bruckner was very much a "late-bloomer" as a composer. Whereas Schumann and Brahms wrote their first masterpieces already at twenty, and Richard Wagner composed his *Flying Dutchman* at the age of twenty-eight, Bruckner was forty years old when, in 1864, he completed his F minor Mass in Linz, the first work in which he developed his own particular style. The numerous works he had produced until then were undoubtedly important for his musical development: through them he learned to master the craft and techniques of composition and the various musical styles. Even so, his early works hardly offer a hint of his later characteristics and originality. For proof of this one need only compare his Missa solemnis in B flat minor, written in 1854 at St. Florian, with the D minor Mass completed ten years later in Linz.

Bruckner composed the Missa solemnis for mixed choir, orchestra and organ for the solemn enthronement (infulation) of the prelate Friedrich Theophil Mayr, which took place on September 14, 1854. Leopold Nowak held that one could look at the Missa as a "summa musica" of the first thirty years of Bruckner's life, and thought he could detect in it both the summation and the difference of diverse styles – Viennese classicism and pre-classicism, Bachian fugue technique, mixed with elements of the Romantic period. The solidly composed work must in any case have impressed the noted Viennese musicologist Simon Sechter, since after having looked through the manuscript in 1855, he instantly accepted Bruckner as his pupil.

Much happened in Bruckner's musical training during the ten years that lie between the B flat minor and the D minor Mass. After the six years of studying music theory with Sechter and the intensive course in composition with Otto Kitzler, Bruckner's encounter with the music of Wagner, triggered by his attending a performance of *Tannhäuser* on February 12, 1863 in Linz, acted like a catalyst enabling him to find his own artistic individuality. In addition, Bruckner began to be interested in the music of Franz Liszt and Hector Berlioz, two further exponents of the "New Music" to whom Otto Kitzler and Ignaz Dorn had drawn his attention.[1] With Dorn, Bruckner studied Liszt's Faust Symphony, which he admired – Dorn even made him a present of his own copy of the work.`[2] How eager Bruckner was to acquaint himself with works by Liszt and Berlioz we can also gather from the fact that in August of 1865 he traveled from Linz all the way to Budapest for the premiere of Liszt's *Legend of St. Elizabeth* and then attended Berlioz's *La damnation de Faust* performed on December 16 in Vienna under the baton of the composer.[3] It is important for Bruckner's artistic development that in writing his great Easter masses during the years in Linz he also sought to orient himself on Liszt's sacred compositions.[4]

In his short, fragmentary essay of 1834, "On Future Church Music," the young Liszt wrote that the church music of his dreams – he called it *musique humanitaire* – should be "solemn, strong and effective," should unite "church and theater in colossal proportions," and should be "at once dramatic and holy, splendorous and simple, solemn and serious, fiery and unbridled, stormy and peaceful, clear and heart-felt."[5] It is safe to say that in his Gran Solemn Mass Liszt essentially realized this youthful ideal. It is no accident that contemporary critics frequently emphasized the "dramatic style" of this mass,[6] as it manifests itself in the conception and interpretation of the text, in strong contrasts, in effects that caused offense to some, fanfares and signals, prominent ostinato rhythms, innovative instrumentation and the use of the leitmotif technique.

We know from August Stradal, a Liszt pupil and confidant of Bruckner's, that the latter dearly loved Liszt's two great masses, the Gran Mass and the Hungarian Coronation Mass.[7] Regrettably, Stradal did not indicate at what time Bruckner first knew these two works. The Gran Mass, which is the one that interests us here, composed in 1855 in Weimar, was premiered on August 31, 1856 in the cathedral of Gran and was performed repeatedly thereafter, in Budapest, in Prague, in Vienna and in Leipzig. The score with underlaid piano reduction was printed in large format at state expense and was published in 1859 by the Austro-Hungarian State Press in Vienna.[8] Bruckner's D minor Mass, as mentioned before, originated only in 1864, his E minor Mass dates from 1866, and the F minor Mass was completed in 1868.

Numerous correspondences and analogies between the Gran Mass and Bruckner's D minor Mass prove that Bruckner knew Liszt's mass before he embarked on the composition of his own. To begin with, it is both striking and symptomatic that an eight-note phrase from the *Agnus Dei* of Liszt's mass recurs in nearly identical form in the Gloria of the D minor Mass:

Liszt, Graner Messe (1855), *Agnus Dei*
T. 114-121

Bruckner, d-moll-Messe (1864), *Gloria*
T. 100-103

Musical Example 1

Perhaps even more significant than this correspondence is the fact that, like Liszt, Bruckner conceives the text at least in part dramatically in his great masses, makes use of the leitmotif technique, and in the concluding *dona nobis pacem* has recourse to motifs from the Kyrie, the Gloria and the Credo.

18th-century mass composition obeys a cyclical conception to the extent that thematic links between the *dona nobis pacem* and the Kyrie are not unique to the masses of Joseph Haydn and Mozart. Among the many innovations that the Gran Solemn Mass introduced all at once, however, is the fact that the final movement not only refers back to the Kyrie but also cites motifs from the Gloria and the Credo. Liszt's intention was poetic in nature, namely to suggest "that the blessing resulting from the prayer heard by God is the strengthening of the faith 'that moves mountains.'"[9] Thus the mass ends on the Credo theme, the concluding falling fifth being nothing other than the very germ of that theme. Bruckner follows Liszt to the extent that in the *dona nobis pacem* of both the D minor and the F minor mass he quotes not only from the Kyrie but also from the Gloria and the Credo.

The realization that Bruckner composes several parts in his great orchestral masses in a dramatic way has confused many a present musicologist;[10] the critics of the masses in Bruckner's own time were a good deal more perceptive. Thus the reviewer for the *Salzburger Zeitung* of September 12, 1870, wrote about the D minor Mass: "Although the work as a whole shares the pronounced standpoint of the new direction in music and pays homage to the throughout dramatic conception and rendition of the sacred text, it can nevertheless be lauded for a unified style and in part also concise musical expression."[11] The *Linzer Zeitung* noted after the premiere of the work in 1864: "After Liszt, we can call Herr Bruckner's Mass in D the most outstanding work of most recent times in the area of church music."[12] The critic of the *Wiener Fremdenblatt*, reviewing the F minor Mass, gave Bruckner credit for immersing himself "with poetic understanding" in the "situations created by the text of the mass" but thought he had to censure him because now and then he let himself be "seduced" by the "dramatic content" of the texts to "verge on the theatrical."[13]

The Credo Settings

Of the plethora of sacred music of the 19th century, only a small amount has stood the test of time, among it Bruckner's great masses from the Linz period and his *Te Deum* – four works that are still heard in the concert hall today. The reason for that is not only their accomplished structure and architectonic but also the quality of their highly original music, their expressive power and, not least, their spiritual depth.

The Credo – the Nicean creed – is the centerpiece of the Latin mass. Newly translated from Greek into Latin in the eighth century, it gives expression to the belief in the Trinity, reviews the principal stations of Christ's Passion, adds the commitment to the Catholic Apostolic Church, and concludes with the expectation of the resurrection of the dead and a life everlasting. The more than a thousand year-long history of Credo settings has been presented more than once, historically as well as analytically.[1] The question, on the other hand, how composers interpreted the theological text musically, has, if at all, been discussed only marginally. It is to be the central question here.

Setting the Credo to music has confronted composers with rather complicated problems, and still does. To begin with, how is one to express the unity of the belief in the Trinity in music? Bruckner may not yet have been aware of this problem while working on the Credo of his Missa solemnis in B flat minor.[2] At all events, the latter clearly divides into four sections, an Allegro moderato in B flat major, an Adagio in F major, an Allegro moderato in B flat major in three-fourths time and an Allegro moderator in B flat major in four-fourths time. Each section is independent in motif and theme: one will look in vain for cyclically recurring, leitmotiv-like elements. To all appearances, Liszt was the first who, in the Credo of the Gran Mass, treated the main subject most ingeniously in leitmotif fashion in such a way that the aimed-at expression of the Trinity is brought home symbolically to the listener. For the succinct orchestral theme that precedes the intonation of the words *Credo in unum Deum* recurs, in different keys and timbres, also in the sections that deal with Christ and with the Holy Spirit. Moreover, it is picked up again in the confession of belief in the Apostolic Church, in a lively measure (Allegro militante in alla breve time), as though to demonstrate the glorification of the *ecclesia militans*.

Bruckner treats the main orchestral theme in the Credo of the D minor Mass in a similar fashion. It is intoned in D major every time the chorus professes its belief in the Father, the Son and the Holy Spirit. Even more persuasive is the treatment of the main theme in the Credo of the F minor Mass. Here the theme, functioning as a leitmotif, recurs every time the chorus sings of the belief in God conceived as Trinity and of belief in a life hereafter. The following table of motifs will illustrate the connections.

Musical Example 2

How can the changing situations of the *Heilsgeschichte* – Incarnation and Birth, Crucifixion, Passion and Entombment, Resurrection, Ascension, Second Coming and Last Judgment – be interpreted musically in the Credo? Both Liszt and Bruckner dramatized the story and transmuted religious images into musical ones, making liberal use of tone symbols.

The incarnation of the Son of God is the fundamental sacrament of Christianity. It is therefore only natural that even before Liszt and Bruckner many composers were impelled to give it a special treatment. Thus in Franz Schubert's Mass in E flat major D950 – a work that Bruckner is likely to have known – the *Et incarnatus est* is intoned three times by three soloists, first by the first tenor, then by the second tenor and finally by the soprano, in such a way that the solo singing gradually becomes a duet and then a trio.

In the Credo of the Gran Mass, Liszt treats the *Et incarnates* relatively briefly. But he emphasizes it by a variety of means: to begin with, by using a bright sharp key, secondly by a soprano solo, which at one point is accompanied by mixed chorus; thirdly by a soloist treatment of the strings, fourthly, by an almost ethereal accompaniment from the woodwinds, which enact hovering eighths repetitions, and fifthly by the markings *dolce* and *dolcissimo*. In this way the music conveys the impression of an extraordinary tenderness.

The key relations are exceptional: The Credo of the Gran Mass is in C major; the key of the *Et incarnates est* is F sharp major. The Credo of Bruckner's D minor Mass is in D major; the *Et incarnatus* is keyed again in F sharp major. But it is the *Et incarnatus* of the F minor Mass (a piece that a contemporary of Bruckner's counted among the most significant works "modern church music has to offer"[3]) that documents most impressively how extensively Bruckner was inspired by the Gran Mass. The section *Moderato misterioso* is in E major, while the basic key of the Credo is C major. The text is sung as a tenor solo, which in some passages is supported by the female voices of the mixed chorus. The strings pause, except for a solo violin and viola, which recite highly expressive figurations *dolce*. The woodwinds accompany hoveringly in eighths repetitions. Two excerpts will illustrate the similarity in composition.

Christ's becoming human does not constitute a separate section in any of the three Linz masses; instead, the music of the *Et incarnatus est* is further developed. The mystery of God becoming human finds its appropriate expression mainly in the dynamics (*piano* or *pianissimo*) and in the, at times, audaciously modulated harmonies: both in the D minor and in the F minor Mass, the music modulates from F sharp minor to C major! The recital of the words *homo factus est* is different in the three Credo movements. Whereas in the Credo of the D minor Mass they are sung by the chorus and in the E minor Mass at first by the female voices and the tenors and then by the basses solo and in a very low position, Bruckner in the F minor Mass distributes them over the individual voices, whereby the *pianissimo* of the basses at the beginning is especially memorable.

[Musical notation: Liszt, Graner Messe, Credo, T. 93-96, Sopran - Solo]

[Musical notation: Bruckner, f-moll-Messe, Credo, T. 117-120, Tenor - Solo]

Musical Example 3

Ever since Johann Sebastian Bach, at the latest, composers of sacred music have used chiastic note figures to symbolize the crucifixion, that is to say, characteristic motifs, whose notes are arranged cross-wise (chiastically). Famous instances include the chorus *Laß ihn kreuzigen* from the St. Matthew Passion, the *Crucifixus* of Schubert's Mass in A flat Major D 678, completed in 1822, and the Requiem of Antonín Dvořák (see Musical Example 5d).

Liszt and Bruckner, as far as I can see, did not employ this figure in their sacred music, perhaps because both had a predilection for another cross symbol. In a long note to the score of his *Legend of St. Elisabeth* (completed in 1862 and published in 1868), Liszt indicated that he had used the Gregorian intonation g-a-c in numerous of his compositions as a "tone symbol of the cross." In the *Legend*, for example, it serves as the main motif of the chorus of the Crusaders (No. 3).

From it, incidentally, Liszt fashioned the theme of the fugue *Cum Sancto Spiritu* in his Gran Mass. I have shown elsewhere that several prominent composers of the 19th century (besides Bruckner also Wagner and Mahler) paid close attention to this tone symbol of Liszt's and employed it in their compositions in the same or a similar function.[4]

The Legend of St. Elisabeth premiered on Tuesday, August 15, 1865, in Budapest, under Liszt's direction. Another indication of how strongly Bruckner was interested in Liszt's music is the fact that he traveled all the way to Budapest to attend this premiere. The score of the work was published in February of 1868 by Christian Friedrich Kahnt in Leipzig, but a piano reduction had appeared there already in March of 1867. Remarks made by Bruckner to his students at the university indicate that he had studied the work in detail.

Bruckner uses the tone symbol in a manner all his own, including it in exposed positions in his movements, preferably intoned by the trumpets in double or triple *forte*. Whenever it accompanies, or is directly intoned by, the chorus, the text sung refers to images like the crucifixion, the resurrection or God the Father in Heaven. The symbolic motif plays a special role in the Adagio of the Ninth Symphony (1894), where it is sounded by the trumpet at the first two climaxes of the movement (at A and H) – not just once but several times in a row!

Musical Example 4

The three *Crucifixus* settings of Bruckner's Linz period differ greatly from each other. The *Crucifixus* of the D minor Mass has pronounced dramatic features. After a preparatory two-beat crescendo of the orchestra, which is highly turbulent throughout, the chorus sharply declaims, unisono and *fortissimo*, the words *Crucifixus etiam pro nobis sub Pontio Pilato*, whereby no word is repeated. The *Crucifixus* of the E minor Mass, by contrast, is structured like a chorale. Intoned *pianissimo* at first, it sets occasional expressive accents but rarely leaves the *piano* sphere, sounding overall like a prayer. Clarinets and bassoons, supported by the horns, accompany the words *Crucifixus, crucifixus* recited chorale-like. In the *Crucifixus* of the F minor Mass, Bruckner likewise set out from the idea of a chorale, but by means of dynamic differentiation, numerous verbal repetitions, inclusion of a bass solo, entrance of the trombones and a restless syncopated accompanying line in the violins and the celli respectively, developed the section into a miniature dramatic scene.

The passion and entombment of Christ are commemorated laconically with the simple words *passus et sepultus est* in the Credo text. In the D minor Mass, Bruckner lets the chorus recite the word *Passus* twice a cappella. A descending tone sequence is harmonized primarily with the diminished seventh chord, the tone symbol of suffering from time immemorial. In a similar fashion, but not a cappella, the words *passus, passus* are recited by the chorus in the E minor Mass. Far more differentiated and highly dramatic is the treatment of the passage in the F minor Mass. Several cries of *passus* of the chorus are here framed by intonations of the bass soloist. Especially characteristic of the three Linz masses is the fact that the words *sepultus est* are followed by a *pianissimo* intonation of the trombones. This "funeral chorale" is a Bruckner specialty. It is found neither in Schubert's not in Liszt's masses, and it is also missing from his own Missa solemnis of 1854.[5]

Liszt's and Bruckner's dramatic conceptions of the text become fully manifest in the four thematic areas Resurrection, Ascension, Second Coming and Last Judgment. Thus Liszt illustrates the Resurrection by a crescendo that rises all the way to *fortissimo*. In the Credo of his D minor Mass, Bruckner outdoes this expressive device. The entrance of the *Et resurrexit* is prepared for by a mighty and very long crescendo in the orchestra (28 measures), which was quite off-putting to Bruckner's contemporaries. Thus the reviewer of the *Linzer Zeitung* wrote after the Linz premiere of the mass on November 20, 1864:

The *et resurrexit*, too, is full of beautiful musical effect, though we would have preferred a different conception. By commencing with the double basses and then adding instrument after instrument, it takes Bruckner 28 whole measures before he can finally reach the convincing *et resurrexit* in the vocal section, If this conception, which adheres to the new direction in music, might find a defense in the perhaps too literal interpretation of the words, we yet do not believe to be in the wrong when we say that the impression produced is of someone rising up with great difficulty. The passage (the Savior is risen) would be more overwhelming and convincing without these preparatory introductions, which are based on a naturalistic way of thinking."[6]

In the Credo of the F minor Mass, the *Et resurrexit* is prepared for in a like manner, except that the crescendo here is shorter: it is eight measures in length and rises from *pianissimo* to *fortissimo*. But already in his Missa solemnis of 1854 Bruckner had employed unusual means for the *Et resurrexit*. The resurrection is here imagined quasi-pictorially in a five-measure crescendo of the orchestra with the addition of the time-honored anabasis figure: above a fixed pedal point, the violins and violas rise in sixths chords in stringent chromaticism from f^1 to b-flat^2. As one can see, already the thirty-year-old Bruckner liked to experiment with sounds.

A number of motives constitute the Christian representation of the Last Judgment: Christ enthroned in the clouds, the twelve apostles as jurors, graves that open and angels with bright trumps, whom the Son of Man sends out to gather in his elect (Matth. 24:30-31). In Bruckner's musical representation of the Second Coming (*et iterum venturus est*) and the Judgment (*judicare vivos et mortuos*), trombone signals dominate altogether – perhaps for the first time in this passage in the history of mass composition. In addition, Bruckner works in both of the orchestral masses with fanfare-like motifs, tympani rolls and ostinato rhythms (often dotted), all of which have leitmotif significance. He thus reaches a high measure of drama.[7] Signal-like motifs by the trombones, incidentally, occur also in Liszt's Gran Mass, albeit earlier, in the section *Et resurrexit* (Credo, mm. 175-187). Liszt also achieves dramatic effects in the *Judicare* section, not least by an ostinato rhythm in the brasses, intoned no fewer than ten times (mm. 203-212).

The confession of belief in a holy Catholic and Apostolic Church is set to a unisono chorus melody in Bruckner's Linz masses, as also already in the Missa solemnis of 1854 – a tone-symbolic treatment underlining the unity of the church and of some tradition in mass composition. Liszt in his Gran Mass writes a four-part fugue at this point.

The expectation of the general resurrection of the dead is intellectually associated with the resurrection of the Lord in the Credo text. It is characteristic for Bruckner's subtle leitmotivic interpretation of the text that in the Missa solemnis of 1854 as well as in the F minor Mass the section *Et expecto resurrectionem* picks up the music of *Et resurrexit* exactly, thus building a deeply meaningful bridge between the two. There is, besides, an abrupt, uncanny contrast between the *expecto resurrectionem*, on the one hand, and the *mortuorum*, on the other. In both the D minor and the F minor Mass the *expecto resurrectionem* is exclaimed by the chorus in a relatively high register, whereas the alto voices, tenors and basses intone the *mortuorum pianissimo* and in unison in the low register.

Bruckner's dramatic interpretation of the Credo text manifests itself above all in changing images, in the use of leitmotifs and in stark contrasts, for which he had a special affinity and a sure instinct. Sudden contrasts are found repeatedly in his Credo settings. To cite one additional example: in the Credo of the F minor Mass, the visible world is represented differently than the invisible one. While the word *visibilium* is quasi recited by the chorus, *piano* and in unison on the note of d, at the word *iinvisibilium* the whole segment is transposed a half-tone lower and sung *pianissimo*. The effect of this passage can be called shadowy.

Religious Tone Symbolism

> "Everything is after all to be taken only symbolically, and everywhere there is something else behind it."
> *Goethe to Chancellor Müller, June 8, 1821*

The spiritual depth dimension in Bruckner's sacred music is like a vast subterranean plain, on which something new can always be discovered. His Credo settings impress, as we have seen, not only by their mastery of the compositional techniques but also by their dramatic conception and their rich pictorial language. In pursuing this track further, and delving into details, one soon comes upon further connections. Particular intervallic constellations and chord progressions recur both in the masses and in the *Te Deum* like a musical vocabulary with symbolic functions (intentions).

In 1934, the prominent musicologist Robert Haas made some observations about the tone symbolism in Bruckner that deserve our attention. He pointed out that Bruckner must have known and studied two of Joseph Haydn's masses, the Harmony Mass and the Lord Nelson Mass, since he "borrowed" from both. Thus the Kyrie of the D minor Mass contains three "leading musical ideas" that are borrowed from the Lord Nelson Mass, namely the "downward octave leap," the "chromatically filled fourth thesis" and the "diatonic descending fourth."[1]

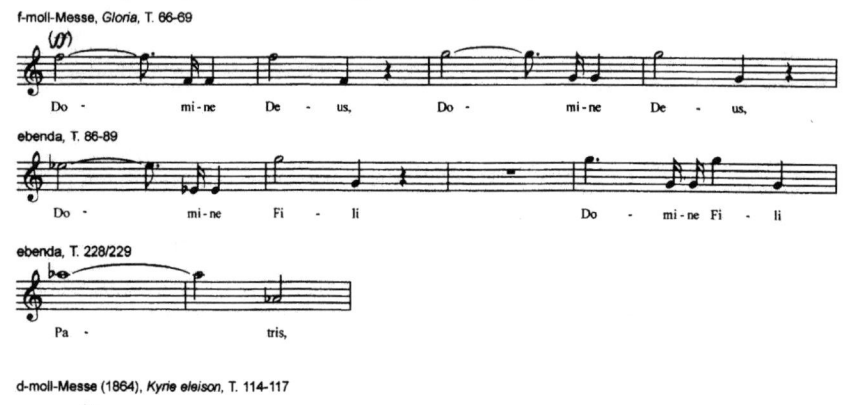

Octave drop as Symbol of "divine grandeur" (Haas)

Potentiated Octave drop

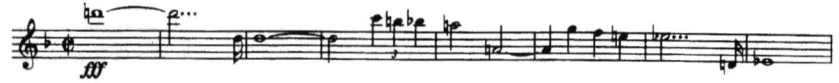

Musical Example 5a

"Fifth-Octave drop" as symbol of majesty
Te Deum, T. 1-5

ff gestrichen

Dritte Symphonie, Kopfsatz, T. 5-7

Variant: Octave drop with upbeat fourth

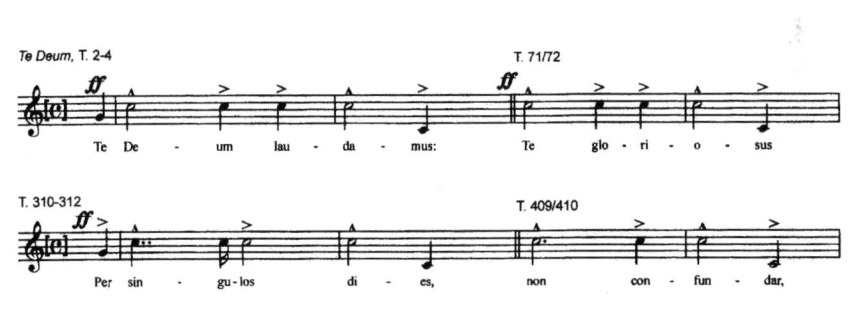

d-moll-Messe (1864), *Gloria*, T. 8-10

lau - da - mus te,

Te Deum, T. 2-4   T. 71/72

Te De - um lau - da - mus: Te glo - ri - o - sus

T. 310-312   T. 409/410

Per sin - gu - los di - es, non con - fun - dar,

Musical Example 5b

The chromatic fourth passage (its technical term is *passus duriusculus*, the somewhat rough passage) is part of the repertoire of musical-rhetorical figures and served as symbol of suffering and imploring entreaties in the music of the 17th and 18th century.[2] Haas interprets it as an "emblem of mercy on human weakness" in Bruckner. Bruckner was also very familiar with other figures, including the anabasis (going up, ascent) and the katabasis (going down, descent) – two figures that one can find in his masses with the words *ascendit* and *descendit*.

Rising and falling minor third
Kyrie eleison – Motive

F sharp major or G flat major as "mystical apparition of Christ"

Musical Example 5c

Haydn uses the interval of the falling octave in the Lord Nelson Mass to set the words *Kyrie, Kyrie eleison.* The memorable interval recurs, as Haas pointed out, not only in the Kyrie, but also in the Gloria and the Credo of Bruckner's D minor Mass, as a symbol of "divine grandeur." In pursuing this investigation, one will encounter the octave drop also in the E minor and the F minor Mass, quasi as an invocation, with the words *Christe, Domine Deus, Domine Fili, Patris* and *Hosanna,* as well as in the *Te Deum* with the words *Te Deum laudamus, Te gloriosus, Per singulo dies, non confundar,* to name only the most striking instances. There can be no doubt that this prime expression serves as symbol of majesty, and it is especially noteworthy in this connection that the main theme of the first movement of the Ninth Symphony is nothing other than a three-fold potentiated octave drop on the basic intervals (d, a and e flat). That this warrior-like symphonic theme also has a religious connotation I regard as certain.

Chiastic Sound Figures as Symbols of the Cross

d-moll-Messe, Credo, T. 177-180
Tenöre + Posaunen

ju - di - ca - re   ju - di - ca - re

Diminished Seventh as Symbol of the Sting of Death

Joh. Seb. Bach, *Matthäus - Passion*

Laß ihn kreu - - - - - - - (zigen)

Franz Schubert, Messe in As-Dur D 678 (1819-1822)
[Grave]

Cru - ci - fi - xus

Antonin Dvořák, Requiem op. 89

Tritonus (*diabolus in musica*) as symbol of the Last Judgment

Te Deum, T. 138-134
Tenöre + Tenorposaune

Tu de-vic-to a - cu - le-o   Tu de-vic-to a - cu - le-o   Tu de-vic-to a - cu - le-o

Musical Example 5d

Along with the octave drop, Bruckner also employs the falling "fifth-octave leap" as a motif with religious connotations. Manfred Wagner pinpointed the semantics here as "symbol of majesty."[3] Typically enough, it plays a prominent role in the *Te Deum,* where it occurs innumerable times in the form of an ostinato figuration, and it returns also in the unfinished finale of the Ninth Symphony, as we will see later in greater detail. It is hardly a coincidence that the famous trumpet theme of the Third Symphony commences with just this "fifth-octave leap."

A further heavily symbolic element in Bruckner's sacred music is the constellation of a rising and falling minor third. Unless I am wholly mistaken, this tone sequence occurs first as *Kyrie* cry in the Missa solemnis of

1854; it is then reused as *Benedictus* invocation in the Benedictus of the E minor Mass and as *Kyrie* cry in the F minor Mass; and it returns finally as a mysterious horn call at the beginning of the first movement of the Ninth Symphony.

Bruckner was, as we have noted, a close reader of the Bible. Nearly all of his mature motifs show that he gave a great deal of thought to the theological meaning of the texts he set to music. Especially revealing in this respect are, to begin with, the three settings of the gradual in the Maundy Thursday liturgy *Christus est factus*, whose text is taken from the Pauline Epistle to the Philippians (2:8-9) and reads as follows:

Christus factus est	Christ was made for us
Obediens usque ad mortem,	obedient unto death,
Mortem autem crucis,	even the death of the cross.
Propter quod et Deus exaltavit illum,	Wherefore God also hath highly exalted him
et dedit illi nomen	and given him a name
quod est super omne nomen.	Which is above every name.

Bruckner's three settings of the gradual differ greatly, both in style and in expression. The first (WAB 9), conjecturally composed in 1844, forms the first movement of the mass for Maundy Thursday for a four-part mixed a cappella chorus. The second (WAB 10) from the year 1873 provides for a large ensemble (eight-part mixed chorus, strings and three trombones). The third (WAB 11), finally, composed in Vienna in 1884 for four-part a cappella chorus and dedicated to Father Oddo Loidol, bears the expression mark *Moderato misterioso*. In both the second and the third setting, Bruckner gives special weight to the final line (*quod est super omne nomen*): in WAB 10 by an immense successive rise from one to eight choral voices, in WAB 11 by a six-fold repetition with constantly increasing expression.[4]

In a study published in 1965, Leopold Nowak was able to show convincingly that in all of his sacred compositions after 1861, Bruckner, by various accentuating means, makes the words *Jesus Christus* clearly stand out from their surroundings.[5] Thus in the seven-part *Ave Maria* (WAB 6), the name Jesus occurs three times in rising dynamics: at first *pianissimo*, then *piano* and finally *fortissimo*. Naturally the name is also accentuated in different ways in the three Linz masses. Robert Haas noticed in 1934 that in the first three movements of the D minor Mass, the music shifts into F sharp major as soon as Christ is the subject, and he spoke not without justice of a "mystic apparition of Christ."[6] Sudden shifts to F sharp major or else G flat major in fact occur also in the E minor Mass (Gloria, mm. 113-115) and in the F minor Mass (Kyrie mm. 67-71), as well as in the *Te Deum* (mm. 121-124), as soon as the name of Jesus Christ is invoked.[7] It is possible that Bruckner got his inspiration for this association of key from Liszt's Gran Mass, where the *Et incarnates* is set in the remote key of F sharp major. In any case, both the bright sharp key of F sharp major and the twilight of the G flat major must have appeared to both Liszt and Bruckner as uniquely suited for musically emblematizing something as mysterious and miraculous as the Son of God becoming Man.

A further example is offered by the gradual *Virga Jesse* of 1885, one of Bruckner's boldest and most beautiful motets. It begins in E minor, modulates though numerous keys and closes in E major. In the course of that, the passage *Virgo Deum et hominem genuit* (the Virgin gave birth to both God and man) is emphasized dynamically by a *fortissimo* and set in the remote keys of G flat major and B flat major. A study of the motets reinforces the impression that Bruckner devised the modulatory plan of his sacred compositions also with a view to the symbolism and semantics of important passages.

The characterization of specific keys has a long tradition that can be traced back all the way to antiquity. At the latest from the Baroque period on, numerous composers have been preoccupied with it. Bruckner once told his listeners at the University of Vienna that he liked the old keys because they had "something mystical about them.[8] Some of his motets are in fact written in the old church modes, thus in the Phrygian (*Pange lingua*, *Tota pulchra* and *Vexilla regis*) and in the Lydian (*Os justi*). All of these compositions Bruckner handles in striking conformity with the rules of the 16th century, at the same time employing cadences and modulations as elements of a musical language with semantic implications.[9] To his private pupil Max von Oberleithner we owe the information that Bruckner had his own definite views about the character of different major and minor keys. According to Oberleithner, Bruckner in 1889 remarked the following: "F sharp minor is yearning, F minor melancholy, D minor solemn, mysterious, A minor gentle, E minor lyrical; D minor I like so well that I am writing my last symphony in it. If a Beethoven has his Ninth in D minor, he will not have anything against it."[10] Regrettably such specifications are only sporadic. In any case, we can presume as certain that the bright and dark tonal effects in his so colorful music are also based on reflections about the character of individual keys.

Viewed as a whole, Bruckner's motet opus exhibits a remarkable variety. While many choruses stand out by their simplicity and are diatonic in their overall tenor, others surprise us by their bold, modern harmonies and a delight in modulation that makes extraordinary demands on the performers. Some pieces include Gregorian or pseudo-Gregorian turns.[11] Others are not free of the spirit of "Caecilianism," a trend aiming at a renewal of Catholic church music by a recourse to the style of Palestrina[12]. This is true especially of the Phrygian *Pange lingua* (WAB 33), which Bruckner wrote already in 1868 in Linz and, in 1885, put at the disposal of Franz Xaver Witt, the founder of the "General German Caecilia Society," for publication as a musical supplement in the journal *Musica sacra*. Above all it is true of the Lydian *Os justi* (WAB 30) of 1879, which Bruckner dedicated to St. Florian's music director Ignaz Traumihler, who was also a Caecilian.[13]

Jubilant and Devout Music

The Credo score of Franz Liszt's Gran Mass contains numerous "performance marks" that provide information about the changing expression of the music and about the intentions of the composer. The initial heading *Andante maestoso, risoluto* conveys a sense of the composition's overall character. The intonation of the belief in Jesus Christ is preceded by "jubilant" figures in the violins and violas. The words *Deum de Deo* (at B) the soloist is to recite "loftily and very expressly." The section that deals with Christ's descent from heaven and his incarnation is headed *Andante con divozione*, and repeatedly uses the marks *dolce suave* and *dolcissimo*. The four measures in which the orchestra introduces the *et homo factus est* are dominated by whole-tone sounds containing tritones and bear the heading *Doloroso flebile* – an indication that Liszt wanted to interpret already the incarnation as a sorrowful event. *Et in Spiritum Sancturm* is to be the sung "loftily and expressly" again. Finally, the words *et unam sanctam catholicam et apostolicam ecclesiam* (the profession of commitment to the Church) is to be presented "very energetically and fierily." These "expression marks" already convey a sense of the expressive scale of music, which ranges over every shade from devotion to rejoicing jubilation.

The music Bruckner wrote for his three great masses is likewise abundant in expressive features, although he is sparing with "expression marks."

One could generalize by saying that his masses range between "jubilant" and "devout" music, whereby the shades in between comprise a whole cosmos of expressive characters. The powerful effect of the music results from the mixture of splendor and devotion, radiance and rapture, drama and inwardness.[1]

The Gloria movements represent the type of "jubilant" music in their purest form. "Devout" music, on the other hand, is found in the Kyrie movements and the *Et incarnatus est* sections. The contrast between the two modes is manifest above all in the dynamics, the sound image and the instrumentation. While the "jubilant" music is naturally loud and requires the full vocal and orchestral apparatus, including horns, trumpets, trombones and tympani, the "devout" music rarely goes beyond the *piano* range, prefers soft sounds and limits itself to a reduced orchestra, leaving out trumpets, trombones and tympani. The contrast between "jubilant" and "devout" music is an aspect under which especially the *Te Deum* and the 150th psalm should be viewed.

The types of "jubilant" and "devout" music can naturally be found as well in Protestant church music. Thus in Johann Sebastian Bach's Christmas Oratorio (BWV 248), the introductory choruses of the first and fourth cantatas, "Jauchzet, frohlocket" ("Jubilate, exult") and "Fallt mit Danken, fallt mit Loben" ("Kneel with thanking, kneel with praising") respectively, represent the type of jubilant music with kettle drums and trumpets, whereas the famous aria "Schlafe mein Liebster" ("Sleep, my beloved") from the second cantata would more likely be called "devout" music. According to a marginal entry in his Bible, Johann Sebastian Bach took "andächtige [devout] Musique" to be music at which "God with his mercy [is] present at all times."

"Let Me Not Be Confounded in Eternity"

The *Te Deum*

> "In thee, O Lord, I put my trust; let me never be put to confusion."
> *Ps. 71:1*

The genesis of the *Te Deum*, the work that would soon become one of Bruckner's most successful, is in some respects unusual. He conceived this new project in the first half of 1881, while he was still working on his Sixth Symphony. Dates on the autograph of the first, incomplete version enable us to determine that work on it progressed quickly: on May 3, 1881, the rough draft was finished, on May 10 he was working on the last part, the *In te Domine speravi*, and on May 17, the choral part was done.[1] He then laid the draft aside and returned to the Sixth Symphony, whose scherzo was completed by June 17, the Finale three months later, on September 3, 1881. Twenty days after the completion of the Sixth, he commenced composing the Seventh, which occupied him for two years. Only then did he resume work on the *Te Deum*, and this time he was able to complete the score, in its now second and final version, by March 7, 1884. It was a time when the witch hunt against him was reaching a climax. When one of his many antagonists asked him sneeringly: "But why on earth did you strike up your *Te deum laudamus* just now?" he is said to have answered: "In gratitude to God, because my persecutors have still not succeeded in killing me off!"[2] The authenticity of this anecdote is beyond doubt: Bruckner himself told his protector Hermann Levi on May 10, 1885, that he had dedicated the *Te Deum* to God "to give thanks for the many afflictions overcome in Vienna."[3]

Since the 5th century, the *Te Deum* hymn has served as a song of praise to conclude the morning service, the so-called Matins. The question as to the author of the hymnal text remains unresolved: the earlier ascription to St. Ambrose turned out to be spurious. Of the three parts into which the hymn can be divided, the first (ll. 1-13) serves the praise of God the Father. The second (ll. 14-21) turns to Christ and issues in a prayer of intercession. The third part (ll. 22-29) consists of a number of glorifying verses from the Psalms and concludes with the plea *In te Domine speravi, non confundar in aeternum* ("In you, O Lord, I have put my trust: let me never be put to confusion," or: "let me not be confounded in eternity") – a plea that may have been taken from either Psalm 25:2 or Psalm 71:1.[4]

Since no written or oral statements have come down to us as to how Bruckner understood the text, this question can be answered only through a close look at the way it is set. Bruckner composes the text in blocks and loves contrasts, often in close proximity. He carefully scrutinizes the textual details but never loses sight of the larger context. His music ranges between the poles of the "jubilant" and the "devout." Its originality results from a happy synthesis of heterogeneous styles: the archaic melds with the modern, Gregorian intonations, modal chord progressions and bold, progressive harmonies are made to be compatible. Song, declamation and recitation alternate. Full-voiced, full-sounding choral sections, which occasionally expand to eight voices, alternate with solos and unison passages that faintly suggest Gregorian tones.

Unlike the traditional hymn, Bruckner's work is divided into five movements, which should not be marked off by long pauses. In the first movement, Bruckner combines the praise of God and of Christ, transmuting the separate theological statements into contrasting pictures. "Jubiant" music alternates constantly with quietly intoned, meditative sections, while the ostinato-like and sometimes varied fourth-fifth figuration in the strings serves as a kind of bracket guaranteeing the unity of the composition.

Several things contribute to the jubilant effect of the opening (*Te Deum laudamus!*): in addition to the fullness and strength of the chorus singing in unison, there is full orchestral instrumentation, whereby trumpets and trombones underscore the choral melody. The latter, upon closer inspection, turns out to be a psalmodic formula with flexa, meditation and finalis[5] – albeit with one major difference: the section, which is basically set in C major, ends strangely enough in a B tonality. A parallel example of this kind of formation is found in Liszt's Mass for Male Chorus (second version of 1870).[6] It is not known whether Bruckner knew Liszt's mass when he composed his *Te Deum*. In stark contrast to the jubilant hymning is the soft sound of the song of the heavenly hosts (angels, cherubim and seraphim), which Bruckner entrusts to three soloists (soprano, tenor and alto).

The *Te Deum* also includes the text of the Sanctus. Bruckner sets it in a differentiated manner, in that the chorus declaims the first two *Sanctus* exclamations *pianissimo* or at least *piano* in mysterious-sounding harmonies and then, at the *Sanctus Deus Dominus Sabaoth*, the jubilant music abruptly sets in *fortissimo* and even *piu fortissimo* in a new version. At the *Te gloriosus Apostolorum chorus,* the music of the beginning sounds at first without change. This is followed (starting with the *Te Martyrum candidatus laudet exercitus*) by a 16-bar period of likewise jubilant music that modulates into the B flat tonalities. The section *Patrem immensae majestatis* (starting at F) constitutes once more a *piano* island, whose monophonic choral melody is unmistakably Gregorian in tone. The invocation of Christ (*Tu rex gloriae, Christe*, letter G) returns to the jubilant style, whose turn to G flat major is particularly striking.

The passage dealing with the overcoming of the sting of death and the opening of the kingdom of heaven (*Tu devicto mortis aculeo*, from letter H) deserves special attention, not only because the volume is reduced here but because the music is shadowy in effect. Largely based on a pedal point with kettle drum roll, it makes a weak impression at least at first. Interestingly enough, the three-fold intonation of the words *Tu devicto aculeo* in the leading voices of the tenors (reinforced by the tenor trombone) is constructed from the intervals of the diminished seventh chord – similar motif formations occur in the Judicare of the D minor Mass (see p. 81). At this point, sharp dissonances will set the listener to prick up his ears. Evidently Bruckner here had the Last Judgment in mind, and we know that he was familiar with the symbolic meaning of the tritone as the satanic interval (*diabolus in musica*).[7] The last section of part one (*Tu ad dexteram Dei sedes*, letter L), which harks back to the beginning and is set in the C major tonality, concludes, as to be expected, in the affirmative diction of the "jubilant" music.

In stark contrast, the second part (*Te ergo quaesumus*) is throughout calm and "devout" in tenor. The movement is divided into four periods (plus a short coda), which are constructed climactically, so that the second and fourth periods transpose the music of the first and third, respectively, to a register that is one whole tone higher. At the end of each period, the melody of the leading tenor solo receives a confirmation from a brief interjection by he three other soloists. Apart from a concluding intonation of the trombones and the tuba, the orchestra is reduced to the strings and the first clarinet. The hovering figurations of the solo violin, which come to the fore at N, are among the earmarks of this prototypically Brucknerian "devout" music, which maintains an intimate character throughout, and which also plays a prominent role in the symphonic oeuvre, specifically the slow movements of the "Nilth," Third and Eighth Symphonies.

The brief text of the third part gives expression to the plea to let the faithful partake of the eternal glory along with the saints: *Aeterna fac cum sanctis tuis in gloria munerari*. Bruckner composed this text not as an entreaty but as a minuscule dramatic scene. The expression of the music is not jubilant but massive and urgent. In the autograph, the movement is headed "Allegro, Moderato. Solemn, with power." The key is D minor, partly D Dorian. In the first section (mm. 213-236), pressing ostinato choral motifs – which at the end seem like cries, owing to the very high pitches of the sopranos (similar effects occur in Carl Orff's *Carmina burana*) – are followed by a diatonically falling line, covering a twelfth (a^2 to d^1), of the monophonic chorus. In the second section (mm. 237-256), which is arranged in part as a climax, we notice above all the chromatically rising chord sequences. The music reaches its culmination in mm. 248-251 with two *piu fortissimo* diminished seventh chords, as though it tried to contradict the meaning of the word *gloria* uttered here.

The text assembly of the fourth part gives expression to several things: a plea for salvation of the people; guidance and uplifting of the people in eternity; again the jubilant praise of the Lord; and finally a plea for mercy and compassion. In complete coincidence with these themes, Bruckner set the text in several contrasting segments, which partly make use of music from the preceding parts but also contain newly composed portions. Thus the first segment (*Salvum fac populum tuum*, mm. 257-291) represents a kind of varied reprise of the second part *Te ergo quaesumus*. The second section (*Et rege eos*, mm. 291-310) adopts a tone that audibly echoes the Recordare of Mozart's Requiem, a work that had strongly impressed Bruckner early on and that he studied time and again.[8] The third section (*Per singulos dies*, mm. 311-330), directly take up the "jubilant" music of the first part. The fourth section (*Dignare, Domine*, mm. 331-353), largely *piano*, is newly composed, whereby the passage *Miserere nostri* is again modeled on Mozart's Requiem. For the fifth section (*Fiat misericordia tua Domine*, mm. 354-371), Bruckner almost exactly reused the music of mm. 146-160 from the first part. In this way he established a meaningful conceptual link between the hope for the Lord's mercy and the earlier statement about overcoming the sting of death.

Bruckner based the fifth and last part of his composition on a single psalm verse, the brief *In te, Domine, speravi, non confundar in aeternum*. In Luther's translation, this reads: "Herr, ich vertraue auf Dich; laß mich nimmermehr zu Schanden werden" (roughly "come to ruin"), though the King James Version reads, more accurately, "In thee, O Lord, I put my trust: let me never be put to confusion." This sentiment of confidence, which has also been adopted for the funeral ceremony of the Protestant Church, occurs likewise in Johann Sebastian Bach's cantata *Nach dir,*

Herr, verlanget mich (BWV 150). The four segments into which Bruckner divides this part comprise an introduction by the four soloists, to which eventually the chorus is added, a fugue, a chorale-like section and finally a jubilant sort of coda. Already in the introduction (mm. 372-401) the chorale-like theme of *non confundar in aeternum* is intoned from m. 388 on – at first *mezzo-forte* in G major, then *forte* in A major and finally *fortissimo* in B major. The independent subject of the fugue (mm. 402-448) is boldly worked and developed according to all the rules of art (in mm. 425-433, the sopranos strikingly sing a line rising chromatically from g^1 to g^2). Upon the entry of the trombones and the tuba in section three (mm. 449-490), the distinctive variant of the chorale-like theme is intoned in several waves of increasing intensity, first in A flat major, then in B flat minor and then again *fortissimo* in B major and in C sharp major. In section four (mm. 491-513), after the chorus has "trumpeted" the *non confundar in aeternum* in unison, the work closes, with jubilant music and jubilant fanfares by the trumpets, in radiant C major.

Along with the Seventh Symphony, the *Te Deum* was the work of Bruckner's that gained acceptance relatively quickly, and the one that added much to the belated spread of his fame also abroad and even beyond the oceans. Although the first performance with two pianos, on May 2, 1885, in the Viennese Academic Wagner Society, which Bruckner conducted in person, had but a moderate echo, the regular premiere on January 10, 1886, in the *Musikvereinssaal,* in a society concert under Hans Richter, became a great success. In his review in the *Wiener Fremdenblatt*, Ludwig Speidel called it a "consistently enthusiastic work" and wrote: "As by storm, as in a whirlwind, [Bruckner] raises up his Lord. But then, after such storm and stress, for which no means is deemed too strong, the depths of Heaven, the depths of the spirit, open, It is a rapturous seeing and hearing of the mysteries of faith, their heights and abysses."[9] Bruckner's friends congratulated him enthusiastically on the event. Rudolf Weinwurm referred to the "immense significance" of the work,[10] and Bruckner's old Linz supporter, Betty von Mayfeld, wrote on January 23, also in her husband's name:

Bored by Schubert and Schütz, I felt cold shivers run down my back from the first notes of the Te Deum, and the effect of it on me and Moritz was powerful, we were swept away in true enthusiasm, and the assembled public felt the same. You are understood, you are recognized, even in Vienna, and no one surely rejoices more in your triumph than the old couple from the province.[11]

The premiere was followed in rapid succession by performances in Brünn (Brno), Linz, Munich, Christiania (now Oslo), Berlin, Amsterdam and at length also Hamburg and Cincinnati.

Gustav Mahler had a special predilection for the *Te Deum*. As his wife Alma reported, he had thickly lined out the words "for chorus, soloists and orchestra, organ ad libitum" in his personal copy of the work and written in their place: "For the tongues of angels, the godly, tormented hearts and souls cleansed by fire."[12] It makes sense that the *Te Deum* should have been the first major work of Bruckner's that Mahler performed. He conducted it, together with Mozart's Requiem, on Good Friday (April 15), 1892, in Hamburg, where since the end of the 1890/91 season he held the position of First *kapellmeister* at the Municipal Theater, The performance was a triumphant success, and Mahler was able to write to Bruckner on the very next day: "Yesterday (Good Friday) I conducted your magnificent and powerful *Te deum*. Both the musicians and the entire audience were deeply moved by the mighty structure and the truly sublime thoughts. [...] You would have been delighted with the performance: I have rarely witnessed an ensemble work with such enthusiasm as yesterday. [...] 'Bruckner' has now made his victorious entrance into Hamburg."[13] Joseph Sittard, the reviewer of the *Hamburgische Correspondent*, also praised the work: "Bruckner is made to stand out," he wrote, "by two peculiarities that stamp him as an original composer: the sharp divisions in the structure of the periods and the wealth in harmonic means of expression. He is a master of instrumentation."[14] Two days later, Wilhelm Zinne told the composer that the work had been "instantly rousing" in its effect, "especially by its final chorus sweeping one along with irresistible force."[15] It is surely owing to the success of this premiere that Mahler performed the *Te Deum* again in 1893 and 1897 in Hamburg, each time on Good Friday.

Moreover, the impression these performances left on Mahler must have been a sustained one, as numerous observations add up to the thesis that Mahler must have had Bruckner's *Te Deum* in mind while he was designing the first part of his Eighth Symphony. Both works are based on religious Latin texts, both call for a large ensemble – vocal soloists and organ along with a large orchestra and chorus (or choruses) – in both the prevailing tenor is jubilant and "affirmative," and in both more or less homophonically conceived passages alternate with contrapuntally worked ones. Characteristically, Bruckner's work culminates in a four-part fugue, which Mahler bettered by an eight-part double fugue.[16]

The overwhelming success of the *Te Deum* may be ascribed to the work's originality, its expressive strength and wealth of contrasts, its peculiar fusion of splendor and worship, rejoicing and rapture. The musicologist Rudolf Louis observed justly already in 1918 that the "supposed deficiencies" that have been criticized in this work – that the power in the expression of jubilation at times borders on the "brute and uncouth," and that the accents of "dread, doubt and despair" also crowd "unduly" into the foreground – are the very things that are so eminently characteristic of Bruckner:[17]

The genre of the *Te Deum* has undergone a remarkable development. In the course of time, it separated itself from its original, strictly liturgical function and, especially in the 18th and 19th century, frequently acquired a political accent. Many of the settings of that time were played at coronations and oaths of allegiance, victory and peace celebrations, consecrations of bishops, weddings, baptisms or name day festivities in noble families.[18] Hector Berlioz's famous *Te Deum*, composed in 1849 and, according to the composer's wish, designated for the enthronement of Napoleon III. in 1852, received its premiere only in 1855, in a concert in the church of St. Eustache on the occasion of the opening of the Paris World's Fair. According to a report by Maurice Bourges, it was meant to be part of "a half-epic, half-dramatic work of the most colossal dimensions designed to glorify the warrior fame of the First Consul."[19] After one performance of the work (probably on May 24, 1884 in the municipal church in Weimar), Bruckner is said to have remarked that it was not "ecclesiastic."[20] About his own *Te Deum* Bruckner told in a letter to Arthur Nikisch of July 17, 1884, that court *kapellmeister* Joseph Hellmesberger wanted to perform it "at court."[21] It never got to that. It is questionable to what extent Bruckner's *Te Deum* can really be called "ecclesiastic." In the fullest sense of the word, it is a confessional work.

Music as Song of Praise

Psalm 150

> "There are still songs to be sung
> beyond humanity."
> *Paul Celan*

In December of 1891, Bruckner was occupied with thoughts about a Ninth Symphony, when Richard Heuberger sent him an inquiry shortly before Christmas, if he would be willing to compose a hymn or cantata for mixed chorus and orchestra for the opening ceremony of a planned "Music and Theater Exhibition."[1] Already on January 2, 1892, Bruckner agreed to contribute a cantata for mixed chorus with "brass harmony," that is, without strings. Heuberger suggested two texts for the work: Psalm 98, "Sing unto the Lord a new song" or Psalm 150, "Let everything that hath breath praise the Lord." Bruckner chose the 150th Psalm "because of its special solemnity," but had to tell Heuberger on March 31, 1892, that "despite steady industry," he would be unable to finish the work in time for the opening of the exhibition and suggested to schedule the performance for the closing ceremony instead. Although his health at this time was no longer the best (he complained about swelling in his feet), he succeeded in completing the work, which, contrary to his original intention, he executed for mixed chorus and full orchestra. The premiere on November 13 in one of the Viennese society concerts did not have the great success he had dreamed of. But the next performances, in Dresden and Chemnitz, of the cantata, which Bruckner himself later called his "very best festival cantata,"[2] were triumphs.

On the outside, the *Te Deum* and Psalm 150 have a good deal in common: the instrumentation (mixed chorus and large orchestra), the basic key (C major), the even meter; besides, both conclude with a spacious fugue. Intrinsically, however, they are quite different, because the hymnal texts on which they are based differ substantially. Whereas in the *Te Deum* the problems of existence, of the abyss, of man's dread of finitude are given expression along with the hymnal praise, the tone of the psalm is throughout one of unclouded affirmation. Bruckner's settings take account of that. Besides the jubilant music in major keys, the *Te Deum* also contains passages of devotion in minor keys. In Psam 150, on the other hand, the major mode dominates over large stretches. Ernst Kurth therefore speaks of the "radiant light effect" of the psalm, of "measureless tonal splendor" and of the "brightness" of the music.[3] Both works impress by their bold harmonic turns, unusual progressions and, in places, a systematic use of a chromaticism rich in dramatic tension.

The psalm setting ("Rather slow, solemn, strong") consists of a main part (164 measures) and a fugue plus coda (83 measures). The principal part is clearly divided into five sections, which are arranged in the form of an arc (ABCBA), with "jubilant" and "devout" music alternating repeatedly. In the first part (mm. 1-22), the chorus intones the word *Hallelujah* six times, the first three times accompanied by the full orchestra, the second three times a cappella. The melisma-filled initial motif commences first on the tonic, then on the third and finally on the fifth. This first, hymnal part is strictly diatonic and never departs from the basic key of C major. At the end, the wind instruments intone an octave drop in unison – this salient interval will be sounded time and again in preparation for the pithy fugue subject.

The second section (mm. 23-75) centers on the praise of the Lord in His essential attributes, as set forth in the psalm verses:

Praise God in his sanctuary:
Praise him in the firmament of his power.
Praise him for his mighty acts:
Praise him according to his excellent greatness.

Structurally, the four segments of the setting here are determined mainly by modulatory processes. The first segment modulates from A flat major to D flat major, the second from A major to D major, the third from F sharp major to B flat major and the last from B major to E flat major via F major and a fifth-sixth chord. The respective target keys D flat major, D major, B flat major and E flat major are thus assigned to the concepts holiness, power, acts and greatness or glory.

The subject of the third section (mm. 75-108) is praise with instruments: trumpets, psaltery and harps, drums, strings and pipes and finally "high-sounding" cymbals. The idea of praising the creator also with instrumental music must have greatly animated Bruckner, for he shaped this section into a kind of small instrumental concert along with jubilant song. Characteristically, the opening choral song "Praise him with the sound of the trumpet" is introduced by a duple, rhythmic intonation of the trombones, which will recur twice later on, the last time by the horns. The entire section is erected on a pedal point of g with a nearly uninterrupted tympani roll. The violins are assigned a constantly developing eighths figuration, which bears some resemblance to the *majestas* figure in the *Te Deum*. The harmony is supported by tremolos in the violas and cellos, while flutes, oboes and clarinets take part in the "concert" with partly independent figures. Bruckner uses neither harps nor cymbals to correspond to the "harp" and "loud-sounding cymbal" of the text, because these instruments were scorned by the leading Viennese critics as being part of the repertoire of the "New German" orchestra and Bruckner's fear of Hanslick in this respect, too, is well documented.[4] One of the boldest traits of this section is the climactic wave of mm. 89-96 on the basis of the stringently chromatic line of the sopranos rising from g^1 to g^2.

Like the second section, the fourth (mm. 109-142) again represents the type of "devout" music, corresponding with the second without being identical with it. The harmonic progression is different, and a violin and a soprano solo come to the fore here. The textual basis of this section is the final verse of the Psalm, "Let every thing that hath breath praise the Lord" – a line that also underlies the fugue finale.

The fifth section of the main part (mm. 143-164), finally, constitutes an almost exact reprise of the first: a six times repeated *Hallelujah*.

The subject of the concluding fugue displays a notable similarity with the finale of the Fifth Symphony. In both instances, two octave leaps, a falling and a rising one, constitute the "head" of the theme. In his masses as well as in the *Te Deum*, Bruckner employs the falling octave as a symbol of divine grandeur. In Psalm 150, as the all-embracing, pure interval, it emblematizes the creation praising its creator. The fugue itself is clearly divided into an exposition with five theme entries (mm. 165-183) and a development, in which the subject, appearing in its original form as well as in inversion, is worked in close succession (stretto) and otherwise artfully wrought. Reduction of the theme to the two octave leaps and consequent octave shifts makes for boldly harmonized and contrapuntal chromatic lines that entail climactic sequences (mm. 190-198, 199-212). A short year after the completion of Psalm 150, Bruckner wrote to Franz Bayer: "Counterpoint is not genius but a means to an end"[5] – a significant statement that also applies to this Fugue. Psalm 150 reaches its peak in m. 229 with its C major fourth-sixth chord in triple *forte*. While the chorus intones the *Hallelujah* three times, the trumpets blare out fanfares – the work concludes resplendently with "jubilant" music.

Critics were divided in their opinions following the premiere of November 13, 1892. Hans Paumgartner described the work as "altogether unnatural, pretentious, without an inner cause," even as "operatic,"[6] whereas Robert Hirschfeld lauded the "grandiose conception," the "fullness of sound" and the "wealth of combinations,"[7] and Hans Puchstein called it a "highly significant occasional work."[8] Robert Haas, in turn, apostrophized both the *Te Deum* and the 150th Psalm as "flourishing testimonies of the master's religious enthusiasm, swept along by an inner momentum, which in its primeval strength rises up monumentally and almost fearfully"[9] – a pointed, if slightly overstated judgment.

PART THREE

The Symphonies

The Fiction of "Absolute Music"

> "The artist Anton Bruckner presents, in both life and work, a firm unity of being of such extraordinary and sharply defined attitude of mind that its import extends far beyond the merely musical."
>
> *Robert Haas*

One of the oddest stereotypes in Bruckner research is the frequently argued and still not altogether silenced notion of the supposed discrepancy between his life and his work. In 1919, the journalist Julius Bistron went so far as to maintain that Bruckner as a man was "not only unimportant in the ordinary sense of the word but all but inconsequential." As a result, it was difficult "to find one's way back from such a human being to the idea of a significant art."[1] Fifty years later, the feature writer Karl Grebe thought along similar lines. His 1972 popular-science monograph opines the following: "The description of Anton Bruckner's work cannot be incorporated into a narrative of his life. Life and work reveal nothing about each other. His life says nothing about his work, and his work says nothing about his life: any presentation has to start from this awkward fact."[2] Even today many commentators confess to being at a loss when it comes to establishing any closer relation between Bruckner's personality and his oeuvre.[3]

In an attempt to find a way out of this aporia, several writers in the 'twenties, including Erich Schwebsch, Oskar Lang and, later, Ernst Kurth, stylized Bruckner s a "metaphysician" and a "mystic." One can see why, as the empirical person is quite secondary in a "mystic," and troubling questions about intelligence and literary education recede into the background. Bruckner's disinterest in literary and philosophical matters may also be a reason why he was made into an "absolute" musician. The notion that his symphonies were pure music was generally accepted for a long time and still lives on untroubled in the Bruckner article in the new edition of the encyclopedia *Musik in Geschichte und Gegenwart.* The paradox here is that there is no unambiguous definition of "absolute" music. It is not clear what one should understand by that. According to Carl Dahlhaus, the idea of absolute music originated around 1800 as the notion that "because music is disconnected from the visual and even from the affective, it is therefore a revelation of the absolute."[4] Wilhelm Seidel, to whom we owe an objective, carefully considered article on the subject, writes:

Ever since [the publication of Eduard Hanslick's treatise *Vom Musikalisch Schönen* in 1854] music is called absolute if it is independent of any so-called extra-musical elements and is grounded solely in itself. At the same time, the attribute *absolute* frequently proves to be twofold in meaning. On the one hand, negatively, it refers to music that is independent of anything outside the realm of musical sounds – of any ecclesiastical or social function, of prosaic reality, of a specific affect or object, of dance, of language, of a program, of any speculation regarding the audience, let alone a specific audience, of applause, of emotional effect. Secondly, and often simultaneously, the attribute *absolute* denotes, positively, any music whose subject, in terms of the Romantic metaphysics of instrumental music, is the Absolute.[5]

Assuming this definition to hold true, Bruckner's music is virtually the opposite, exactly because it is visual and the affective component is particularly strongly developed. It has been fully demonstrated that in conceiving his Third, Fourth, Eighth and Ninth Symphonies Bruckner was beset by pictorial, extra-musical ideas.[6]

In spite of this, Dahlhaus tried, in a tendentious, hair-splitting article, to cast doubt on the results of my research, to all appearances in order to yet rescue the beloved idea of "absolute" music.[7] The time has come to ask the question: Is there *any* music in the 19th century that is detached from the "affective"? Three things can be said of any significant music: that it is no mere play of sounds but has a psychological, a spiritual and a social depth dimension; that it always has a human substratum; and that in most cases it reflects the personality as well as the intellectual world of its creator.[8] That is true not only of composers like Beethoven, Schumann, Chopin, Berlioz, Liszt, Richard Strauss and Mahler, but also of Anton Bruckner. His music is an expression of his spirituality and his "inner" world.

Originality and Modernity

> "Unfamiliar music gets me all unhinged."
> *Bruckner*

To this day, opinions are divided about the significance of Bruckner's symphonies, which are still often regarded as outlandish. Many of his contemporaries, including those who were sympathetic to him, could not find their way in his music. Even his pupils did not always recognize the inherent laws of his symphonies, their stringent structural logic.

As paradoxical as it may sound, the secret of Bruckner's "outlandishness" lies in his great originality and the modernity of his musical language. Even Bruckner, of course, is not "without precedent" historically. Certain traits of his symphonic work are traceable to Beethoven, Schubert, Wagner, even to the programmatic composers Berlioz and Liszt. Nevertheless, Bruckner as a symphonist is an incommensurable phenomenon. He exists in isolation, "alien and unrelated in an altogether heterogeneous world," as Rudolf Louis rightly saw already in 1904.[1] It is not inappropriate to describe him as an "erratic boulder." Add to this that his works, seen in historical perspective, are simply astounding in their novelty. In relation to contemporary symphonic composition, they constitute the avant-garde. Already the first symphonies are no less "progressive" in their use of technical means and the boldness of their musical language than the symphonic poems of Franz Liszt, with which, of course, they have nothing externally in common. It is only natural that such music would have to overcome considerable obstacles to be accepted.

Several motives can be cited for the polemic of Eduard Hanslick, as spokesman for the Brahms party, against Bruckner: personal animosities, practicalities of musical politics, ideological and aesthetic considerations. But certainly Bruckner's "outlandishness" also played a role in this. Hanslick, Brahms and their followers would not and could not understand Bruckner. The symphonic music he represented was irreconcilable with their aesthetic principles, it departed fundamentally from the generic norms they deemed inviolable. Time and again they reproached Bruckner with monstrosity, formlessness, lack of musical logic, epigonic Wagnerism and unnaturalness. The prevailing tenor of this criticism was that Bruckner, in a fatal transgression of the symphonic genre's natural limits, had transferred the Wagnerian style to the symphony.

Hanslick and his like-minded cohorts were simply not up to the monumentality of Bruckner's symphonic designs and the modernity of their musical language. They failed to see the symphonies' strict tectonics and meaningful organization. They only saw disorder, arbitrariness and chaos where in fact a stringent logic ruled – a logic sui generis, to be sure, that differed in many points from the laws of Classic-Romantic music. They took badly Bruckner's use of modern harmonies and of a new type of instrumentation. At certain places in his work they angrily heard a quasi-Wagnerian idiom. They took umbrage at Bruckner's pathos-laden, emphatic language and felt unsettled by a new, unfamiliar tone they regarded as theatrical and bombastic. Yet even musicians who were close to Bruckner did not approve of his music unreservedly. Gustav Mahler, for example, one of Bruckner's most energic champions, admired the grandeur and the wealth of invention in his work but found fault with the "disjointedness" of its form.[2] And it seems like an irony of cultural history that, of all people, a Bruckner supporter like Hermann Levi should have given currency to the false slogan of the "stereotypical nature" of Bruckner's music. In a letter to Joseph Schalk of September 30, 1887, he remarked that what shocked him the most in the (first version of the) Eighth Symphony was its "great similarity to the Seventh," the "almost stereotypical nature of the form."[3]

Posthumously, Bruckner found eloquent apologists like Rudolf Louis, August Halm, Max Auer and Ernst Kurth, who corrected the distortions in his image and praised his formal mastery. Especially August Halm regarded him as the "most universal musician" ever, as the founder of the "first universe of music" and of a new "music culture."[4] Even so, many of the old prejudices continued to flourish. As late as 1941, Alfred Einstein wondered whether Bruckner's much-discussed general pauses were "really charged with form" or at any rate to be regarded as "not merely empty."[5] And Wilhelm Furtwängler noted in 1939 that there was a lack of understanding for Bruckner in many countries – that especially listeners in Romance countries time and again spoke of formlessness. "Musicians take exception to the excessive use of sequences, to the stereotypical endings, etc."[6] Much, of course, has changed since that statement was made. Today there are Bruckner communities even in Romance countries.

Matters of Style

> "With Bruckner, song has finally come back into the world, along with a good conscience. He has learned from Wagner, but the overheated manner, the 'bloody' score is gone. There is now active mobility and a self-transforming aura of an intellectual kind, of intellectual essentialities, of a swaying calm, though drawn by Bruckner more from the 'cosmic' than from the 'intelligible' realm."
>
> *Ernst Bloch*

If one wanted to put into words the impressions that Bruckner's symphonic music makes on the listener, one would above all have to speak of a grandiose union of opposites: rigor and opulence, simplicity and ecstasy. anxiousness and solemnity follow each other in quick succession. Add to that a fairly singular synthesis of the archaic and the modern, which lends this music its unique character and determines its special position. In Bruckner, as in virtually no other composer, the archaic and the modern, the Baroque and the Romantic, the old-fashioned and the futuristic are fused and integrated.

The spectrum of stylistic influences in his music is a wide one. Besides the special affinity with Wagner, diverse relations to the music of the 16th century, to the Baroque, to Beethoven, Schubert, and even the programmatic symphonists Berlioz and Liszt, can be recognized.

Yet Bruckner's art has nothing in common with eclecticism. What is so admirable is that even received stylistic means are completely assimilated, thanks to his strong, rugged personality, so that no break is felt anywhere. Everything bears the handwriting of the composer. Assimilation of the traditional and the adopted to such a degree is a phenomenon one rarely meets elsewhere.

Fairly early on, Bruckner came into contact with the polyphonic vocal music of the 16th century. Among others, he got to know works by Palestrina and Giovanni Gabrieli. His "elective affinity" with these composers may explain why modal, richly gradated harmonies are fairly frequent in his music. His symphonies occasionally contain stretches that remind of Palestrina,[1] while not infrequently, passages in the brasses recall instrumental *canzoni* by Giovanni Gabriele in their severe splendor – as, for example, in the first and last movements of the Fifth Symphony.

Bruckner's special predilection for polyphonic writing and counterpoint points, secondly, to the music of the Baroque. Clearly Baroque in origin are, for example, the frequent sequence formations, which he loved and for which he was often faulted. Even his manner of treating the orchestra and its instruments like a giant pipe organ with its registers bears Baroque traits.[2] During his many years of study with Simon Sechter, Bruckner learned to master counterpoint composition in all its nuances.

It is symptomatic for his symphonic work, however, that he put these compositional skills in the service not of any kind of historicism but of the search for new modes of expression.

Another very important component of Bruckner's orchestral music is the symphonic style of Beethoven. Several of his symphonies are indebted in structural detail to Beethoven's Ninth Symphony. The special scherzo type, the rondo-like design of many of his adagios, the shape of many of his themes and climaxes, numerous *unisono* passages, the "flashback technique" at the start of the Finale of the Fifth Symphony – all of this would be unthinkable without the model of Beethoven's Ninth.[3]

To get, thirdly, at the specifically Austrian element in Bruckner's symphonic work, one has to refer to Franz Schubert. The monumental design of the symphonies, the obligatory trinity of Bruckner's theme complexes, the disposition of keys in some of the expositions, the lied-like shape of many of his "song periods," the regular inclusion of trombones, the fondness for landler-like passages in the scherzi and trios – all of this can be traced ultimately to the Schubertian model, especially the Schubert of the "Unfinished" and of the Great Symphony in C major.[4]

Especially revealing are also the (hitherto overlooked) relations to Liszt and Berlioz. Bruckner admired Liszt's Faust Symphony and carefully studied its technique of using linkages, quotations and reminiscences. He also received important impulses from Berlioz's method of the contrapuntal intertwining of contrasting themes for the purpose of programmatic characterization. In addition, the *pizzicato*-accompanied chorale of the *Pilgrims March* from Berlioz's Harold Symphony became a model for the composition of several of Bruckner's "chorales," specifically in the Adagio of the Second Symphony (at B), the Finale of the Third (at T), the Andante of the *Romantic* Symphony (at C) and the opening movement of the Fifth (at C).[5]

All-powerful, finally, was the influence of Richard Wagner. It is well known that Bruckner literally idolized Wagner and found his own way as a symphonist only after he had encountered *Tannhäuser* and *Lohengrin* in 1863 and 1864 in Linz. Bruckner was the first major symphonist of the 19th century to incorporate numerous elements of the Wagnerian music drama (stage music) into the symphony. Wagner's influence on Bruckner shows itself also in numerous quotations and echoes, in Bruckner's orchestration and instrumentation, in his richly modulated harmonies and in the famous climactic waves, his frequent signals and fanfares, his predilection for elements of recitative and arioso, abrupt contrasts and, not least, a novel conception of form that was met with complete incomprehension on the part of most of his contemporaries.

What does this conception consist in? Ernst Kurth attempted to answer this question by saying that Bruckner was a "dynamist of form," the leading representative of a novel principle of form constituted by the concept of "becoming" and "inner dynamics." For clarification he distinguished between the form principle of the classicists and that of Romanticism by saying the former was "predominantly static" while the latter was "predominantly dynamic." For Bruckner, he went on to say, form was without exception defined in terms not of stasis but of tension, which "constantly bears a live becoming within.[6]

The more one studies Bruckner, the clearer it becomes that this insight of Kurth's, which is based on theories of Richard Wagner, identifies an essential characteristic of Bruckner's music.[7] Bruckner's principle of form differs indeed fundamentally from that of classicism. It s not static but dynamic and in its essence resembles the principle of dramatic music. The powerful climactic waves which largely determine the formal processes in his work, correspond to affective curves, which, ascending steeply, reach one or several climaxes and then fall off, for the most part abruptly.

Clarity of organization and logic of structure are not diminished by the dynamics of such processes. The talk about Bruckner's supposed formlessness is thus wholly unfounded. The monumental movements of his symphonies are tectonically strictly organized and well-proportioned down to the smallest details, and everything is consequentially developed. The development sections are restricted to the themes and motifs of the exposition: new elements are generally not introduced. With all the modulalory mobility, the harmonic disposition remains purposeful and perspicuous, contrasting tone pictures are integrated to create a diverse but throughout unified whole. Each thematic complex is structured in a special way and exhibits an unmistakable expressive character, while the individual complexes are linked associatively. The result is a wealth of different expressive modes: the cosmos of Bruckner's symphonic oeuvre comprises the profane and the sacred, the intimate and the ceremonious, the Romantic and the religious, the lyrical and the dramatic, the march and the funeral march, the landler as well as the chorale.

Each of the symphonies has its own fully developed character, each displays a physiognomy of its own. The notion that Brucknerian symphonies are spitting images of each other is simply not true. If, to test this, one compares the Third Symphony with the Fourth, or the Eighth with the Ninth, one will notice fundamental differences already in their basic attitude. Bruckner's musical language developed substantially over time: his symphonies are subject to stylistic change to an extent not readily paralleled by the music of Johannes Brahms. Setting the Second Symphony (1871/72) side by side with the unfinished Ninth will reveal an immense stylistic change: it is hard to believe that a mere twenty years lie between the two works.

How Bruckner Came to the Symphony

Anton Bruckner's encounter of the *kapellmeister* Otto Kitzler was fateful in that it had undreamed-of consequences for his artistic development. It is no exaggeration to say that the training in the science of form, in instrumentation and composition that Bruckner received from Kitzler in Linz between December of 1861 and July of 1863 opened the way to the symphony for him. Kitzler had envisioned two years for the course: Bruckner needed only nineteen months to complete it.[1] Kitzler based his instruction on Ernst Friedrich Richter's treatise *Die Grundzüge der musikalischen Formen und ihre Analyse* (Fundamentals of Musical Forms and their Analysis) and Adolph Bernhard Marx's theory of instrumentation. In addition, Bruckner studied the first two volumes of Johann Christian Lobe's theory of composition, which he owned.[2] The "comparative basis" of the instruction, Kitzler later recorded in his *Musikalische Erinnerungen* (Musical Memoirs), was supplied by Beethoven's piano sonatas, "and Bruckner always took special pleasure in coming upon any musical turns or formations that ran counter to his earlier compositional studies with Sechter."[3]

In setting Bruckner compositional tasks, Kitzler proceeded methodically. First he made him write a sonata movement for piano, then a string quartet, and only then orchestral pieces, an overture and a symphony. The composition of this earliest symphony, a sizable work in F minor, occupied three-and-a-half months, from February 15 to May 26, 1863.

In his *Musikalische Erinnerungen*, Kitzler also speaks of this symphony, saying that it was more of a "homework," for which Bruckner was "not particularly inspired," so that he (Kitzler) could not give him "any particular praise" for it. "He seemed hurt by my reserve," Kitzler continues, "something that surprised me, considering his infinite modesty. Later, he confessed to me, with a laugh, that I had been right after all."[4] To specify his own estimation of the work in writing, Bruckner himself, in a copy preserved in the Vienna Municipal Library, furnished all four movements with the note "school work."

It is, however, also typical that although he regarded these early orchestral works as studies only, he did not omit to show some of them to the Munich court *kapellmeister* Franz Lachner during a trip to Munich in September of 1863. Lachner thought they were distinguished by their 'flow of ideas, order and noble bearing" and intimated to Bruckner that he was not disinclined to perform the Symphony in F minor the following year.[5] The planned event did not materialize, however.

What place can this "school work" be said to occupy in Bruckner's artistic development? The answer is that even here Bruckner created an architectonic type capable of further elaboration. Both the opening movement and the finale each contain three themes and an epilogue. Of the three subjects, the second – as in the later symphonies – is songlike (cantabile), while the third is massive or energetic in character. Importantly also, the typically dynamic formal principle is already established here. It manifests itself in numerous crescendos, which admittedly do not have as much staying power as in the later symphonies but do point forward to the famous later climactic trains. Other aspects are still conventional. Thus the design of the middle portion of the Andante as a *minore* is a sole exception in Bruckner.

The harmonies exhibit much that can be called "Brucknerian," such as the predilection for the major-minor (as in the Andante), for the Neapolitan sixth chord and for altered chords, and especially the predilection for chromatic progressions, half-tone shifts and modulating transpositions. At the beginning of the development section of the Finale, it takes him only one chord to modulate from A flat major to A major.

Impulses for the composition of this work came to him from the assiduous study of Beethoven's symphonies. The development section of the F minor Symphony's opening movement reveals a clear familiarity with Beethoven's technique of working themes and motifs. The musical idiom, however, that Bruckner speaks in this his very first symphony is not the musical language of Beethoven, but that of High Romanticism. He may have studied symphonic works of Robert Schumann and Felix Mendelssohn at this time.[6] It is demonstrable, at any rate, that he received a lasting impression from Carl Maria von Weber's opera *Der Freischütz*.[7]

During his years in Linz, Bruckner had the good fortune to win the friendship of the art-loving couple Moritz and Betty von Mayfeld. Moritz von Mayfeld (1817-1904), a high-ranking civil servant, who combined a political career with artistic interests, was also active as a writer, painter and musician, wrote musical critiques and composed.[8] His wife Betty, née Lady Betty von Jenny (1831-1098), was an excellent pianist: no less an expert than Clara Schumann voiced praise for her piano-playing. The Mayfelds frequently played Beethoven symphonies four-handed on the piano for Bruckner. In his old age, Bruckner was in the habit of saying: "It was Mayfeld who drove me into the symphonic."[9] Mayfeld, who facilitated a performance of Bruckner's D minor Mass on December 18, 1864, in Linz's Redoubt Hall, published a lengthy review in the *Abendbote*, in which he praised the great originality of the composer, predicted a great future for his creations, and prophesied "that he is bound to cultivate the field of the symphony in the very near future, and do so with the greatest success."[10]

Soon after the appearance of this review – in January of 1865 – Bruckner began work on his First Symphony in C minor, which was completed in 1866 in Linz and premiered there two years later. Viewed historically, it must be called a highly original and bold work. Bruckner's unique symphonic style already shows in this symphony, which he subsequently declared to be the first "valid" one, in such a developed form that the question of models is of entirely secondary importance.

This is true above all with regard to the powerful climactic waves that largely determine the formal processes, especially in the outer movements, and to the triads of themes and their capacity for development, with respect to the elementary rhythmic energy of the G minor Scherzo, to the tendency toward a dense polyphonic style and, finally, to the individual instrumentation and peculiar relation of the diatonic and the chromatic. At the same time, differences to most of the later symphonies cannot be ignored. The outer movements are only vaguely related in subject, chorale-like themes are absent, and there are none of those structuring pauses that, starting with the Second Symphony, as a rule divide the various thematic complexes from one another.

Most surprising, next to the boldness, is the impetuosity of expression. The creative urge, long damned up during the long apprenticeship years, here erupts with such violence that Bruckner himself was startled by the work, which he later deemed one of his "best and most difficult," calling it the "brash little broom," and evidently then made an effort to achieve greater "comprehensibility" in the Second. An example of such audacity in the concisely shaped opening movement (Allegro) is the grandiose idea of the trombones at C (in the score of the Linz version), which follows upon the march-like main subject, the lyrical second theme and the climactic section at B. No less bold is the main theme of the Adagio, whose key of A flat major, veiled at first, becomes overt only in measure 20. The Finale, too, is remarkable, which despite an extensive tectonic organization also has aspects of improvisation and is rich in dramatic moments.

In 1895 – one year before his death and prior to the move to the Belvedere apartment – Bruckner undertook a critical sifting of his youthful work and destroyed many a manuscript. One piece that escaped the autodafé was the symphony in D minor, preserved in the estate (WAB 100), which wanders wraith-like through Bruckner criticism under the cognomen "Die Nullte," "The Nilth." After his death, and in accordance with his wishes, his executor, Dr. Reisch, bequeathed the autograph to the state museum of Upper Austria in Linz. The manuscript, still preserved there, bears the title "Symphony Nr. 2 in D Minor," but many entries in Bruckner's handwriting make clear indubitably that Bruckner annulled the work. He himself marked it as the "Nilth," as "rejected," and individual movements as "invalid" and "wholly void."

The leading Bruckner biographer August Göllerich was the first to advance the thesis that Bruckner composed the "Nilth" in 1863/1864 upon the completion of his compositional studies with Otto Kitzler,[11] basing his theory on a remark of Bruckner's that he work originated in Linz. The numerous annotations in the autograph, however, document that the symphony in its extant version originated partly in Vienna and partly in Linz in 1869, more precisely in the period between January and September of that year.

Much of the confusion about this posthumously published Symphony in D minor is apparently due to the title "the Nilth." According to Max Auer, Bruckner called it that in 1895 in order to make clear that it should be ranked ahead of the symphony now legitimated as the First:[12] the somewhat odd nomenclature was to secure the correct historical placement. But that is a misinterpretation. The term "Nilth" is to be understood not in terms of a chronological lineup but as signifying annulment. Bruckner thereby signaled his intention not to include the work in the series of nine symphonies that he deemed valid.

Yet the "Nilth" bears throughout the stamp of Bruckner's manner, the unmistakable handwriting of the composer. It differs substantially from the First, to be sure: in design, character, individual traits, in the structure and development of the themes. But that does not mean that it must represent an earlier stage of artistic development than the First. What is especially important is that many features of the "Nilth" point forward to the Third and even to the Ninth Symphony – two works with which it shares not only the key.

Probably shortly after his move to Vienna in the fall of 1868, Bruckner established contacts with leading musicians of the Danube metropolis, and showed them some of his works. Especially the first Symphony of 1865/66 seemed exceptionally daring to them. Much later Bruckner confessed to Hans von Wolzogen that in the beginning he had gotten "quite scared off" in Vienna.[13] According to a report by August Göllerich, he had the "Nilth" played privately during his earliest time in Vienna. The court *Kapellmeister* Otto Dessoff failed to detect any developed head theme and, nonplussed, asked Bruckner: "But where is the theme?" Bruckner is said to have replied: "I didn't have the spunk no more to write up a reg'lar theme."[14] Dessoff's objection is understandable when one considers that the formation with which the "Nilth" commences is highly original in every respect: it springs from the conception of a weaving or wave of sound that describes a crescendeo-diminuendo arc and in a second attack realizes a full crescendo.

Newly made observations let the "Nilth" appear in a different light. Hitherto overlooked connections to the Mass in F minor, which originated in 1868 in Linz, prove that the "Nilth" was conceived and elaborated only in 1869 – after the First! To fully comprehend these connections one has to remember that in composing this mass Bruckner had made many discoveries and in every respect opened new territories. So when he took up work on the "Nilth" on January 24, 1869, he was still under the spell of the F minor Mass, specifically the highly dramatic music of the Credo. A study of the opening movement and the Andante of the "Nilth" helps us to realize that he was here partly transferring the conceptions of sound he had developed during the composition of the mass to the symphonic realm. Thus we find in the opening movement of the symphony those same rousing climaxes, ostinato figures in the strings and ostinato rhythms in the trumpets, and those prominent signal-like motifs that characterize the portions of the Credo dealing with the Resurrection, the Ascension, the Second Coming and the Last Judgment; and the Andante is religious, even devout in nature. The second theme complex of the movement, moreover, is modeled after a type that Bruckner first tried out in the *Et incarnatus est* of the Credo of the F minor Mass. The Scherzo and the Finale of the symphony are likewise distinguished by many original features.

If one looks at the "Nilth" retrospectively, it appears as an early stage of the Third Symphony. The two works are related to each other like a rough draft to a finished, fully developed, mature composition. Once he had completed the first version of the Third in 1873, Bruckner must have come to regard the "Nilth" as an obsolete stage in his compositional development. It was thus consequential that he should annul the D minor symphony and dismiss it as a mere "experiment."

After his move to Vienna, he turned away from the sacred music he had hitherto cultivated and concentrated in a notable way on the symphony. Apart from the *Te Deum* and the 150th Psalm, the years in Vienna produced merely a few motets.

A number of reasons present themselves for this conspicuous new focus on the symphony. After the move to Vienna, at the latest, he must have come to realize that the symphony was the sole medium in which he could really speak out as a composer, express his feelings and ideas. He probably also let himself be swayed by the model of Beethoven, whom he knew principally as a symphonist. Besides, the symphony was regarded in the 19th century as the highest, loftiest genre of instrumental music bar none. He now felt as a symphonist and referred to himself as such. On the occasion of the honorary doctorate he was to receive from the University of Vienna, he noted that the term "symphonist" should by all means be set down on the certificate, persuaded, as he was, that it was the only term that could accurately designate his "life's calling."[15]

A report of his pupil Dr. Franz Marschner casts additional light on this matter. When, profoundly impressed by Bruckner's magnificent organ-playing, he once asked him if he would not also write compositions for the organ, he is supposed to have answered irately: "No, the world is too corrupt, I write nothing for the organ."[16] That might mean that in his view organ music, and sacred music generally, in addition to its religious function, also had an ethical mission. Perhaps, also he was of the opinion that in the mundane Viennese metropolis he could not expect any appreciation for such music and resolved for that reason as well to present himself in Vienna principally as a symphonist.

Autobiographic Elements in the Second and Third Symphony

> "I wrote the mass in Linz as a sick man, being as unwell then as I am now. "
> *Bruckner, on November 5, 1894, on the F minor Mass*

In what sense can one speak at all about autobiography in the work of Anton Bruckner, a composer whom Peter Raabe once described as the "most absolute of absolute musicians"?[1] It might have been difficult to argue about that if Bruckner had not left some hints about it himself. As an old man he told his confidant Theodor Helm about the genesis of the Benedictus in the F minor Mass, one of his most personal works. On Christmas Eve of 1867, after an hour of intense devotion, the melody had come to him of the movement with which he, who had been close to madness, had found himself again. As a way of giving thanks for the delivery from spiritual death, he had taken a passage from the Benedictus over into the Adagio of the Second Symphony.[2]

When he moved to Vienna in 1868, he met rather conservative musicians there, who made him unsure of himself and who regarded his First Symphony as "too audacious." Together with the telling formulation, "In Vienna I had gotten quite scared off at first,"[3] the Second Symphony, completed there in 1872, seems to prove that he had taken the advice of those musicians after all. Compared with the First, the "brash little broom," in any case, the second appears in many respects smoother and more "classicistic." In this work, which also struck Richard Wagner as somewhat "tame," Bruckner seems to be at pains to achieve greater "intelligibility," as revealed already by the numerous general pauses between the individual complexes. They were to clarify the formal organization and bridge abrupt contrasts – with the result that they earned the work the nickname "pause symphony."

Nevertheless the Second is of fundamental importance for the development of the Brucknerian symphonic type. The dimensions have already been expanded to gigantic size – its performance takes about twenty minutes longer than does that of the First – the themes cluster together into entire complexes, the outer movements are linked for the first time by common motifs, and for the first time chorale-like elements crop up, especially in the Adagio.

Now between the F minor Mass and the Second Symphony there are most remarkable connections. The Symphony's Adagio, a predominantly lyrical-hymnal movement, exhibits a five-part structure, after the schema $ABA^1B^1A^2$, plus coda. Two contrasting thematic nexuses alternate in rondo fashion, whereby each return constitutes not only a variation but also an intensification. Bruckner quotes the Benedictus of the F minor Mass (mm. 97-102) twice (before K and at O). The first quotation, which is not exact but has more nearly the character of an allusion, follows immediately upon the B^1 part. The second, "literal" quotation occurs at the beginning of the coda and (in the first version) is separated from the preceding A^2 part by a general pause. Its start in F minor, is, to be sure, carefully prepared for by modulation, and it is immediately followed by the "head" of the main subject in A flat major.

Musical Example 6

These Benedictus quotations have an eminently personal significance and are meant as a thanksgiving for recovery and regained creative energy.

According to Robert Haas, Bruckner finished the drafting of the Adagio on July 19, 1872.[4] Shortly before, on June 16, he had performed the F minor Mass with the orchestra of the court opera in the church of St. Augustine in Vienna.[5] These dates highlight the connection between the mass and the symphony and help us understand what gave Bruckner the idea to quote the Benedictus in the Adagio. Several observations, moreover, strongly support the presumption that this movement has a religious import, independent of the quotes. The Adagio of the Second is the first symphonic movement that bears the marking "feierlich" (solemn), exhibits the so-called "St. Mary's cadence" and contains a chorale accompanied by *pizzicato*.[6] Last but not least, it is in the key of A flat major, the key of the Benedictus of the F minor Mass.

The close connection between the Second Symphony and the F minor Mass reveals itself also in the Finale of the symphony, where a passage from the *Kyrie eleison* of the mass is quoted twice (after F and after U). The first quotation occurs at the end of the exposition and forms the sharpest contrast imaginable to the preceding third theme complex, from which it is separated by a general pause of nearly three measures in length. The climactic wave in which the third theme complex crests in a triple *forte*. After the general pause, the Eleison quotation commences *sempre pianissimo*.

The second Eleison quotation occurs at the end of the reprise. Here its dynamic contrast to the preceding third theme complex is toned down, even leveled out in that the latter itself, after a triple *forte*, concludes with a *pianissimo* passage. It is highly instructive that the climax of the third theme complex (mm. 533-538) exhibits diverse analogies with the climax of the Kyrie movement (mm. 113-121): dynamically (*piu fortissimo*), motivically and harmonically (culmination on the C flat major triad). There can thus be no doubt that Bruckner had several passages from the F minor Mass in mind during the composition of the Adagio and the Finale of the Second Symphony.

Compared with the Second Symphony, the Third, completed in 1873 and repeatedly reworked, is distinguished by numerous "progressive" features.

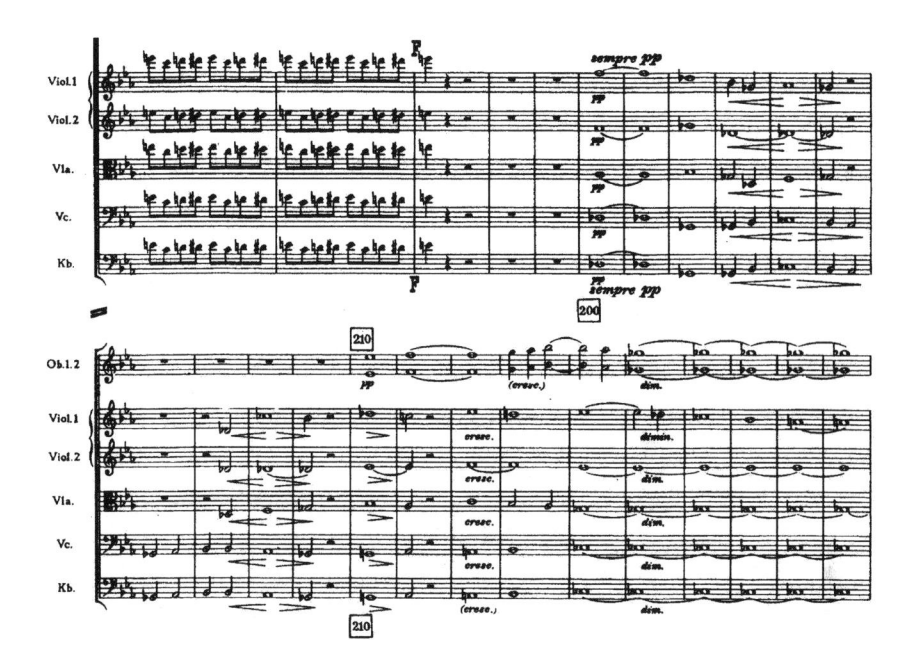

Musical Example 7

It is thus understandable that Richard Wagner preferred the latter when Bruckner showed him both symphonies in Bayreuth in September of 1873. For many Bruckner fans, as well as for many conductors, the Third is really the first symphonic work that represents the unmistakable, idiosyncratic style of the master. Among the early symphonies it is the one with the strongest contrasts. Compared with the Second, not only do the individual movements stand out more strongly from each other but the themes appear more graphic and differentiated. Stark motivic and dynamic contrasts crowd each other more frequently. One example is the conclusion of the opening movement's development section. Even the Adagio, which exhibits a strong affinity with Bruckner's church music, does not dispense with such effects. Again, there is great tension between the generally uncanny dynamism of the Scherzo and the tender, landler-like Trio. But it is in the Finale that the contrasts become dramatically acute. Bruckner himself called the contrapuntal interweaving of two such heterogeneous figures as the polka-like string and the chorale-like brass statement in the second theme complex a union of opposites – "the joys and sorrows of the world."

Like many other composers before and after him, Bruckner, too, was given to endowing his music with extra-musical meaning through the use of quotations, whether from others or from himself. A further example of that is the end of the exposition of the Third Symphony's opening movement, which exists in three versions. Here[7] the high woodwinds and later the horns quote, four times and nearly note for note, a *Miserere* phrase from the Gloria (mm. 100-103) of the D minor Mass of 1864.

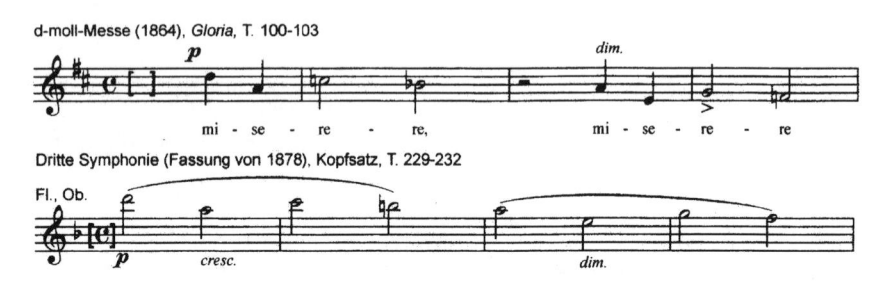

Musical Example 8

The significance of the passage as a plea for mercy becomes immediately plausible once one notices that the entire end of the exposition is replete with religious semantics: quasi at the summit of the exposition (second version of 1878, mm. 201-207), the trumpets intone a melody that is marked "chorale."[8] Upon closer inspection, the melody turns out to be a paraphrase of the first line of the Catholic chorale *Crux fidelis inter omnes*, and specifically a paraphrase of the form in which the line is sounded toward the end of Franz Liszt's symphonic poem *Die Hunnenschlacht* (The Battle against the Huns):

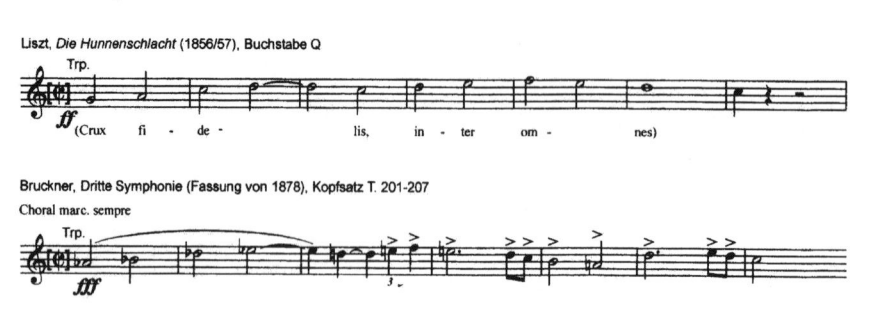

Musical Example 9

And that's not all: in the second version, the solo flute plays a melody marked "mysterious," and the exposition closes with quasi modal chord progressions that remind of Palestrina.

Especially suitable for semantic investigations is the Adagio of the Third Symphony, a movement whose shape is modeled on an arc (ABCB^{1}A^1). Each of the parts has its own distinct tempo or expression mark. Here is the architectonic schema of the second version of 1878:

Bewegt, quasi Andante	(Part A)	mm.1-40
Andante quasi Allegretto	(Part B)	mm. 41-72
Misterioso, langsamer [slower]	(Part C)	mm. 73-111
Andante quasi Allegretto	(Part B^1)	mm. 112-171
Langsamer (= reminiscence of the *Misterioso*)		mm. 172-181
Andante	(Part A^1)	mm. 182-251

This Adagio is one of the movements of Bruckner's about the occasion of whose genesis we have specific knowledge. Late in life, Bruckner told his young friend Josef Kluger that he wrote the "Andante" in this Adagio (he meant the second theme complex) on October 15, 1872 in memory of his mother Theresia (whose name day he always celebrated with a mass on that date). On the following day, the theme of the Misterioso of the third theme complex had come to him.[9] Numerous observations about semantic elements in Bruckner's music confirm this statement and help us to realize that the Adagio of the Third Symphony (like that of the Second) has to be viewed against a biographical background.

In terms of both tonal language and style, the Adagio is distinguished by a happy synthesis of archaic and modern elements. Phrases from the sacred music of the 18th century, sighing *Tristan* motifs and boldly modulated harmonies are perfectly integrated. And many details show plainly the connections between the movement and Bruckner's own sacred music. To cite a few examples:

The main subject of the Adagio exhibits a hitherto overlooked resemblance to the theme of the Benedictus from the Mass in C major written in 1842 in Windhaag (WAB 25).[10] The Benedictus theme seems practically like an archetype of the differentiated Adagio subject:

Messe in C-dur (um 1842) WAB 25, Benedictus, T. 1-6

Be - ne - dic - tus qui ve - nit, qui ve - nit in no - mi - ne Do - mi - ni,

Dritte Symphonie (Fassung von 1873), Adagio T. 1-8
1. VI. Feierlich

Musical Example 10

An attentive listener will not miss the twofold abrupt contrast between a *fortissimo* and a *piano* passage right after the main subject (1873 version, mm. 9-19): the *piano* passage is a somewhat stereotypical cadence stemming from the music of the classical period, which Bruckner loved.[11]

The Adagio's second theme complex – the very passage about which Bruckner spoke to Josef Kluger – is constructed after the type of "devout" music that Bruckner developed first in his masses and, ever since the Adagio of the "Nilth," also adopted in his symphonies. The third theme of the Adagio, marked *Misterioso*, also has the characteristics of a chorale.[12] Towards the end of the Adagio (at N), Bruckner quotes the sleep motif from Wagner's *Walküre*, surely no coincidence: my sense is that the quotation refers to the memory of the deceased mother, conveying the concrete meaning of "Rest in peace."[13]

Kurt Singer[14] and Hans Heinrich Eggebrecht[15] called Bruckner a "preacher." Preaching means elucidating the Biblical text, lecturing, exhorting at length to virtue, edifying. Bruckner's music does none of that. Most appropriately it can be called subjective, existential, religious confession.

The Allegiance to Richard Wagner

Everyone knows that composers at times receive decisive impulses from their colleagues. Mozart's preoccupation with the music of Bach and Handel in Vienna in 1782 had unlooked-for effects on his own creation, and Johannes Brahms's encounter of Robert and Clara Schumann in Düsseldorf in October of 1853 was fateful for him. Even so, Bruckner's enthusiasm for

Richard Wagner and his art seems something unique. Bruckner was 38 years old when he first heard and saw *Tannhäuser* on February 12, 1863, in Linz. This initial encounter with Wagner's new kind of music stirred him deeply and became a kind of catalyst, enabling him, who until then had known only traditional music, to find his own distinctive style. It is no exaggeration to say that Bruckner would not have become so original a symphonist if he had not been confronted with the music of Wagner.

He had seen the score of *Tannhäuser* in December of 1862. Otto Kitzler drew his attention to the beauties of the work and to the novelty of its instrumentation,[1] making him a Wagner enthusiast from then on. In May of 1865, he traveled all the way to Munich to witness the premiere of *Tristan und Isolde* – which, he found to his regret, had to be postponed. But on May 18 he met Wagner in person, who dedicated his photograph to him. On June 19, he was finally able to attend the third performance of the epochal work and was totally fascinated by it. Especially the love duet in the second Act, he said, had a "huge effect" on him.

Three years later, on April 4, 1868, Bruckner conducted the final chorus of Wagner's not yet performed opera *Die Meistersinger von Nürnberg* on the occasion of an inaugural concert of the singing circle *Frohsinn* in Linz. For some time he seems to have attached some hopes for an improvement of his own professional situation to Wagner. On July 20, 1868, in any case, he asked Hans von Bülow, who was then *kapellmeister* at the court of Ludwig II., if there was a chance for him to become court organist or "vice-court-conductor," expressly mentioning Wagner as his "lofty ideal."[2]

In August of 1873, Bruckner traveled to Marienbad in Bohemia for a health cure and there was able to finish sketching out the Finale to his Third Symphony. There also, at the latest, he conceived the idea of dedicating the work to Richard Wagner. Early in September of 1873, he traveled to Bayreuth, with two symphonies, the Second and the Third, in his luggage. Wagner received him in the Villa Wahnfried, and Bruckner asked him if he could dedicate the Third to him. After having looked through the score, Wagner accepted the dedication. In a letter written to Hans von Wolzogen after Wagner's death, Bruckner described in vivid colors the details of this, to him, unforgettable encounter: "Rather shyly and with a pounding heart, I then said to the fervently loved master: Maestro, I have something on my mind that I don't dare to say to you! The master said: Out with it, you know how dear you are to me. Then I came forward with my request, but only on condition that the master would be more or less satisfied, as I did not want to desecrate his Highly Renowned Name."[3]

Returned to Vienna, Bruckner drafted the text of the dedication to Wagner[4] and engaged the Linz engraver Josef Maria Kaiser to print the dedicatory page. Both the text and the detailed instructions he gave to the engraver reveal the limitless admiration he had for Wagner.

Symfonie in d moll
 sn Hochwohlgeboren
Herrn Herrn
Richard Wagner
 dem unerreichbaren
weltberühmten und erhabenen Meister
 der Dicht- und Tonkunst
  in tiefster Ehrfurcht gewidmet
   Von
    Anton Bruckner

(Symphony in D minor, dedicated in profoundest reverence to the Honorable Richard Wagner, the unequalled, world-famous and sublime master of the arts of poetry and music, by Anton Bruckner.) Bruckner's instructions about the graphic design of the dedicatory page cast a bright light on his own modesty and his idolatrous veneration of Wagner. While his own name was to be signed very simply, without any decoration, Wagner's "renowned name" was to "shine with every expenditure of pomp" "in gold." He was ready to make "any sacrifice" for Wagner.[5]

When composers dedicate works of theirs to colleagues, they often quote or at least allude to themes or motifs of the dedicatee. There are hundreds of examples of this, one of the most famous being Johann Sebastian Bach's *Musical Offering* (BWV 1079), which is based on a theme by Frederick the Great. Bruckner was familiar with this custom. Shortly after Wagner had accepted the dedication, he decided to weave two characteristic Wagner motifs into the opening movement and the Finale of the Third Symphony, namely the *Liebestod* motif from *Tristan und Isolde* and the Sleep motif from the *Walküre*. In the opening movement they occur in mm. 463-468 and 479-488 at the end of the development section, more precisely within the transition to the recapitulation. Bruckner quotes the motifs freely, not note for note, and probably from memory: one could therefore also speak of allusions. His concern was not with the kind of scholarly meticulousness so highly valued by some musicologists of the present.[6]

The Wagner quotations in the first version of the Third Symphony should be understood as a homage and as demonstration of allegiance. Significantly, Bruckner joined the Viennese Richard Wagner Society on October 16, 1873[7] – about the time that he inserted the Wagner motifs into the Third – and thereafter let no occasion go by to profess his fealty to the "New German" camp. In diverse petitions which he submitted to the ministry and to the Philosophical Faculty of the University of Vienna in the course of 1874, he referred to Wagner's and Liszt's favorable attitude towards him, as well a to the fact that Wagner had accepted his dedication of the Third Symphony.[8]

When he reworked the symphony in 1876/1877, he deleted the Wagner quotations (except for one in the Adagio), probably primarily in an effort to tighten the work. For several reasons Bruckner thought he had to shorten the work at all costs (the second version is shorter by 241 measures). But he left the *Walküre* quotation in the Adagio (the Sleep motif) untouched (mm. 266-269 in the 1873 version, mm. 237-240 in the 1878 version), evidently because it is, unlike the others, organically integrated into the music.

In the spring of 1874, Bruckner sent the dedicatory copy of the score to Wagner. The latter found no time to thank Bruckner in person but asked his wife Cosima to forward "his warmest thanks and his appreciation of your fine work."[9] "He has," Cosima continues, "gone through your symphony together with music director Hans Richter and taken uncommon pleasure both in the work and in the dedication." As a token of his gratitude, he invited Bruckner "most cordially" to the planned performances of the *Ring des Nibelungen* tetralogy. Bruckner actually attended the first performances of the *Ring* in August of 1876 and continued to be a regular visitor to the Bayreuth Festival until 1892.

Bruckner always spoke of Wagner with reverence and in superlatives. He loved and venerated him. In a letter to Eva Wagner, the youngest daughter, on April 10, 1885, he called him the "ardently loved, immortal master of all masters," the "immortal imperator of music."[10] Whenever he was in Bayreuth, he visited Wagner's grave at Villa Wahnfried, prayed fervently there and wept.[11] Undoubtedly he saw in him also a powerful protector and supporter. In several letters he referred to the fact that Wagner had promised him in 1882 in Bayreuth to perform all of his symphonies.[12]

In August of 1884, in St. Florian, Bruckner composed his Prelude for Harmonium in C major (WAB 129), known under the name *Perger Präludium*. The 27-measure piece is developed from the Sleep motif of *Die Walküre*, which recurs repeatedly in different transpositions. A comparison shows that the quotation is quite faithful: Bruckner uses it in the form it has in Act III (scene 3), where it accompanies Wotan's words *In festen Schlaf verschließ ich dich* ("In fastest sleep I lock you now"). Bruckner quotes not only the chromatically falling melodic line but also partly takes over the chord progressions, though he varies them in a few places (see Musical Example 11).

On the train to Bayreuth in August of 1884, Bruckner had met the leather merchant Josef Diernhofer of the town of Perg. The latter had asked for a small composition for his harmonium as a souvenir of their joint stay in Bayreuth.[13] The prelude thus is both a homage and an expression of allegiance to Wagner. The quotation of the Sleep motif, moreover, lets it be known that the prelude was conceived as a memorial composition.

One of the most common prejudices about Bruckner is the allegation that he experienced Wagner's magnificent art, so immensely rich in poetic intentions, purely musically, without paying any attention to the intellectual background of the music dramas.[14] For the Munich performance of *Tristan*, which he attended on June 19, 1868, he is said to have used a textless piano reduction of the work for his guide, and frequent reference is made to a malicious report according to which, on the occasion of a performance of *Die Walküre*, he supposedly asked why on earth Brünnhilde gets "burned."

Supposedly, then, he did not have the faintest idea what Wagner's dramas were about. On the other hand, he did not miss details of the action by any means. Thus upon coming out of a *Lohengrin* performance bathed in tears, he is said to have exclaimed over and over: "Why, why did she ask him?" His remarks about the "purest" Parsifal among the Flower Maidens and about the "nymphs" in *Rheingold* (he liked the Rhine Maidens' trio) also show understanding.

What fascinated him in Wagner's art was the heroic and the sublime and lofty. To Karl Waldeck's question, which three compositions he ranked highest, he replied: the Requiem of Mozart, Beethoven's *Eroica* and the funeral march from *Götterdämmerung*. Of Wagner's music dramas, *Siegfried* was his favorite. As August Stradal reports, he once shed tears at the scene where Siegfried broods about his mother. Numerous remarks about the function of counterpoint, the use of dissonances and other matters also make it clear that he was quite familiar with the art-theoretical maxims of Wagnerism.

Musical Example 11: Prelude in C major – Solemnly slow

The Triad of the Middle Symphonies

Of the altogether eleven symphonies (to the nine familiar ones one must add the "student symphony" and the "Nilth"), seven are in minor keys (one in F minor, three in C minor and three in D minor) and only four are in major keys. Obviously Bruckner had a predilection for the minor mood. The fact that he wrote three in C minor and three in D minor must be unique within the genre for the 19th century. It is important to know that he associated C minor with seriousness and heaviness (*grave, gravissimo*), and that D minor had a special meaning for him because Beethoven had written his Ninth in that key.[1]

In his voluminous monograph, Ernst Kurth discussed the symphonies not in the expected chronological order, but according to other criteria. To begin with, he turned to the Fourth and the Ninth – two works that, in his view, represented "certain developmental psychic poles": "in one [the Fourth] his most pronounced turn outward to a radiant, natural affirmation of life, in the other [the Ninth] then the most complete turn away from life."[2] The first three symphonies, he thought, served to describe Bruckner's "road" to the Fourth.

Written in 1874 and radically reworked between 1878 and 1880, the Fourth Symphony has always been Bruckner's most popular. Even in his lifetime it was, next to the Seventh, the one performed most frequently. Already the Vienna premiere on February 20, 1881, was a great success – one to be rated all the more highly after the spectacular flop of the Third – and Bruckner himself regarded it as the "most comprehensible" of his works.[3] No doubt the popularity of this symphony is due as much to its stylistic fabric as to its range of expression, as much to the immediacy of its melodic ideas as to the intense glow of its colors.

Already a look at certain technical compositional details will suggest that the *Romantic* Symphony represents in many respects a turning point in Bruckner's symphonic oeuvre. It is not only his first symphony in a major key (the preceding five symphonies are all in minor), but also the first symphonic work in which the alteration of major and minor, and above all the mingling of the moods so characteristic of Romantic harmonies, is adopted on principle.[4] The affinity with the early Romantic sound world of Franz Schubert and Carl Maria von Weber is strongly developed here, while on the other hand the influence of Richard Wagner cannot be missed, especially in the outer movements.

Why did Bruckner give the Fourth the characteristic epithet "the Romantic"? What did he mean by that concept? Wagner's "romantic opera" *Lohengrin* was for him the quintessence of the Romantic, with which he associated feelings of wonder, of the mysterious, religious and pure, and a good deal of this imaginative world also entered into the Fourth.[5]

Bruckner greatly admired the Allegretto of Berlioz's *Harold Symphony*. The second movement of his *Romantic* – an Andante – is, like Berlioz's Allegretto, a nocturnal pilgrims' march. Of its three themes, the elegiac first is strongly march-like in character. The second is a four-line chorale in large note values, while the third consists of yet another, differently structured, six-line chorale with pizzicato accompaniment. The main subject has two climaxes, of which the second greatly exceeds the first in intensity.

In the revision of 1878, the Scherzo and Trio of the original version were replaced by entirely new compositions. The somewhat impressionistic Scherzo of the final version is now devised as a hunting piece, as the horn fanfares at the beginning already signalize; Bruckner himself labeled the landler-like Trio in G flat major *Dance tune during a meal at the hunt.*

The Finale exists in no fewer than three different versions. In the final revision of 1880, the movement was so radically restructured, that the cheerful character of the first version was altogether lost. Not only were a number of the original melodic ideas replaced by new, at times dramatic elements, but even several of the original sections were given a new face by means of a darker coloration. In this final version, the movement is marked by strong contrasts and enormous tensions.

Each of Bruckner's symphonies has its own physiognomy, its own distinct character and unique mode of expression. This becomes especially clear if one compares the Fifth Symphony of 1875/76 with the *Romantic*. Though both are written in major keys, they are worlds apart. While the Fourth is distinguished by its great radiance and opulence, the Fifth, despite its colorfulness, sounds more severe and austere. It is the only one of Bruckner's symphonies that begins with a slow "Introduction," one that recalls models of sacred music and comprises three contrary structures: a shadowy first idea, an enormously emphatic fanfare and a chorale statement.

The three theme complexes of the following Allegro are also sharply distinguished from each other. The main theme, strongly modulated and enveloped in tremolos, is first cited by the violas and cellos and then presented *fortissimo* by the entire orchestra. The second thematic complex (Bruckner's "song period") is developed from an eight-bar chorale-like idea, which the strings recite *pizzicato*. The third theme is of a propulsive nature and brings about the climax of the exposition. In typically Bruckneresque fashion, the Epilogue dies away in a triple *piano.* The development section illustrates Bruckner's predilection for abrupt contrasts.

Two themes provide the basis for the rondo-like Adagio of the second movement. The first, introduced by the woodwinds and supported by the strings with ghostly unison pizzicatos, is a "sad tune." By contrast, the fully harmonized second theme takes a turn toward the hymnal and ecstatic. Both themes undergo grandiose climaxes in the course of he movement. The Adagio and the following Scherzo are closely linked not only by the same key (D minor) but also by their themes. Most of the motifs of the first Adagio theme return in the Scherzo, along with new ideas. The second Scherzo theme contrapuntally links a landler-type melody with alphorn-like phrases.

The Trio in B flat major is distinguished by numerous "Romantic" traits: a peculiar major-minor mode; a lingering in the *piano* region, which only the recapitulation steps beyond abruptly; the leading role of the horns; and above all the expression of tender dreaminess and an inclination toward the mysterious. Of special significance in this Trio is the minor sixth. A lengthy, accentuated G flat played by the horns introduces the first three phrases of the piece and partly determines the harmonic disposition: immediately after the establishment of the theme (at A and E), the key deviates to G flat major.

As noted before, Bruckner had a special affinity with Ludwig van Beethoven. He never tired of studying and analyzing the latter's symphonies. How strongly he was impressed by Beethoven's famous "flashback technique" at the beginning of the Finale of the Ninth Symphony is proven by the way he opens the Finale of his Fifth.[6] Here he quotes note for note the beginning of the symphony, the main subject of the opening movement and the first Adagio theme (along with its accompanying voice). After each quotation, the clarinet intones the head motif of the first Finale theme. These prominent reminiscences and quotations remind the listener of earlier events and at the same time prepare him for the spiritual atmosphere of the grandiose final movement.

The Finale of the Fifth constitutes an artful synthesis of the sonata and the fugue forms. In the exposition, no fewer than four themes are presented: the striking main subject, which is worked in *fugato* manner, the *cantabile* side theme, the propulsive third theme and a chorale-like fourth one. In the development section, the first and fourth themes are interwoven. The double fugue thereby created is monumental in design and worked out down to the smallest detail – a polyphonic construction that exhausts virtually every possibility of contrapuntal combination. Without exaggerating, Bruckner called the Fifth his "contrapuntal masterpiece." Ernst Kurth went even farther when he asserted that the conclusion of the symphony ranks among the most sublime things music, or even the human spirit generally, has produced.[7]

Bruckner never heard his Fifth. Already mortally ill, he had to miss the premiere, which took place, fifteen years after the completion of the work, in Graz on April 8, 1894, under Franz Schalk. His happiness, when he received news of the sensational success of the performance, was all the greater. Franz Schalk wrote on April 10, 1894: "Honored Maestro! You will surely have heard already by word of mouth about the immense impact your great, magnificent Fifth has had here. I can only add that the evening will for the rest of my life count among the most magnificent memories I could ever be blessed with. I felt profoundly moved, walking in the blessed fields of eternal greatness. Of the shattering power of the Finale no one can have the least idea who has not heard it. So I lay, my fervently revered maestro, the greatest sum of all my admiration and my most devout enthusiasm at your feet and hail him who could create such things."[8] Graz, to be sure, did not get to hear the Fifth in the authentic form in which we know it today but in a greatly edited version, wherein Bruckner had approved Schalk's suggestion to execute the final chorale with reinforced winds.

Highly successful were also the first performances in Vienna under Ferdinand Löwe (in March of 1898 and on April 15, 1899), Gustav Mahler (February 24, 1901) and Felix Mottl (November 20, 1904). The influential Viennese critic Gustav Schönaich wrote about the celebrated work: "Of all the symphonies of the master, it is perhaps the one that reflects his unique world of thought and feeling most purely and clearly and speaks the most eloquent language about the voluptuous happiness to be found there."[9] Schönaich was one of the first to point out the basic religious mood of the Fifth.

Robert Haas distinguished three creative phases in Bruckner's oeuvre and had the third commence with the String Quintet and the Sixth Symphony.[10] For several reasons, however, it seems more accurate to regard the Sixth, written in 1880/1881, as the final link in the chain of the three middle symphonies. The stylistic connection between it and the Fourth and Fifth is in every respect exceptionally close, while there are weighty differences to the last three symphonies, which especially in their harmony and instrumentation reveal a new outlook.

Several writers in the 1920's celebrated Bruckner as a mystic. Ernst Kurth was of the opinion that the Sixth Symphony marked one of the moments "of greatest blinding" on Bruckner's way "toward the light," a "rich, radiant shining" being the basic coloration of the work.[11] Strictly speaking, however, this view applies only to the opening movement, whose coda, for example (in the score from W on) exhibits indeed a fascinating palette of shimmering sounds. By contrast the middle movements exhibit far less radiant colors, and the by no means straight development of the Finale, which commences in minor keys, makes clear that the triumphant A major effects of the conclusion had to be laboriously "fought for," as it were according to the motto *Per aspera ad astra* – through the night to the light.

One can best grasp the peculiar character of the Sixth Symphony by holding it against the Fourth and Fifth and realizing how different these works are. It is as though Bruckner had aimed at a kind of balance between the largely divergent tendencies of the two preceding works.

This is especially apparent in the opening movement, whose first and third theme complex, both marked by intense color, implement ideas that Bruckner had first developed in the head movement of the *Romantic*: the mysterious beginning, the dialogical structure of the main subject and, not least, the mixing of major and minor, that being the code of the opening. Altogether different is the intensely expressive second theme complex, where polyrhythmic traits and the characteristic sevenths steps are especially striking. The proximity to the body of ideas of the sublime Adagio of the Fifth is unmistakable.

The Adagio of the Sixth represents the type of solemn music. The three theme complexes of the movement contrast as powerfully as one can imagine. If the first theme voices a tone of lament (the expressive sighs of the oboe are especially eloquent), an ecstatic upswing is unmistakable in the second complex, while the third theme has altogether the character of a funeral march.

Altogether new features are observable in the A minor Scherzo with its Aeolian coloration. Its effect is not dance-like as in most of the earlier scherzos of Bruckner, but more nearly eerie. The fantastic nature of the design manifests itself, among other things, in the contrasts between softly scurrying passages and rigid *fortissimos.* The C major Trio, with its pizzicatos in the strings and fanfare-like sounds of the horns, is Romantic in mood.

Abrupt contrasts, finally, determine the shape of the Finale. They occur not merely between the individual theme complexes but even force a division within the first complex and become more acute in the development section. The movement is designed in such a way, however, that the symphony closes in splendor.

The reception of the Sixth was rather peculiar. After the Viennese premiere of the middle movements on February 11, 1883, Eduard Hanslick, in the *Presse*, called Bruckner a "wild composer," who had "gained some discipline but lost nature" and reproached him with having transferred Wagner's music-dramatic style to the symphony. "During the Adagio," he wrote, "interest and disconcertment still maintained a balance in the audience, which went along, albeit hesitantly. But at the Scherzo, captivating solely by its oddness, the horse, as the sportsman would say, parted company with its rider."[12]

The verdict of the reviewer for the journal *Signale für die musikalische Welt* was more differentiated. He spoke of strengths and drawbacks, about surprising, brilliant ideas and splendid instrumentation along with "lack of logical treatment and exaggerated spinning-out."[13] By contrast, Josef Scheu's language about the premiere of the complete Sixth under Mahler was downright hymnal, and in Stuttgart, on March 14, 1901, the work was received enthusiastically. Nevertheless the Sixth could never fully assert itself. Like the First, it is performed relatively rarely even today.

The Seventh – a Second "Wagner Symphony"

> "I know only one who comes up to Beethoven, and that is Bruckner."
> *Richard Wagner*

Within reception history, the premieres of the Seventh Symphony mark a decisive turning-point. It was the first work of Bruckner's that really earned him great successes and thus also smoothed the way into the concert halls for the other symphonies. Shortly after the path-breaking performance on March 10, 1885, in Munich, the Seventh started upon its triumphal march through the important metropolises of the world. The story of this performance is so instructive that it deserves to be told briefly.

Bruckner had worked on the Seventh for two years, from September of 1881 to September of 1883. He did not initially think of an orchestral performance. Joseph Schalk and Ferdinand Löw, his most loyal pupils, presented the symphony on two pianos at Vienna's Academic Richard Wagner Society. Schalk conceived the plan of another piano performance in Leipzig and turned to Arthur Nikisch about it, who was then first *kapellmeister* at the Leipzig municipal theater. Nikisch got to know the symphony, caught fire immediately, and promised to perform it in a benefit concert, to take place in April or early May, to help fund a Wagner monument. The concert had to be postponed until September and at Bruckner's urging was put off again until December 30, because Hans von Wolzogen and students had begged him not to let it take place under any circumstances during a time between semesters.[1] The hoped-for big success failed to materialize, but the ice was broken. The symphony came to the attention of the Wagner conductor Hermann Levi, who put it on the program of a concert that took place on March 10, 1885 in Munich. That performance turned into a triumph for Bruckner.

What accounts for the enormous impact of this symphony? At first sight, it hardly seems to differ in its design from the architectonic of the preceding symphonies. The opening movement is of considerable length; the outer movements are based on three theme complexes each; and Bruckner's dynamic form principle manifests itself here, too, in large-scale climactic sequences. On closer inspection, however, one notices a number of subtly unusual qualities. The formal organization is more perspicuous; the motifs impress themselves more readily on the memory; the themes contrast strongly with each other, as always in Bruckner, but are dovetailed so organically that the movement remains fluid at all times. There are, besides, few general pauses – those caesuras that are so prominent elsewhere in Bruckner. Written in a bright D major, the Seventh is distinguished by an increased luminosity – in that respect it is comparable only to the Fourth, with which it also shares a fondness for "Romantic" sound effects.

A closer analysis of the score reveals an astonishing boldness of conception, modernity of the musical language and uniqueness of structural logic. Its boldness and modernity are evident above all in its harmonies. Bruckner is more progressive as a harmonist than Brahms and even the New Germans, to whom he felt he belonged. "More progressive" means that mediantic tone relations (i.e. relations by thirds) play a larger part in his work than, say, in Brahms; that harmonic alterations have a greater importance; that freer and more frequent use is made of chromaticism and certain dissonances; and that Bruckner goes much farther than other contemporary composers in shifting into more remote keys in the key circle.

Secondly, there is the peculiar structural logic. Whereas Brahms was celebrated by the conservatives as a master of "musical logic," Bruckner was charged with illogical, disjointed musical thinking. The reproach stems from the inability to recognize the new. True, Bruckner loved caesuras and extreme, unmediated contrasts. His manner of developing and processing motifs differs fundamentally from that of Brahms, but it is equally logical. While respecting the aesthetic norms of the genre, he transformed the structure of the symphony as it were from within. He created a monumental type of symphony, greatly expanded the dimensions of the movements and embraced a dynamic principle of form unknown until then in symphonic music and characterized above all by the climactic waves.

Several other factors beside its musical qualities contributed to the success of the performance of the Seventh: Munich was then a stronghold of Wagnerism, and Hermann Levi the most committed of Wagner's conductors. Bruckner was known as a fanatical Wagnerian, and word had gotten around that he composed the solemn Adagio as an epitaph for the beloved master. Bruckner himself remarked to the music critic Theodor Helm and his son, who visited him in his apartment on January 26, 1894: "Yes, gentlemen, I really wrote the Adagio on the death of the great, the one and only – partly in anticipation and partly as a funeral march after the catastrophe had taken place."[2] The draft of the Adagio was completed on January 22, 1883; on February 13, Wagner died in Venice. When the wire with the sad news reached Bruckner, the composition had advance to the coda. Bruckner wanted it to be understood that the section for tubas and horns at X, which was written under the immediate impact of the news, was intended as a funeral music in memory of the master's demise.[3] Thematic links to the *Te Deum* reveal that the Christian hope *non confundar in aeternum* is at the back also of the Adagio.

Formally, the movement is designed in rondo fashion with two contrasting themes, whereby the first theme in each reprise is developed intensively in several climactic waves. The last climactic train proceeds in several stages, impresses by its extremely audacious harmonic disposition and reaches a high point in C major. The somber C sharp minor of the beginning and the culminating C major are thus like opposite poles. The boldness of the tremendous arc that Bruckner erects here is unexampled in the symphonic music of his time (or even the time thereafter).[4]

There are significant analogies, in conception, structure and expression, between Bruckner's *funeral music* and Wagner's funeral march on the death of Siegfried in Act III of *Götterdämmerung*. Bruckner marked the Adagio as *Very solemn and very slow* – Wagner wanted the playing of the funeral march to be *solemn*. The parallel in musical progress between the two compositions is noteworthy. Bruckner's funeral music is divided into three distinct sections. The initial tuba and horn section in C sharp minor (at X) is followed by a dirge-like part for violins, flute, oboe and clarinet (at Y), which then concludes with another tuba and horn section in C sharp major. The opening section of Wagner's funeral march with tubas and brasses is similarly followed by a dirge-like section of solo woodwinds (English horn, clarinet, oboe) and horns.[5]

Both compositions obtain their unique coloration from the tubas. The Adagio and the Finale of the Seventh are the first movements for which Bruckner prescribed four Wagner tubas and a bass tuba. Significantly he was unwilling and unable to do without these "Wagnerian" instrumental colors in his subsequent symphonies, the Eighth and the Ninth, as well. This is all the more remarkable since Bruckner was generally very reluctant to expand the apparatus of the Classic-Romantic orchestra, as the New Germans loved to do, so as not to rouse the ire of Hanslick. Thus, as Siegfried Ochs reports, he dispensed with a third kettle drum in the *Te Deum*,[6] and his favorite disciples Josef and Franz Schalk had a world of trouble "wringing" the famous cymbals stroke at the climax of Seventh's Adagio from him.[7]

Bruckner loved alluding to Wagnerian motifs in his symphonies. Thus, one measure before P, the horns in the Adagio of the Eighth Symphony intone a variant of the Siegfried motif, on which he also loved to improvise on the organ.[8] He said expressly that he had included the quotation "in memory of the master."[9] A number of Wagner reminiscences in the opening movement of the Seventh similarly appear to be no accidents but serve as homage to the fervently loved maestro. The so-called *liebestod* motif is sounded several times in the movement as a contrapuntal counter-voice to a motif of the main subject. Then, in the Coda of the movement (mm. 417-420), the two flutes and the first oboe almost exactly "quote" the Sleep motif from *Die Walküre*, the movement being in fact in the E major of the *Walküre*'s conclusion. There Wotan kisses Brünnhilde's eyes, casts her into a deep sleep and leaves her surrounded by a sea of fire, while the music weaves together the Siegfried motif, the Fate motif and the Sleep motif.

The Coda of the Seventh's opening movement (from X on) lingers for 31 measures in the E major key. The motif of the woodwinds, which echoes the Sleep motif, is intended as a counterpoint to the main motif, which is derived from the main subject of the movement (and the symphony as a whole). The violins describe pentatonic-colored tremolo eighths figures that remind of similar formations in the conclusion of the *Walküre*. Dynamically, however, the two conclusions are contrary to each other. In Wagner, the music reaches a *fortissimo* climax at Wotan's last words and then gradually dies down. Bruckner's Coda, on the other hand, describes a powerful crescendo arc, which begins *piano* and *pianissimo* and ends in a triple *forte*.

The sensational success of the Munich performance of the Seventh on March 10, 1885, must have been overwhelming for Bruckner. Perhaps for the first time in his life he experienced a work of his being received with unmixed enthusiasm. With great pride he reported to his supporter Arthur Nikisch, immediately after his return to Vienna on March 15, how Hermann Levi, at an evening ceremony at which Munich's entire artistic world was assembled, had described the symphony as "the most important symphonic work since the death of Beethoven."[10] He was received by Karl Baron von Perfall, the general manager of the of Munich's Royal Court and National Theater, had his portrait painted by Hermann Kaulbach, and was twice photographed at the studio of Franz Hanfstaengl. Heinrich Porges, the music critic of the *Münchner Neueste Nachrichten*, praised him in a lengthy review on March 12 as a composer who had achieved great results "because he did not narrowly close his mind to the development that modern music has undergone primarily through Richard Wagner but also through Berlioz and Liszt, but absorbed it and managed to blend it with his own deeply founded musical nature." Bruckner was a tone poet, "who does not labor in careful sophistry to raise up small and insignificant themes into something large, but from the beginning feels in a truly great manner."[11]

After this success, at the latest, it will have occurred to Bruckner to dedicate the Seventh to King Ludwig II., the friend and supporter of Wagner. In the letter to Nikisch cited above, he mentions by the way that the king will also be "notified."[12] Herann Levi informed him on April 26, 1885, that after repeated consultation with the king's court secretary, his Majesty would "quite surely" accept the dedication of the Seventh.[13] In a highly obsequious letter (Hermann Levi had advised him to write it like that) Bruckner entreated the king, in May of 1885, to accept the dedication most graciously.[14] He hoped that Ludwig would order another performance of the work.

This hope could not be fulfilled, however, because the king became mentally ill and had to be certified.

It strikes one as very odd that Eduard Hanslick called the Seventh, of all things, one of Bruckner's most compact works, a "symphonic python." In a review, he confessed frankly that he could hardly judge the symphony fairly, as it appeared so altogether "unnatural, blown up, morbid and corrupting." He said he shared the opinion of one of "Germany's most respected musicians," who described the symphony "as the ghastly dream of an orchestral composer overstrained by twenty Tristan rehearsals."[15] Hanslick was so completely prejudiced against Bruckner that he saw in him only the Wagner epigone and totally missed his originality. He took umbrage at Bruckner's sometimes pathos- and emphasis-laden language, he felt disturbed by the new, unfamiliar tone, which seemed theatrical to him. "Morbid excess of expression" was, significantly, a reproach he directed at Wagner as much as at Bruckner.

The history of the arts is also the history of critical revision. Posterity, which judges more justly than contemporaries do, began to appreciate, love and admire Bruckner not least for the very aspects of his music that Eduard Hanslick so disliked. What today arouses the enthusiasm of many people all over the world when they hear Bruckner is the intensity and breadth of expression, the fervid ecstasy, his fondness for the solemn, consecrational and visionary, the jubilant conclusions and the loftiness and sublimity of his symphonies.

Secular and Religious

Music is a kind of language. No less an expert than Ernst Bloch hit the nail on the head when he referred to Bruckner's "speaking music."[1] The quasi-linguistic quality manifests itself most clearly in the intonation, the recitative-like passages and above all the character types. By that I mean recurring compositional formulae and genres with prominent characteristics of style and strong expressive values, such as the recitative and arioso, the chorale, the hymn, the march and the funeral march, the pastoral, the scherzo and the landler. For Robert Schumann, a composition has musical character "if a specific frame of mind predominates in it, obtrudes itself so much that only one way of interpreting it is possible."[2] In the final analysis, that means that a specific semantic is immanent in every character, It will be generally agreed without for further ado that the march has a different semantic than the funeral march, that the pastoral has different connotations than the scherzo, or that the chorale has a religious character, while the landler has a worldly one.

One could say that Bruckner's diverse symphonic oeuvre is like a cosmos, in which the secular and the religious, the profane and the sacred, exist side by side. It is as much bound to the symphonic and music-dramatic tradition as it borrows elements from the realm of church music. Our task here is to investigate the means of its tonal language and to examine the various areas of influence. The following table summarizes the results of my researches.[3]

Character Types in Bruckner

INSTRUMENTAL RECITATIVE AND ARIOSO
All the main themes in the opening movements of the symphonies (from the Second on)

CHORALE
Third Symphony (1878 version), First Movement, mm. 201-207
Third Symphony, Finale, second theme complex
Fourth Symphony, Andante, second theme complex
Fifth Symphony, First Movement, second theme complex
Fifth Symphony, Finale, conclusion

MARCH
First Symphony, head theme
Eighth Symphony, Finale, third theme complex
Eighth Symphony, Finale (at N): "March of the Dead"
Ninth Symphony, First Movement, development (at O)

FUNERAL MARCH
Fourth Symphony, Andante, main theme
Fourth Symphony, Finale, second theme complex
Sixth Symphony, Adagio, third theme complex
Seventh Symphony, Adagio (at X): "Funeral Music" in memory of Richard Wagner

PASTORAL
- Third Symphony, First Movement, second theme complex
- Fourth Symphony, First Movement, second theme complex

LANDLER
- Third Symphony, Trio
- Fourth Symphony, Trio ("Dance Tune during the Meal at the Hunt")
- Fifth Symphony, Scherzo, second theme complex
- Ninth Symphony, Scherzo (at E)

MISTERIOSO
- Motet *Christus factus est pro nobis* (WAB 11)
- F Minor Mass, Credo, *Et incarnatus*
- Third Symphony, First Movement: "Moderate, misterioso"
- Third Symphony, Adagio, third theme complex: "Slower, Misterioso"
- Ninth Symphony, First Movement: "Solemn, Misterioso"

SOLEMN
- Adagios of the Second, Sixth, Seventh, Eighth and Ninth Symphony
- Eighth Symphony, Finale
- Ninth Symphony, First Movement: "Solemn, Misterioso"

The manner in which Bruckner shapes many of his themes is dramatic in nature. From the Fourth on, his symphonies pursue the following pattern. Tremolos in the strings provide a tonal background, from which the subject arises. The latter is recited *piano* by one or several instruments at first and then repeated *fortissimo* by the entire orchestra. This unusual opening technique does not derive from the symphonic tradition. It is rather modeled on the monody, on recitatives and ariosos that Bruckner encountered in Richard Wagner's Romantic operas, and which left a lasting impression on him. We may look, for example, at the beginning of the *Romantic Symphony*:

Musical Example 12

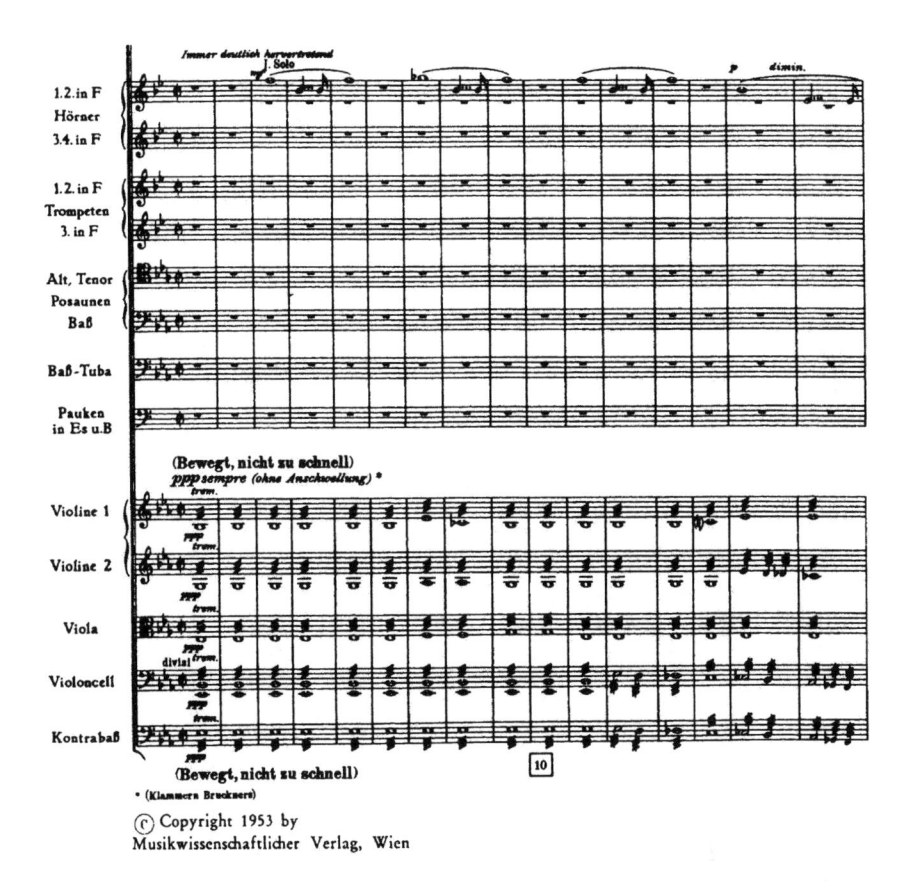

There is a "family resemblance" between the main themes of Bruckner's symphonies (starting with the Fourth). The same can be said of the "second" themes of the outer movements, which are constructed in sonata form. Bruckner's so-called *song periods* represent a type all its own of idyllic, warmly felt music with richly blossoming melodies. Many of these songlike passages – as in the opening movements of the Third and Fourth Symphony – have pastoral features, such as the major modes and the bordoun basses. But they differ from the conventional symphonic tradition by their harmonic wealth, their intensified luminosity, colorfulness and expressivity. Here is the beginning of the song period from the head movement of the *Romantic Symphony*.

Musical Example 13

A family resemblance, finally, exists also between the "third" theme complexes, which – after the relative serenity of the song periods – bring renewed movement and frequently have an tendency to the unisono. A number of these "third" themes are marked by a latent or explicit march character. For an especially vivid example one may cite the third theme complex in the Finale of the Eighth Symphony (starting at the letter I). The tendency toward unison or a heterophonic instrumentation is unmistakable in the first 24 measures.

Musical Example 14

Then the march-like music is replaced by eight measures of a chorale-like idea, marked *Solemn, tender*, while in the eight measures after that (at M), the chorale-like melody – recited by the oboe and later by the flute – is accompanied by a march-like pizzicato rhythm of the strings.

After a further eight measures, the entire orchestra suddenly intones a grandiose march *fortissimo,* which Bruckner, in the well-known letter to Felix Weingartner, referred to as "March of the Dead" – a more fitting description of this music cannot well be imagined.

Those who seek to derive Bruckner's symphonic music from a mystical or metaphysical ur-experience overlook the fact that a weighty "worldly" component exists in his symphonies alongside the religious sphere. It is most apparent in the scherzos and in the many genre pictures included, for example in the *Romantic*. The Scherzo of the latter Bruckner himself wanted to be understood as *Scherzo of the Hunt*; the landler-like melody of its Trio he described in the "side autograph" as "Dance Tune during a Meal at the Hunt."[4] Even the Scherzo of the Ninth Symphony – undoubtedly the eeriest scherzo Bruckner ever wrote – surprises by a landler-like melody reminiscent of Schubert.

Musical Example 15

Bruckner's symphonic language not only stands in the zenith of his time but points to the future. Paradoxically, however, it is not without a number of archaic elements, which I believe must be ascribed to his decades-long preoccupation with church music. Here one may mention above all the modal, gradual harmonies to be observed on occasion, his predilection for sequences ("rosalias") frowned upon by many of his contemporaries, and certain technical peculiarities such as ligatures. One also must take into account the fact that during the long years at St. Florian, Bruckner had ample opportunity to hear and study works by Palestrina and masses by Joseph Haydn and Franz Schubert. Besides, he intimately knew Mozart's Requiem Mass, a work whose compositional technique he still analyzed as late as 1877. Reminiscences to that work are noticeable in several of Bruckner's movements, and it is entirely possible that the strange *Introduction* to the Fifth Symphony with its characteristic ligatures is an echo of his preoccupation with the Requiem.[5]

In 1962, Leopold Nowak argued in favor of distinguishing between a "symphonic" and a "church" style in Bruckner.[6] In principle one must agree with this view: Bruckner's symphonic music and his sacred compositions have to be seen as basically independent spheres. Nevertheless there are interconnections: Bruckner himself at times bridged them.

Bruckner's symphonies are rich in chorales and chorale-like constructions that have religious connotations. Of special interest are two passages to which he himself expressly attached the note *Chorale*. A four-line jubilant chorale, intoned in triple *forte* by the brasses, forms the conclusion of the Fifth Symphony of 1875/76. It is a chorale melody borrowed neither from the Catholic nor from the Protestant liturgy but freely invented. Likewise marked *Chorale* is, secondly, a melody that the trumpets intone quasi at the climax of the exposition in the first movement of the Third Symphony (second version of 1878), mm. 201-207. It is noteworthy that the marking is absent from the corresponding (and variant) passage in the first version of 1873.

Why did Bruckner label these two passages by the word *Chorale*? In considering this question one should note that Franz Liszt's symphonic poem of 1856/67, *Die Hunnenschlacht* (The Battle of the Huns) centers around the chorale *Crux fidelis inter omnes*. In the course of the composition, it is sounded first by the trombones (14 mm. after C), then by the trumpets and the trombone (8 mm. before D), later by the organ (10 mm. after I) and finally by the entire orchestra (at Q). At three points in the score, the term *Chorale* appears. The poetic idea of the symphonic poem, inspired by Wilhelm von Kaulbach's monumental staircase painting, is the ghostly battle between the fallen Huns and Christians outside the gates of Rome and the victory of Christianity. The ancient liturgical melody, the foreword to the composition states, serves as a symbol of the triumph of Christianity and of the light radiating from the *victorious cross*. In a letter to Walter Bache of May 25, 1879, Liszt himself explained the poetic idea of the work:

Kaulbach's world-famous painting depicts two battles: one on the ground, the other in the air, in accordance with the legend that the warriors continued to fight endlessly even after their death. In the center of the picture appears the cross and its mysterious light; to this my *symphonic poem* adheres. The gradually developing chorale *Crux fidelis* makes clear the idea of the ultimately victorious Christianity in effective love of God and men.[7]

A careful comparison of the *Hunnenschlacht* with the passages referred to above leads to the conclusion that Bruckner must have known Liszt's symphonic poem and is likely to have received decisive impulses from it.

One might note in this connection that both the *Hunnenschlacht* and Bruckner's Fifth close affirmatively and apotheosizing with a chorale. Bruckner's freely invented chorale is structured altogether differently than the tune of *Crux fidelis*, but the instrumentation and handling of the chorale melody in the two works are similar. The powerfully harmonized chorale is recited in Liszt (from Q on) by the wind instruments, in Bruckner specifically by the brasses. In both cases the spaces between the individual chorale lines are bridged by brief "intermezzos." In the *Hunnenschlacht*, the strings interject fanfare-like motifs, which are to be played *pomposo*. In Bruckner, dotted ostinato rhythms in the woodwinds and eighths figures in the high strings swirl about the actual chorale. There is much to suggest that in designing the Finale of his Fifth Symphony, which has become known under the cognomen *Glaubenssymphonie* (Faith Symphony), Bruckner had the triumphal conclusion of Liszt's *Hunnenbschlacht* in mind. It needs no saying that the monumental conclusion greatly exceeds Liszt's symphonic poem in sublimity and power.

In speaking of the religious elements in Bruckner's symphonic oeuvre, one must not forget to mention that in composing the *Et incarnatus est* of his F minor Mass of 1868 he had created a type of devotional music to which he was to have repeated recourse in his symphonies. The compositional model according to which that *Et incarnatus* is constructed became, as it were, the archetype for the shaping of the "second" themes in the Andante of the "Nilth" Symphony and in the Adagios of the Third and Fifth, as well as of the String Quintet.

It is significant for our reflections here that the *Et incarnatus* of the F minor Mass bears the momentous marking *Moderato misterioso*. We find the same heading in the motet *Christus factus est pro nobis* of 1884 (WAB 11) – a work meant, as we know, as a gradual for Maundy Thursday. Everything points to the probability that Bruckner chose the description *Misterioso* in the sacred works referred to consciously and deliberately in order to suggest that his music should be understood as the expression of religious miracles, and we will hardly be mistaken in the presumption that this so characteristic denomination has a similar semantic in the symphonies.

The opening movement of the Third Symphony is headed *Moderate, Misterioso*. The third theme complex (at C) in the Adagio of the same symphony is marked *Slower, Misterioso*, and the expression mark at the beginning of the Ninth Symphony, which is dedicated to the "Good Lord," is *Solemn, Misterioso*. All these so named parts have a mysterious quality about them. One might also mention in this connection that in reworking his Third Symphony in 1878 Bruckner added a flute melody toward the end of the exposition of the first movement (mm. 242-246), to which he expressly attached the note "p mysterious."

Musical Example 16

In November of 1896 – only weeks after Bruckner's death – the Viennese critic Theodor Helm published a lengthy article that stands out for its many excellent observations. In it he celebrated Bruckner "as the specific master of the Adagio" and praised the "majestic breadth and solemnity" of his music.[8] A solemn expression is indeed unique to many of Bruckner's movements, and not a few bear the marking *feierlich* (solemn) – specifically the Adagios of the Second, the Sixth, the Seventh, the Eight and the Ninth Symphony.

This momentous label is not to be found in either Beethoven, Schubert, Mendelssohn or Brahms, masters, that is, who all used the Italian performance marks. It does occur, however in the fourth movement of Schumann's Rhenish Symphony, a movement initially headed *Im Charakter der*

Begleitung einer feierlichen Ceremonie – "in the character of an accompaniment to a solemn ceremony."[9] But it was Richard Wagner who had a special predilection for the term and the kind of "solemn" music it marked. In his music dramas, we find it mostly in places where the music gives expression to a situation of exceptional gravity, as, for example, the funeral march on the death of Siegfried, the "funeral ceremony" for Titurel in *Parsifal*, the death announcement in the second act of *Die Walküre*, and the mortally wounded Siegfried's imagined farewell to Brünnhilde in *Götterdämmerung*..

What exactly does the term "feierlich" import in Bruckner? Let us consider three instances.

The marking "Sehr feierlich" of the Adagio in the Seventh Symphony becomes immediately obvious when one recalls that Bruckner devised this movement as an epitaph for Wagner.

We spoke earlier of the musico-dramatic means employed in Bruckner's symphonies: one example of their use is presented by the Finale of the Eighth Symphony, whose conception, according to Bruckner's letter to Felix Weingartner, was prompted by an event in world politics – the encounter between the Emperor Francis Joseph I. of Austria and the Russian Czar.[10] The terse hermeneutic notes Bruckner supplied for this movement may seem naïve to unconditional adherents of "absolute" music. Nevertheless, they precisely describe what happens in the music. Bruckner interpreted the powerful horn and trombone sounds of the first theme as "military music," the pounding accompanying rhythms in the strings as "ride of the Cossacks," the striking trumpet fanfares as "meeting of the majesties." It seems likely that images of a solemn ceremony stimulated his imagination and also dictated the Finale's marking of "Solemn, not fast."

To the head movement of his last symphony, Bruckner assigned the exceptional and singular double marking of *Feierlich, Misterioso*. The religious connotations of the movement are suggested not only by the portentous adverb *Misterioso* and, above all, the mysterious character of the beginning, but also by the intonations of the horns, which seem to recall the *Kyrie-eleison* cry of the early Missa Solemnis in B flat minor (WAB 29).

In a conversation with his biographer August Göllerich in 1891, Bruckner made a statement that proves that he was not the simpleton he is often thought to have been. One marvels not a little upon first reading how he interpreted the strange intertwining of a polka-like string passage with a chorale-like statement by the wind instruments in the Finale of the Third Symphony (second theme complex, at B): "You see," he said to Göllerich, "here, in the house, a great ball – next door, in the penitentiary house (*Sühnehaus*), the master [cathedral builder Schmidt] on his bier! That is how it is in life, and that is what I wanted to depict in the last movement of my third symphony: the polka signifies the humor and mirth of the world – the chorale its sadness and pain."[11] This utterance indicates again that Bruckner's symphonic oeuvre constitutes a sounding universe, in which both the secular and the sacred have their part. He sharply distinguished between the things of the world and the religious sphere, as his remarks about dedicating the Ninth to the "Good Lord," the "majesty of all majesties" prove. His terse hermeneutic elucidations of the Fourth and the Eighth Symphony, however, enable us to realize that in his conception the worldly and the religious were not so very far apart from each other. To his mind, the world was embedded in an order that was firmly anchored in the religious.

Imaginations - Bruckner's Associations in the Eighth

Like many other creative individuals, Bruckner firmly believed that he had a mission on earth to fulfill. A feeling of responsibility for his creations shaped his life. He saw in his compositional work a task imposed on him from on high. This is suggested by his repeatedly documented utterances about the talent given him by God and the parable of the talents. Time and again he professed that he owed his music to God, that much of it had come to him for the glory of God, even that the "good Lord" Himself had inspired many a theme in him.[1]

During a conversation with Richard Specht, Gustav Mahler once said about his Eighth Symphony how he had "never before, perhaps, worked under such duress," like a "lightning-like vision" the whole had instantly stood before his eyes, so that he only had to write it down as if "dictated" to him.[2] Similar utterances are known of Bruckner, who indicated about several of his inspirations that he had received them in his sleep. Thus he claimed that a violist had played the main subject of the Seventh Symphony to him in a dream; that his old composition teacher Ignaz Dorn had dictated the main theme of the same symphony's Finale in a dream; and that Ludwig Spohr had exhorted him in a dream to write down the *Te Deum* as dictated by him. Evidently Bruckner regarded inspiration as a gift from on high; but he ascribed no less relevance to the execution. He was in the habit of saying that he worked very slowly, rethinking everything that was to be considered in the process.[3] He was – as Friedrich Klose once formulated it – "a hard laborer, who had to wrest every blessing from his God in fervent prayer."[4]

As already mentioned, Bruckner, in conversations and also in letters, furnished hermeneutic commentaries to two of his symphonies, the *Romantic* and the Eighth, which however were not taken seriously, were even ridiculed, for a long time. People made fun of his linguistic awkwardness, the muddled quality of his utterances and their lack of logical stringency. Their authenticity was questioned, and some thought they were irrelevant because they had been given *ex post facto*.

In my book of 1980 about Brahms and Bruckner I showed that these commentaries are authentic and that in composing his symphonies Bruckner was beset by mental pictures that largely determined his musical shapings. I pointed out, however, that his associations were not to be understood as worked-out or tightly organized programs but rather resembled sequences of "strung-together genre pictures."[5]

Psychology defines imagination as "series of fantasies," which resemble dreams and can be located in a no man's land between the conscious and the unconscious.[6] In that sense, Bruckner's creative associations and mental pictures may frequently be called imaginations. It is significant in this connection that in a copy of the first version of the *Romantic Symphony* Bruckner personally entered the cues "night," "dreams," and "confused dreams."[7] Every human being has thoughts of, and ideas about, death, presentiments, fears and terrors of death. After the Bayreuth premiere of Wagner's *Ring of the Nibelung* in 1876, many contemporaries were greatly impressed by the *Todesverkündigung*, the Death Annunciation scene in *Die Walküre* (II.iv), in which Brünnhilde, against her own wishes, tells Siegmund that he will soon die and be gathered into Valhalla. The renowned "solemn" scene owes its fame not least to the dark coloration of the beginning with its tubas and muffled tympani strokes. The scene must have left an indelible impression on Bruckner, inasmuch as in the opening movement of the Eighth Symphony, completed in its second version in 1890, he realized it in an entirely new and highly dramatic way. At the climax of the recapitulation (at V), the horns and the trumpets jointly intone ten times in a row, *fortissimo*, the dotted rhythm of the main theme – a passage of truly elemental force, which Bruckner, in a letter to Felix Weingartner, referred to expressly as "die Todesverkundigung."[8] A general pause then marks an abrupt break, followed by three tympani rolls, *pianissimo*. Then commences the epilogue, taking up, dirge-like, the head motif of the main subject and dying away in a triple *piano*. Bruckner interpreted the passages as "resignation," but also as ""tolling bell'and as "death clock" (deathwatch).

Gustav Mahler all his life stood under the spell of Richard Wagner's music dramatism. Thus it does not come as a surprise that he, too, was familiar with the concept of the "Todesverkündigung." The final three movements of his posthumous Tenth Symphony were written in the summer of 1910, at a time of severe crisis. In my book about Mahler's symphonies I voiced the surmise 25 years ago that Mahler conceived the short third movement – *Purgatorio* – after having read the notorious letter of Walter Gropius to Alma, in which the young artist begged Mahler's wife to leave everything behind and come to him. Mahler feared he might lose Alma to Gropius and composed the *Purgatorio* in a state of pain and agony[9] – a hypothesis that has been confirmed by more recent researches.[10] In a more recently published particello sketch for this eerie movement, the word *Todesverkündigung* appears written in Mahler's hand above mm. 95-97[11] – a hint that for Mahler the news of his wife's infidelity must have felt like his own death sentence.

A different conceptual sphere in Bruckner includes the legendary figure of the "German *Michel.*" As we know from several sources, Bruckner wanted the Scherzo of his Eighth Symphony to be understood as a portrait of the "German Michel." Thus he wrote to Theodor Helm on March 26, 1892: ""The Michl [sic] refers to the Austro-German one, and no joke"[12] (*Scherz*).

The figure of the "German Michel" had political overtones in the 19th century. From a time no later than the 17th century, St. Michael, as the embodiment of heroism and strength, was regarded as the patron saint of the German nation. His image preceded warriors into battle and brought victory. Later – it is uncertain exactly when – St. Michael morphed into the figure of the "German Michel" – an embodiment not only of courage and bravery but also of "high-mindedness." According to the researches of Carl Rademacher, Michel is patient, bears humiliations and insults with a smile. At the crucial moment, however, he turns into a "berserk, who assaults his slanderer with irresistible rage and spreads fear and trembling about him."[13] Many in the 19th century thought they recognized much of German nature, even the essence of the German people, in this figure. The Michel figure connoted hope, disappointments and anxieties: the hope for the creation of a German Reich, the disappointment about the political lethargy of the

Germans, and the anxiety about losing out in the political game of the global powers.

In the Upper Austrian town of Steyr, where he dwelt often and with pleasure, Bruckner had many supporters, who furthered him in every respect. One member of his closest circle of friends was the influential manufacturer Carl Almeroth (1852-1906), who was indefatigable in championing him. Bruckner esteemed him not least for his straightforwardness and sincerity and saw in him the personification of the German Michel. In the sketches to the Scherzo of the Eighth, which he plotted in July of 1885 in Steyr, he significantly jotted down the name of Almeroth at one point, as a way of indicating the theme of the movement (see the facsimile, below).[14]

Figure
Sketch for the Scherzo of the Eighth Symphony (dated July 26, 1885). The name of his friend Carl Almeroth serves as a cue for identifying the theme (Clar.).

Especially interesting in this context is that Bruckner himself was caricatured as the German Michel in 1892 by Ferry Bératon. The drawing bears the caption *Anton Bruckner's Victory Allegory* and shows him seated in the form of the German Michel, with peaked night cap, woolen gaiters and mountain boots, peering out into the landscape, while at his feet snakes, hatching from their eggs, dart their tongues up at him.[15] According to a report by August Stradal, Bruckner was "very annoyed" about the drawing.[16] That does not preclude the possibility that he identified with the mythical figure of the German Michel and secretly hoped he would yet live to see the ultimate victory of his art.

The Ninth - Bruckner's "Farewell to Life"

According to an old tradition, music has an affinity with magic, with sorcery, with Astrology, with Fate and with superstition. At the end of the 19th and the beginning of the 20th century, the concept of a Ninth Symphony had ominous overtones for several major composers. In Gustav Mahler's mind, as we learn from his wife Alma, a superstition had taken root that no great symphonist could get beyond a Ninth.[1] It was for that reason that after the Eighth Symphony, he composed *Das Lied von der Erde* (*The Song of the Earth*). Of Bruckner, too, it is reported that he was timid about working on his Ninth. During a walk in St. Florian, he is supposed to have said: "I don't like to even start on the Ninth, I am scared to, for Beethoven, too, concluded his life with the Ninth." [2]

The exceptionally protracted genesis of his last symphony seems to prove that there is a kernel of truth in this report. After having drafted several themes already in August/September of 1887, he interrupted the work for several years. Only in February of 1891, he began with the execution of the opening movement, whose first, provisional score was completed on October 14, 1892.[3] There were external reasons for the interruption: for a long time Bruckner was intensively preoccupied with reworking his Third, Eighth and First Symphony. Besides, during the years 1892 and 1893, he composed no fewer than four vocal works, frequently for occasional purposes: the motet *Vexilla Regis* (WAB 51), the *Deutsche Lied* (German Song, WAB 63), the 150th Psalm (WQB 38), and finally *Helgoland* (WAB 71).

Ever since 1892, at the latest, Bruckner had presentiments of death, as testified to by his Hamburg admirer Wilhelm Zinne, who visited him in the summer of 1892 in his apartment in Vienna and noticed loose score pages at the open grand piano – the opening movement of the Ninth. Even then Bruckner referred to the Ninth as his "last" symphony and remarked he would not live much longer.[4] At that time he already suffered from cardiac and renal insufficiency, shortness of breath and dropsy. On November 13, 1893, he made his will. Even so, he did not stop composing. The first movement of the Ninth was finished in December of 1893, the Scherzo, which has come down to us in two versions, in February of 1894, and by the end of November, the score of the Adagio, too, was complete.

When Bruckner began the latter in April; of 1894, he had been ill for two years. His condition improved temporarily, only to get worse again thereafter. On April 13, he wrote to his friend Ludwig Oblat: "I was ill again; my heart denies me breath."[5] Although the growing recognition of his work did not remain unnoticed by him, and he took pleasure in it at times, he often suffered from depression. To his Viennese pupil August Stradal he complained about the hostilities of the Viennese press, and even about the Viennese Wagner Society, where, although he had done much for it, he was dismissed as a Wagner epigone, which, he observed, was quite "incorrect," although he worshipped Wagner like a god. When Stradal tried to console him by saying that the battle had been necessary and that he was entering into victory, he replied: "Yes, the victory is death."[6] Significantly, he wanted the tuba passage in the Adagio at letter B to be understood as a "Farewell to Life." No less telling are the musical quotations contained in the movement. A *Miserere* cry from the Gloria of the D minor Mass constitutes the principal element – a kind of four-part *cantus firmus* – from which the secondary theme is formed. The movement also quotes from the Benedictus of the F minor Mass, the Adagio of the Eighth and the opening movement of the Seventh Symphony. All this leads one to conclude that in the Adagio of the Ninth Bruckner gave touching artistic expression to his presentiments of death, his religious faith and his hope in divine mercy.[7] The movement dies away *pianissimo* with an elegiac retrospect.

Crucial information about the spiritual conception of the Finale we owe to Richard Heller, the physician who treated Bruckner from December of 1894 until his death. Three points in his report deserve our attention. First, the information that Bruckner was dedicating his last symphony to the "good Lord," the "majesty of majesties," in the hope that He would grant him enough time to complete the work and that his gift would be received graciously.

Musical Example 17
Grail motif, Cross symbol + Dresden Amen. – "Yearning motif"

Secondly, the statement of Bruckner's that he would bring back the Hallelujah of the second movement at the conclusion of the Finale, "so that the symphony" would end "with a song of praise to he good Lord," to whom he owed so much. And thirdly, Heller had the impression that Bruckner "believed he had made a contract with the good Lord, who would surely grant him life until he was able to lay his completed work at His feet."[8] Heller's formulations provided fresh nourishment to the old prejudices about Bruckner's simple-mindedness. But they can also be interpreted differently, if one considers that artists of genius frequently place their existence in the service of a work of theirs.

151

Being his last symphony and unfinished to boot, one can understand why the Ninth is enveloped by a special nimbus. Soon after Alfred Orel had edited the autograph material to the Finale preserved in Viennese libraries, under the title *Entwürfe und Skizzen* (Drafts and Sketches), for the Complete Edition,[9] numerous attempts were undertaken to render the torso performable.[10] None of them were very successful, perhaps because Orel's edition, on which they were based, was neither free of errors nor complete. For Orel had not always arranged the various score pages in the correct order, and had not been able to make use of the drafts to the Ninth kept at the Prussian State Library in Berlin, which the widow of Ferdinand Löwe had sold to that library in 1933. These were evacuated in 1941 and rediscovered only in the 'seventies – at the Biblioteka Jagiellonska in Cracow.[11] It was thus only in 1983 that Nicola Samale and Giuseppe Mazzuca could begin to compare Bruckner's autographs with Orel's edition in order to produce a valid performance version. The Australian scholar John A. Phillips studied Bruckner's way of working during his late years, and it is to his credit to have presented a facsimile edition of all the then known sources to the Finale of the Ninth.[12] It contains both the complete particello sketches and all the score sheets, as well as the "movement trajectory drafts" so characteristic of Bruckner's way of working.

Bruckner began work on the Finale in May of 1895 at the latest. One of his calendars bears the note "24. Mai 1895. 1mal, Finale neue Scitze"[13] – a formulation that might suggest that he had already earlier given some thought to the conception of the Finale. As isolated dates in the autographs indicate, he made fairly good progress with the sketching of the movement, since already by mid-December he was busy with the composition of the fugue with which the recapitulation begins. He sketched both the varied recapitulation and the coda, the latter probably in May of 1896. Immediately thereafter he will have begun with the instrumentation, which got as far as the development section. Phillips rightly pointed out that the extant music material is by no means a mere "compilation of sketches," but rather constitutes "a series of particello drafts, which preceded a formal, continuously written orchestra score written on consecutively numbered sheets."[14] Unhappily, not all the sheets have been preserved. Of the conjectural 600 measures, of the original particello sketch, 172 are completely instrumented. This voluminous material Nicola Samale, John Phillips, Giuseppe Maszzuca and also Gunnar Cohrs have made the basis of their "Reconstruction of the autograph score" – a completely orchestrated score comprising no fewer than 687 measures.[15] That attempt at a reconstruction deserves recognition. To do it justice, one needs to keep in mind that the four authors were forced, over long stretches of the monumental movement, to complete and complement a great deal at their discretion and in accordance with their sound knowledge of Bruckner. That goes both for the recapitulation and above all for the coda, to which there are only isolated notations.

Upon first looking at the formal structure of the Finale, it seems to reflect the conditions well known from Bruckner's other final movements. Here, too, we find the obligatory triad of theme complexes, the division into exposition, development (called "second part" by Bruckner), recapitulation and coda, as well as suggestive extended climaxes, grandiose peaks and strikingly frequent contrasts. Along with these, however, we encounter also features that seem uncommon and even singular. Above all, the motivic linkage between the "song period" and the main subject is unusual: Bruckner transposes the first few bars of the main theme a fifth lower, thereby obtaining the head motif of the "song period," which he repeats ostinato both at the outset and again later.

In the particello sketches, he designates the passages several times and expressly as "Gesangsperiode." [16] But what is songlike here is above all the lower voice in half- and quarter-notes, which accompanies the dotted notes of the upper voice an octave lower. Interestingly enough, he had originally written out an extended, diatonically progressing chorale melody for the song period, which he later rejected.[17] In an effort to utilize as much as possible of Bruckner's sketches in their reconstruction, the authors of the "performance version" have included this melody in the recapitulation.

In his attempt to interpret the Finale of the Ninth, John A. Phillips came fairly close to the results of my researches as to the latent programmatic content of Bruckner's symphonic oeuvre, although he felt the need to distance himself from them.[18] Already in 1980, I proposed the thesis, in my book on Brahms and Bruckner, that in composing his symphonies Bruckner often set out from images and extra-musical conceptions, which had a decisive influence on the formal and musical shape. That is also true of the conception of the Finale of the Ninth. The music is full of images and intentions, which Heller's statements impressively confirm.

If one follows the trajectory of the movement as a listener,[19] one gets the firm impression of a frequent alteration between dramatically tense and more serene sections. Structurally, this contrast manifests itself above all in the harmony, which his dominated, on the one hand, by complex sound combinations (tritone relations, chromaticism, diverse four-note chords and now and then sharp dissonances) and, on the other, by diatonicism and mostly pure triads. Especially striking in this Finale is also the abundant occurrence of figures and elements that unmistakably derive from the sphere of church music. These include the *Te Deum* figurations, the section marked *Chorale*, the grand fugue, the allusion to *Christ is risen* and the planned Hallelujah at the end.

Everything points to the conclusion that Bruckner projected ideas he developed in his sacred music, and especially in his psalm settings, into the symphonic conception of the Finale o the Ninth. Characteristically, nearly all of the psalms he composed are designed as songs of praise,[20] and they have notable traits in common: all of them contain a fugue, in four of them Hallelujah settings play a prominent role, and regular chorales occur in two of them. A straight line seems to lead from these psalm settings to the Finale of the Ninth, which, indeed, was conceived as a symphonic song of praise.

In studying the 47 pages of the particello sketches more closely, one observes that Bruckner's thoughts initially appear to have concentrated on tritone relations. For in several places, such relations are explicitly referred to by means of tonal letters below the notes.[21] And that is not all: Bruckner drew up entire tables of such relations. Thus he wrote down, in notes, numerous tritonic chord relations, which clearly reveal that he took as his model the linking of the Neapolitan sixth with the dominant, e.g.:

E-flat$_6$ – A, D$_6$ – G-sharp, D-flat$_6$ – G, C$_6$ – F-sharp.[22]

The relevance of these chord combinations becomes evident when one notices that the introduction to the movement is based on an entire chain of such chordal relations:

Musical Example 18

As one can, see the four-note head motif is transposed downward in several steps and harmonized with tritonic chord relations (D-flat$_6$ – G, C$_6$ – F-sharp$_6$, A-flat$_6$ – D$_6$). It then plays an important role in the development, where it appears in free inversion and in rising transpositions, again grounded with tritonic chord combinations (F$_6$ – B, G$_6$ – C-sharp, A$_6$ – E-flat, C-flat$_6$ – F).

In addition, Bruckner uses it in the function of a "developmental motif" in the transition between the song period and the onset of the chorale at the summit of the exposition, in a grandiose climactic wave, which here, however, is harmonized, not with tritonic sound combinations, but with chromatic shifts and chords related by thirds.

Might these conspicuous tritone relations have a concrete semantic? As we have shown, Bruckner was familiar with the traditional view of the tritone as *diabolus in musica*. Fortunately, we have a clue for the answer to this question in the sketches. For in one of the drafts,[23] Bruckner notes, on four systems, besides the freely inverted head motif and its tritonic harmonies, eight times at different levels a descending chromatic motif (see Musical Example 19).[24]

In the left margin, the note "VIII!" is written in an unknown hand and with an exclamation mark. In all probability, Bruckner regarded the descending chromatic motif as a variant of the final motif from the opening movement of the Eighth Symphony – a striking passage, which on diverse occasions he identified as "resignation," "tolling bell" or "death clock" ("death watch"). Once, when he was playing the movement for his pupil Friedrich Eckstein, he said: "That is the death clock. It strikes relentlessly, without cease, until everything is over ...!"[25] And in a conversation with August Göllerich, he remarked: "This is like someone lies dying, and across from him hangs the clock, which, while his life is ending, keeps ticking uniformly: tick, tock, tick, tock ..."[26]

The introduction to the Finale of the Ninth is therefore conceived from the notion of the "death clock," the fantasy of a person who is lying on his deathbed, and from that vantage point the astonishing regularity of the arrangement also acquires a deeper meaning. In devising the passage, Bruckner was consciously leaning on the end of the first movement of the Eighth Symphony, and everything points to the conclusion that the tritonic passages in the Finale of the Ninth represent the associative field of death – the negative pole, so to speak, of the movement.

Musical Example 19

When Bruckner began working on the Finale of the Ninth in May of 1895, he was already seventy years old. His state of health was fragile, he was sickly and had to reckon with the possibility of not being able to finish the movement. Early in July of 1896, he came down with a serious pneumonia, had high fever and was frequently unconscious for hours on end. By the 17th of July he had improved sufficiently to be able to resume work on the Finale. Some important data about the genesis of the Ninth were provided by Ernst Schwarza, one of his students at the University of Vienna, On November 5, 1894, according to Schwarzara, the day of his last lecture, Bruckner remarked the following:

Three movements of my Ninth Symphony are already finished, the first two already completely, only the third still needs some nuancing. With this symphony I burdened myself with another heavy job. I shouldn't have done it, what with my advanced age and my sickliness. [...] If I die before the completion of the symphony, my Tedeum is to be played in lieu of the fourth movement. I have already given instructions about that.[27]

The accuracy of this report is beyond doubt: several witnesses confirm it.

In light of that, the note *Te Deum* in the autograph draft of the score acquires special significance. It is found at the end of the exposition on a page on which the conclusion of the E major chorale is jotted down.[28] A little later, at the beginning of he development (here the note "2nd pt." appears), Bruckner writes out the head motif of the *Te Deum* four times in the part of the first flute. From then on it appears repeatedly in several different manifestations, both in the original form and its inversion, but also in augmentation, and even in "developing variation," to use a term of Arnold Schönberg's. That this motif has a religious connotation and provides a link to the *Te Deum* will be obvious to everyone. If one compares the Finale with the first movement, one discovers something that has hitherto been over looked, namely, that the four-note *Te Deum* motif appears already in the opening movement. The first time it is intoned *piano* by the oboe, at the transition from the second to the third theme complex (mm. 153-156). From it, the main motif of the third theme complex is then formed (Moderato at F), and it is unmistakable that Bruckner originally planned to likewise base the epilogue to the exposition on this motif (mm. 219-223). Later he decided, however, to give a different, more differentiated, shape to that passage. It remains undecided whether the motivic link between the outer movements sprang from a conscious intention.

From his youth, Bruckner had a special predilection for the Protestant chorale, which had long since been introduced to St. Florian. In 1848, at the age of twenty-four, he set a Maundy Thursday hymn in the style of the chorale.[29] Already here the typical characteristics of the genre are unmistakable: division into lines, even meter, plain, diatonic melodies, even rhythm and homophonic harmonization.[30] All of these features are found in the Psalm 114 composed at St. Florian in 1852 (WAB 36), which commences with a four-line chorus to the words *Alleluia*. A four-line chorus a cappella likewise concludes Psalm 22 (WAB 34), composed very probably also around 1852 at St. Florian.

As he had done in the opening movement of the Third, Bruckner also shaped the climax of the exposition of the Ninth's Finale as a chorale. Here, to be sure, we have an ornate chorale complex, intoned at first by the brasses (12 bars), then by the woodwinds (8 bars) and then again by the brasses (12 bars). Already in the sketches, E major is designated as the principal key.[31] Cadencing, however, is not done in E major: the chorale concludes with a deceptive cadence.

In the recapitulation, the chorale is set in D major – a further indication that the symphony was to conclude in the key of Beethoven's Ninth. It is especially remarkable that the chorale's wind instruments are grounded by the *Te Deum* figuration in the strings, as though to underscore the confidence in, and firmness of, religious belief.[32]

Bruckner highly valued craftsmanship and aspired to mastery in compositional technique, but he put his art in the service of expression. That is the sense of the weighty statement, already cited, in the letter to Franz Bayer of April 22, 1893: "Counterpoint is not genius, but a means to an end." In my view, that applies also to the summit achievement of contrapuntal writing, the fugue. Long before his studies with Simon Sechter, Bruckner had been writing fugues. It can be said of the fugue that it constitutes an indispensable, integrating component of his sacred music. All of his psalm settings include a fugue, and in his masses we find at least two fugues each, once even three. In choosing the parts of the texts for setting fugally, he generally followed hallowed tradition: in the Requiem of 1848, for example, the words *quam olim Abrahae promisisti* are in fugal style, as they are in Mozart,[33] and the *et vitam venture saeculi* at the conclusion of the Credo is almost obligatorily set in fugue form.

Bruckner used the fugal technique also in some of his symphonies.[34] Fugal sections or fugatos occur in the Finales of the so-called "Nilth" and the Eighth Symphony, longer, fully worked-out fugues, on the other hand, only in the Finales of the Fifth and the Eighth.

Is there such a thing as a semantic of the fugue? Put differently, does the fugue in a so-called autonomous conception serve merely as crowning conclusion to a contrapuntal movement, or should it be understood as the expression of a collective? In my opinion, Bruckner had the tradition of sacred music in mind, when he wrote fugues for the Finales of the Fifth and the Ninth Symphony. There is much to suggest that the fugues in both cases had a religious connotation.

Musical Example 20

To all appearances, the fugue in the Finale of the Ninth was planned from the beginning. After Bruckner had sketched it twice, he executed it and placed it at the beginning of the recapitulation.[35] By a small modification, he derived the fugue theme from the main subject, and planned from the start to develop the fugue theme both in its original form and in inversions in numerous keys.

When, in the 19th century, there was talk of a ninth symphony, one would inevitably think of Beethoven's Ninth and its choral finale. According to a report by August Göllerich, the question of a choral finale was once discussed in Bruckner's circle of friends. Rudolf Weinwurm proposed to use the church hymn *Christ ist erstanden*, "Christ has (or is) risen" – an idea that Bruckner appeared to like[36] It never happened. It is interesting, however, that at one point in the Finale, an allusion to the old hymn *Christ ist erstanden* is written in unison:[37]

T. 467-470

Musical Example 21

This Gregorian or pseudo-Gregorian intonation confirms that in conceiving the Finale of his Ninth Bruckner was moving in a religious circle of ideas.

When, on October 4, 2001, I gave a paper about my researches at the Bruckner Conference "On the History of Bruckner Research," I could not guess that in the following discussion my observations about the *Christ ist erstanden* would receive an unexpected confirmation from Elisabeth Maier, who pointed out that the old church hymn crops up also in Bruckner's prayers around Easter during his last years.[38] Thus Bruckner prayed it several times during Holy Week in April of 1895, specifically in the version *Der Heiland ist erstanden*, "The Savior is risen."[39] As Meier noted, the text of the final two strophes of this "Easter song" turns around the motif of the *Non confundar*:

Mein Glaube darf nicht wanken,	My faith, it must not waver,
O tröstlicher Gedanken!	O comfort when I quaver!
Ich werde durch sein Auferstehn	That through His resurrection brave
Gleich ihm aus meinem Grabe gehn.	I, too, shall go from out my grave.
Halleluja!	Hallelujah!
Halleluja, Halleluja!	Hallelujah, Hallelujah!
Haleluja!	Hallelujah!
Wie Du vom Tod erstanden bist,	As Thou didst from Thy death arise,
Lass uns erstehn, Herr Jesu Christ!	Let us arise, Lord Jesus Christ!
Halleluja!	Hallelujah!

Like the Adagio of the Ninth, the Finale, too, is a composition that must be viewed against an autobiographical background. Bruckner conceived this movement in the knowledge of approaching death, as it were *sub specie aeternitatis*. To nearly every element of the musical shaping a specific associational field can be assigned: that is one of the results of the semantic analysis. Motivic figures in the Introduction, conspicuously harmonized by tritonic chordal relations, chromatic shifts or thirds-related chords stand for death, mark the "negative" pole. The *Te Deum* figurations, the chorale, the fugue and allusions to *Christ ist erstanden*, on the other hand, all carry religious overtones, represent the "positive" pole. In the Finale of the Ninth Symphony, Bruckner countered his fears of death, which had him in their clutches, with the hope for salvation by the mercy of Him, whom, in his letter to Ludwig II., he had referred to as the "Eternal." As Joseph Schalk told his brother Franz in September of 1896, Bruckner's religious zeal acquired during his last months traits of a "religious mania."[40]

The Adagio of the Ninth ends by dying away. Ernst Kurth rightly spoke of this conclusion as of a "process of release."[41] Several of Gustav Mahler's movements will later end similarly – *morendo*. But it is highly characteristic of Bruckner that he intended to end his last symphony not with a music of farewell but with a praise of God. He was thinking, as Richard Heller testifies, of a symphonic Hallelujah. A jubilant Hallelujah also concludes his settings of Psalm 146 and 150.

Reflections on the Bruckner Interpretation

Günter Wand, Eugen Jochum, Sergiu Celibidache

> The most important thing in music
> is not what is written down.
> *Gustav Mahler*

Hans Swarowsky, my teacher in conducting at the Vienna Music Academy, was in the habit of remarking ironically that the compositions of the Vienna classics, especially those of Haydn and Mozart, were so fabulously constructed that even the worst interpreters could not do any damage. The same can certainly not be said of Richard Wagner's music dramas or the symphonies of Bruckner and Mahler. To that extent, Theodor W. Adorno was right when he insisted that interpretation was the "salvation of the work of art."

For both conductors and musicologists, the interpretation of Anton Bruckner's symphonic works poses special problems, for which there are no comparable instances in the more recent history of music. It would be no exaggeration to call the history of Bruckner interpretation unexampled and downright bizarre. For Bruckner was the only major symphonist of the 19th century whose works all the way into the 1940's were frequently heard not in their original form as created by the composer but in deforming abridgments and radical adaptations with at times totally altered instrumentations and doctored dynamics, agogics, phrasing and articulation. Bruckner's own versions were frequently regarded as unplayable. It was only when, on April 2, 1932, Siegmund von Hausegger juxtaposed Löwe's until then solely known arrangement of Bruckner's Ninth with the original that people began to recognize the superiority of the originals and a growing number of voices began to call for a Complete Edition.

Today we have that Complete Edition, thanks to the meritorious life's work of Robert Haas and Leopold Nowak. The dubious editions of Schalk and Löwe are forgotten, and orchestras everywhere play Bruckner's original versions, and not only the latest but also the earlier ones. The musical world got to know the "genuine" Bruckner, it admires his feeling for form, the originality and beauty of his orchestration.

The secret of a good interpretation seems to me to lie in the art of the nuance, in the interpreter's ability to realize the sound stream conceived by the composer in such a way that it is communicated to the listener both acoustically and intellectually. A key task of Bruckner interpretation is to make the architectonics of the movements transparent, to find the "right" tempi and the "right" relations between them and, not least, to show off the expressive and cantabile quality of his music to advantage.

Anton Bruckner is one of the composers with whom Günter Wand (1912–2002), the one-time honorary conductor of the North German Radio Orchestra, has wrestled longest and most intensively. Already in his youth he felt drawn to Bruckner's grandiose symphonic conceptions. As early as the 'forties, he performed several Bruckner symphonies – the Seventh, the Fourth and the Eighth – with the Gürzenich orchestra, and from then on his occupation with Bruckner's scores was continuous. "It took me a long time," he once remarked, "not only to recognize the grand arcs in the architecture of Bruckner's works – even that took time – but to have the composure to make them available in interpretation. What move me in an almost unreal way in Bruckner's oeuvre, with those gigantic blocks of which the architecture of his symphonies is formed, is [...[something like the reflection of a cosmic order in this music, something not measurable on a human scale.."[1]

No less an authority than Gustav Mahler formulated the aperçu in the epigraph that the most important thing in music is not what is on the page – an aperçu, whose somewhat obscure meaning Günter Wand explicated as follows: "If I see to it that the musicians follow the score with the utmost precision, that is, of course, by no means all. It is difficult enough and takes many rehearsals. But I have always made an effort to recognize and convey in interpretation what is *behind* the notes, the idea of a work, its musical character, the 'spirit of the music,' if you will. Fidelity to the work, therefore, means to me first and foremost recognition of the work, an insight into the rightness of the choice, and the proportion, of the compositional means."[2]

What distinguishes Günter Wand's Bruckner recordings? What are its unique qualities, and how do they differ from other recordings? Their persuasiveness, it seems to me, can be traced to three factors, the coherence of the interpretation, its high emotionality and its exceeding sonority.

Of basic importance for the right interpretation is the choice of tempi. Günter Wand was of the opinion that there is no such thing as an absolutely correct tempo. A tempo of a rendition is persuasive, he thought, "when the relations between the individual tempi are right, both within a movement and between movements." "Only thus a meaningful connection is created, and then the layman, too, will have the feeling of 'rightness.'"[3]

All of Bruckner's symphonies are gigantic, the dimensions of the individual movements are immense. By studying them, one can discover a system of fine agogic gradations. Thus the main subjects of the outer movements are differently nuanced in both character and tempo than the second theme complexes, the so-called "song periods." The architectonic conception of the movements can therefore be made audible only if the tempi are attuned to each other. Günter Wand said in this connection: "The reason why Bruckner's greatness still goes unrecognized by many today may be that his compositional architecture is of an entirely different kind than that of the Viennese classicism, where the symphonic form is developed *thematically*. That is altogether not the case with Bruckner. In his music the architectonics becomes 'visible,' that is, recognizable to the listener, in the clear juxtaposition of blocks of sound, tempi and rhythms that do not merge into each other but stand side by side like building blocks. That is why it is so important for me for the tempi to have the right relations."[4]

Günter Wand's principal objective was to make the musical architecture audible, to grasp the music as it was "meant" by the composer, to represent the idea of the work. Next to the correct relation of the tempi, expressiveness in performance was a predisposition for an adequate interpretation. Franz Schalk, who was familiar with Bruckner's own ideas about the interpretation of his works, tellingly thought that the soul of his music was "song." The prime demand for an effective rendition was therefore "to raise the expression of every singing voice to the point almost of *articulate* speech and to permit nowhere an indifferent cranking out or 'ripieno' playing."[5] Of many of Günter Wand's Bruckner recordings it can be said that their badge, from beginning to end, is the *Espressivo*.

In talking about Bruckner's symphonies, one inevitably will have to confront the problem of the different versions. Bruckner is fairly unique in having reworked several of his symphonies – some of them radically. The First and the Eighth Symphony exist in two versions, the Third and Fourth even in three. Much has been speculated about the reasons for this proceeding. What is certain is that Bruckner undertook some of these revisions from his own impulse, others upon well-meant advice from pupils and friends – specifically Josef and Franz Schalk and Ferdinand Löwe. What is without example in the music history of the 19th century is that during his lifetime Bruckner's symphonies were not printed and performed in their original form but mostly in distortive adaptations. Adapters would make numerous cuts and even radically change the original instrumentation in places, in order to approximate it to the then fashionable ideal of the Wagnerian sound.[6] When there was talk about these bowdlerizations, Günter Wand would fly into a rage and did not shy away from calling them "crimes."[7]

Within the last thirty-five years, Bruckner's early versions of his symphonies have come to occupy the center of attention. A number of scholars and interpreters never grow tired of pointing out the boldness and originality of the early versions – some even make no secret of their preferring the early versions to the later ones. Günter Wand did not share this view. For him, the authoritative versions were the late ones sanctioned by Bruckner, the so-called original versions of the last hand. Thus he conducted the Viennese version of he First, and the third versions of the Third and Fourth. The Eighth is a special case: Wand here followed the edition by Robert Haas, which mingles, not without problems, the first and the second version.[8]

In a historical perspective, Bruckner's symphonies appear astonishingly progressive today, not only because of their gigantic dimensions, their boldness and their new, unaccustomed tone, but also on account of their sound. Even to many of his pupils, Bruckner's new sound seemed audacious, robust, untamed, and too voluminous. By taking numerous liberties with his orchestrations, they hoped to domesticate his unusual sound picture, to adapt it to the acoustic ideas of the time. In Günter Wand's renditions, this new, original sound picture shows to particular advantage. We did not know before how expressive Bruckner's music can be in spite of its severity, how voluminous his symphonic manner is, and how jubilant and affirmative his endings can sound.

Between 1958 and 1966, Eugen Jochum (1902-1987) recorded all of Bruckner's symphonies (except for the "Nilth") in Munich's Hercules Hall and in the Berlin Philharmonic Hall, partly with the Berlin Philharmonic Orchestra and partly with the Orchestra of the Bavarian Radio. His recordings, which appeared separately to begin with, and later jointly in a box under the label of the Deutsche Grammophon,[9] right away evoked great interest and for a long time were regarded as exemplary – and no wonder, since Jochum had an exalted reputation as a Bruckner conductor. Already in 1950, the International Bruckner Society made him president of its German section, and four years later he was awarded the much sought-after Bruckner medal. Already in his youth, Jochum had an affinity with Bruckner. He received his first formative impressions from Bruckner's church music, and from childhood on, he was familiar with the organ – Bruckner's instrument. The publicist Karl Schumann once explained Jochum's close relation to Bruckner as follows: "Shaped by the German Romantic tradition, Eugen Jochum is by nature an adherent of content aesthetics. He essentially starts out from the content, the expression, the metaphysical sense. The specific, unique character of Eugen Jochum's Bruckner interpretation, however, is the way he nevertheless – or, perhaps, therefore – masters the wide-flung and often loose-jointed form, how he brings various tempi into relation with each other, develops wide arcs serenely, without haste, and even at the first note of the symphony already thinks of the last. Bruckner is made for content aestheticians; the spiritual/intellectual background of his symphonies touches on ultimate religious questions."[10]

Like Oskar Lang, Fritz Grüninger or Ernst Kurth, Jochum regarded Bruckner as one of the great metaphysicians in German music. Günter Wand, too, saw in religiosity the prime fountain of Bruckner's oeuvre, but he thought that the latter was not only the composer of solemn, sacred moods but above all a great symphonist, "one of the greatest of all."[11]

Many, besides, thought Jochum's special merit was that he brought about a general acceptance of Bruckner's work already in the 'fifties. For Bruckner's symphonies had long a reputation of being long-winded, unwieldy, lacking in tension, even tedious. Unquestionably, Jochum was one of the first conductors who succeeded in largely doing away with this prejudice by using brisk tempi and a tension-filled manner of performing.

There is also this: even at first hearing, Bruckner's grandiose movements stand out by their frequent general pauses – caesuras not known from the symphonies of Felix Mendelssohn, Robert Schumann or Johannes Brahms. Eugen Jochum managed outstandingly to "bridge" these tension-filled caesuras in such a way that the well-ordered current of sound was nevertheless perceived as a continuum.

Those interested in comparative interpretation should turn particularly to Jochum's and Wand's recordings of the Fifth Symphony, a work that both regarded as central. Jochum wrote an extended essay about this work, which Bruckner himself called his "contrapuntal masterpiece."[12] In 1973, Günter Wand had also immersed himself for months in the study of this symphony. His friend Bernd Alois Zimmermann had urged him to come to grips with this work in particular, because he had come to regard Wand was uniquely suited to performing it.[13]

Of this so-called Faith Symphony, Jochum rightly held that all of its first three movements, seen from the perspective of the conclusion, seem almost like a vastly laid-out preparation for the climax of the Finale. His recording makes apparent that he staked everything on a fluid, nuanced performance. The listener gets the impression that Bruckner's music is stripped of every bit of heaviness: a beautiful rounded sound is the ideal that is paid homage to. Jochum attains a particularly high luster in the final chorale by reinforcing the brasses, following the precedent set by Franz Schalk, with eleven additional brass instruments: four horns, three trumpets, three trombones and a bass tuba.

Günter Wand, by comparison, placed greater emphasis, by means of tempo contrasts, to the differences between the various thematic characters, thus making the architecture of the symphony more clearly audible. Wand's ideal is not the beautiful but the massive Bruckner sound. The result is a greater prominence of the music's expressive qualities.[14]

In 1979, Sergiu Celibidache (1912-1996), who as a young man had led the Berlin Philharmonics through part of the post-war period, took over the direction of the Munich Philharmonic Orchestra, where especially his Bruckner performances regularly caused a sensation. Time and again, audiences were fascinated by the extraordinary staying power and intensity of his interpretations, which despite their length never permitted a moment's tedium.

It is not inessential in this connection that Brucker himself had a predilection for rather slow tempi and his music often calls for stately speeds. His pupil August Stradal reported that he played organ works by Johann

Sebastian Bach much more slowly than later organists.[15] Early on already he must have observed with pain that conductors took his music too fast, inasmuch as, from the Third Symphony on, he frequently furnished the tempo markings of his outer movements with retarding additions like "moderate," "moderato," maestoso," "not fast" and so forth. Celibidache attends to this.

Celibidache regards Bruckner as a representative of German music. In his view, however, the German musical spirit and sentimentality do not go together. He consequently did not tolerate any ritenuti or rubati – the sort of thing one knows from the piano music of Frédéric Chopin – in performances of Bruckner's symphonies. These convictions coincided with the statements Franz Schalk made on the subject. "Nothing was more repugnant to the master," he wrote, "than the little, all-too personal accent ripples of performers, which had the effect of tearing either the tempo or the expression, or, as most often, both, into bits. He demanded that the tempo (principal speed) was to be maintained, especially within the great periods, and forbade all nervous and hysterical rubati, which were contrary to the epic character of the symphony and to the German musical sensibility in general."[16] As one can see, Celibidache was able to invoke an authentic tradition of Bruckner interpretation.

In line with this tradition is also his demand for clarity, for transparency of the sound picture. Celibidache always took great care that a proper balance between the various instrumental groups was maintained – in other words, that thematically important voices – especially if they were not strongly orchestrated – would come duly to the fore.

The opening movement of a recording of the *Romantic* by the Munich Philharmonic under Celibidache radiates great calm.[17] It lasts no less than 22 minutes – other conductors "manage" it in much less time. What is most impressive is how artfully and deliberately Celibidache modifies the basic tempo. In the third theme complex it is sped up – an acceleration prepared for by an elaborate stringendo. Especially notable in this recording is the systematic distinction between "heavy" and "light" measures.

In a recording with the Symphonic Orchestra of North German Radio, Günter Wand requires only 18 minutes for the first movement of the *Romantic.*[18] Here, too, the relation between the tempi is very even. That this recording is nevertheless stirring is due to the fairly brisk basic tempo, which makes it possible for the musicians to shape their parts in a highly cantabile manner.

The Progressive

The notion of progress in the arts – an idea that fired many artists in the 19th century – has lost much of its attraction since then. Even so, the question is still frequently raised, whether, and in what sense, an artist contributed to the "progress" of musical art, whether he should be ranked among the "progressives" or the "conservatives." The idea of progress played a considerable role in the thinking of Arnold Schönberg and his disciples Anton von Webern and Alban Berg, as well as in that of artists close to them.[1] Their writings make clear that they endeavored to comprehend the path of the New Music that had led all the way to Schönberg and the dodecaphonic system as a consistent and necessary development, to which several composers had been contributing forerunners. These included above all Bach, Wagner, Mahler and Johannes Brahms. In his famous essay of 1933, Schönberg apostrophized Brahms expressly as the "Progressive."[2] Two years earlier he had named as his "teachers" primarily Bach and Mozart, secondly Beethoven, Brahms and Wagner, and he professed to have also learned a great deal from Schubert, Mahler, Strauss and Reger.[3] He did not mention the name of Bruckner in this context.

Was Bruckner really less "progressive" than Brahms? Can it be that Schönberg, Webern and Berg failed to recognize Bruckner's historic achievement, the modernity of his music? By what criteria did they judge music, and what did they mean by the term "progress"?

The premise from which Schönberg sets out in his Brahms essay is the idea that Mahler, Strauss, Reger and Schönberg himself take their departure from Wagner and Brahms, and that Brahms was as path-breaking an innovator as Wagner. Schönberg seeks to demonstrate his thesis through numerous references to the complexity of Brahms's music – a complexity that manifests itself, in his view, largely in Brahms's techniques of motivic working, metrical irregularity and rich harmonies. The reference to the latter may seem puzzling, especially since Wagner is generally regarded as a bolder harmonist than Brahms. Schönberg, too, however, concedes that" Wagner's harmonies are "richer" in secondary sounds and vagrant chords and richer in the free use of dissonances, especially of unprepared ones.[4]

What, however, did Bruckner mean to Schönberg? Judging from the latter's hitherto published writings, he appears to have regarded Bruckner as a far less important precursor of the New Music than Brahms. That is indirectly apparent from his 1946 essay *Kriterien für die Bewertung von Musik* ("Criteria for Evaluating Music"). Here Schönberg advances the thesis that "higher" and popular art were two entirely different things, and that advanced music had of necessity to exhibit a greater degree of complexity. He exemplifies this by referring to the device of the unchanged repetition, which he expressly calls "cheap." What should replace the unaltered repetition was the procedure of the developing variation, a procedure that would at the same time ensure musical logic.[5]

Schönberg's admiration for Brahms and his supposed progressiveness results from his belief that Brahms had anticipated the procedure of the developing variation. He contrasts this procedure to the technique of sequence- cum-transposition, and he likes to think that one can see in the contrariness of the two techniques a telling difference between the schools of Brahms and Wagner. Whereas Brahms and his followers "repeated phrases, motifs and other structural components only in a varied form," Wagner, "to make his themes rememberable," had to "alter sequences and semi-sequences, that is to say, unchanged or only slightly varied repetitions, which do not differ in any essential way from their first occurrence, except for being transposed exactly to other pitches."[6]

Schönberg admits that in his early years he stood under the influence of Wagner, paid homage to his leitmotif technique and wrote sequences like his contemporaries. But after a time he deviated from Wagner. The technique of sequences and transpositions seemed to him "less meritorious" than the variation – he does not hesitate even to call it "a more primitive method," of which all of Wagner's followers, and even some of his opponents, had availed themselves, including Anton Bruckner, Hugo Wolf, Richard Strauss and even Claude Debussy and Giacomo Puccini. We can thus understand why Bruckner, in Schönberg's view, did not rank among the composers who had accelerated progress in music.

Schönberg's statements tell us a good deal about his own compositional development. But I have to confess that to me his arguments do not seem cogent, his substantiations not reasonable. In lieu of a more extended discussion, I pose the following questions for consideration:

1. Wagner's sequence-cum-transposition technique, as everyone must admit, resulted in an extraordinary harmonic enrichment. Can this technique really be called a "more primitive method" than Brahms's variations technique?

2. Schönberg cites the opening of the Prelude to *Tristan and Isolde* as an example of Wagner's transposition technique. Can one seriously main-

tain that this composition is less precious than the best orchestral works of Johannes Brahms?

3. Bruckner undeniably avails himself of Wagner's sequence and transposition technique. His predilection for the so-called "rosalia" was notorious. Yet can one really say that his symphonies have a lesser degree of complexity than the music of Johannes Brahms?

In the winter of 1941/42, Karl Amadeus Hartmann took some lessons from Anton Webern. In a letter to his wife, he mentions that Webern rejected Bruckner. "He [Webern] does not believe," he writes, "that Bruckner had done anything for the evolution of music." Hartmann counters with the question: "Is Bruckner really so distant from his [Webern's] beloved Mahler?"[7]

Webern himself spoke in some detail about Bruckner in a lecture he gave on April 3, 1933, in Vienna. Like Schönberg, he, too, is concerned to trace the path of the New Music and to find proofs for the legitimacy of composing with twelve interrelated tones. He sets out from the premise that two elements, above all, had led to the New Music as Schönberg created it: the "conquest of the tonal realm" and the representation of ideas. As especially important for the latter he cites in particular the cultivation of cyclical forms, the art of deriving everything from one, the technique of variation, the art of an independent accompaniment and polyphonic thinking. Brahms and Mahler, above all, had decisively contributed to this development. Bruckner's historic achievement Webern sees in the "conquest of the tonal realm": Bruckner had transferred the expansion of the latter, which Wagner had brought about, to the area of the symphony. "In other ways," Hartmann continues, "he [Bruckner] was certainly not so very path-breaking, whereas Mahler, again, was. With him we reach modern times."[8]

Other adherents of the Schönberg School also do not seem to have rated Bruckner very highly, at least for some time. An important exception was Alban Berg. We learn from Josef Polnauer that from his youth to the end of his life Bruckner was close to Berg's heart;[9] that he was deeply moved by the Fifth Symphony; that he was also familiar with the Mass in D minor and even worked the Miserere motif from the Gloria of that mass into the bible scene in *Wozzeck* (Act III, sc. i).[10] To Berg applies what Theodor W. Adorno said about his own relation to Bruckner: "To disparaging remarks I made about Bruckner he did not object anything, although he surely saw the immaturity of my views. He left their correction to my development:

that occurred only after his death, under the unforgettable impression of Webern's performance of the Seventh [Symphony] in London."[11]

In considering whether an artist should be regarded as progressive or conservative, it is important to know how he rated himself and what impressions his contemporaries had of him.

The concept of progressivity is contiguous with the semantic fields of boldness, audacity, innovativeness. Bruckner's psychological situation as composer and teacher can be characterized as an odd mixture of authoritarianism and daring. On the one hand, he had an enormous respect for tradition, especially for the symphonies of Beethoven. The diligence and thoroughness with which he studied counterpoint are proverbial. On the other hand, he stands out as a composer by a conspicuous taste for experimentation: he acted consciously as an innovator. Of his Second Symphony he said repeatedly that it was not his favorite one, because it was "too chaste." He permitted himself fewer liberties with it than with the First, his "brash little broom." Of this symphony, written in 18565/66 in Linz, August Göllerich reports: "Goaded on to bold daring, Bruckner still sometimes shrank back from his own audacious musical ideas. Then he sought refuge with [his teacher Ignaz] Dorn, asking him: "My deah Dorn, won't ya take a look at this, dast one write like dat?" To which Dorn replied: "You have to feel completely free ..."[12]

Ernst Schwarzara, a student in Bruckner's lectures on harmony and counterpoint at the University of Vienna, handed down several remarks of Bruckner's that make it clear that the latter did not regard the rules of counterpoint as sacrosanct. Schwarzara tellingly stated that everything that was bold in music gave Bruckner pleasure and lured him into occasional use.[13] Bruckner taught according to the composition theory of Simon Sechter. But he was more permissive than Sechter, as Schwarzara testifies, when it came to preferring a well-sounding combination to the mere consistency of a theorem. He was in the habit of saying that little was permitted in the *strenge Satz* of counterpoint, but he would add mischievously that he who permitted himself more would have more. There is no doubt: he felt as a progressive and liked it when people called him the "heretic of harmony."

The history of Bruckner reception is marked by personal animosities and polemical invective. Perhaps that is why it has often been overlooked that the impression several of Bruckner's contemporaries had of his music was that of boldness. Hans Paumgartner, for example, called both the Fourth and the Seventh Symphony "magnificently bold tone poems,"[14] and Ludwig Speidel lauded the "freedom and boldness" of the String Quintet.[15] To others, the daring of Bruckner's symphonies seemed mere extravagance. Thus August Wilhelm Ambros thought he had to recommend measure, moderation, and self-restraint to Bruckner, and concluded his long critique of the Second Symphony with the sentences: "Our most modern music suffers from excess. And that will in the end be the death of an art grown hypersthenic."[16] Twelve years later, in 1885, Gustav Dömpke reiterated this Cassandra cry. He counted Bruckner among those gifted composers who had the New Music on their conscience, and wrote in his review of the String Quintet: "One of the most important and most difficult questions of future music historians will of necessity be, whether, and if so, which outstanding talents were ruined by the new German school." It was Bruckner's undoing to have walked in Wagner's footsteps. Dömpke closes with the regretful words: "It is incalculable what he might have been to art, had he followed less fallible stars …"[17]

To define progress in music is hardly easy. If one means by progress a higher development in general, then one can find an abundance of progressive elements in Bruckner. One of the most important is what Webern in 1933 called the "conquest of the tonal realm." What precisely that means in detail, Ernst Kurth explained in his massive Bruckner monograph. He rightly pointed out that the late Bruckner had advanced to the very borders of atonality. Kurth spoke of "loosened tonality," of "disruption of the tonal connection as such," of "overcoming of tonality," occasionally even of "atonal harmony" in Bruckner.[18] From today's perspective, the phrase "atonal harmony" may seem overbold. But certainly the tonal space is enlarged enormously in Bruckner, and tonality is taken to its limits. In his *Harmonielehre* of 1911, Schönberg discussed several examples of what he called "pending" and "suspended" tonality.[19] The phenomenon circumscribed by these terms can be exemplified by quite a number of instances in Bruckner's works.

The widening of tonality in Bruckner is most evident in his harmonies, which are as daring as they are "logical." What with their abundance of thirds-related chords, of bold modulations and deviations, of alterations and chromatic shifts, Bruckner's symphonies are among the most "progressive" compositions written in the second half of the 19th century. To prove that Bruckner's harmonies are in many respects more progressive than Brahms's one need only investigate the tonal schemata in the expositions of the two masters' symphonic movements.[20] Even Bruckner's sympathetic critics often objected to his enormous appetite for modulation. Thus Ludwig Speidel, in his review of the String Quintet, emphasized the "freedom with which the composer seems to render the entire tonal system fluid, does as he pleases with keys." The disposition of keys in the String Quintet struck him as "a tonality Odyssey of the most fantastic sort."[21] Count Laurencin d'Armond spoke of a "tone and modulation labyrinth,"[22] and Bruckner's declared opponents naturally went even farther. Gustav Dömpke remarked in 1885 that with Bruckner it was a matter of course to casually pass through all twenty-four tonalities in each and every movement,[23] and Hanslick ironically paraphrased the amazement produced by Bruckner "when for once he has remained in the same key for three bars in a row."[24]

A wonderful example of what Anton von Webern called the "conquest of the tonal realm" in Bruckner can be found in the main subject of the Eighth Symphony, completed in its first version already in 1887. In its neatly articulated five "lines," the 20 measures of the modulation-happy theme contain all twelve tones of the chromatic scale. Though disposed in C minor, it starts with a phrase that unequivocally belongs to the key of B flat minor. In an early sketch, however, the theme also commenced in C minor![25] The sketch likewise documents that the final formulation of the theme cost Bruckner a great deal of effort.

Musical Example 22 early draft – final version

Arnold Schönberg traces the evolution of the New Music toward twelve-tone composition back to two factors: the expansion of tonality and the emancipation of dissonance. By the now famous latter term he meant the comprehensibility of dissonance, which he regarded as equivalent to the comprehensibility of consonance. "A style that rests on this premise," he stated, "treats dissonances exactly like consonances and dispenses with a tonal center."[26] Now it cannot be said of Bruckner that he treats dissonances exactly like consonances. But it is undeniable that he had a special predilection for dissonances, for long-held ninth, eleventh and thirteenth chords, which he was particularly fond of putting into action at the climax of a passage or movement.[27] He explicitly drew the attention of his listeners at the University of Vienna to the fact that he also used sixth chords, saying: "In sixth chords, the third and fifth of the [bass] foundation are usually excluded."[28] Especially characteristic for Bruckner's modernity are the prolonged dissonances in the opening movement and the Adagio of the Ninth Symphony.

Altogether, the Ninth is a work that one should analyze as an instance of New Music. Whoever wants to examine what has been said about the enlargement of tonality in Bruckner and about his rich harmonies can here put it to the test.

The renowned Adagio – Bruckner's last completed composition – has an idiosyncratic five-part layout, erected on two theme complexes of contrasting character, which later are repeated, developed and intensified. The coda at the end is based on both theme complexes, which are combined with each other in a highly imaginative way. If one examines the tonal relations in the individual parts of the movement, one soon sees how extensively the tonal bonds are loosened and how extensively the tonal space has been widened.

The basic key of the Adagio is E major, that is to say, the movement ends in that key. The opening of the movement, on the other hand, is marked by a remarkable tonal liberality. Within the entire first part of the movement, the tonic, the E major triad, appears only twice: in the 7th and in the 34th measure. The first several bars can hardly be assigned to any specific key. Kurth rightly called them "pretonal." [29] In the subsequent course of the movement, too, one often has trouble locating any tonal centers. Several stretches are determined, to use Schönberg's terminology, by a "vagrant" chord structure.

Let us sketch the structure of the first part of the movement. The physiognomy of the first theme, which constitutes the first period of eight measures, is formed by wide intervals, chromatic steps and a paraphrase of the Dresden Amen from Wagner's *Parsifal*. In the second period, a variant of the head motif is developed in the form of a climactic train: a tonal center is not to be made out. This climactic train culminates in a broad plateau of sound, which is constituted by fluctuating, mostly unresolved eleventh chords. An elegiac tuba period forms the conclusion, which Bruckner wanted to be understood as a "Farewell to Life."

The second theme complex – the Brucknerian "song period" – is systematically developed from a four-note phrase, which Bruckner borrowed from the Gloria of the D minor Mass, where it serves as *Miserere* cry. In the Adagio of the Ninth, the phrase is initially introduced in A flat major. For ten bars (mm. 45-54), one has the impression of being in a firm tonal region. But then the A flat major is replaced by other tonal centers (G flat major and A major), and the complex closes with a striking "whole-tone" four-note chord.

In the third and fourth part of the Adagio, the two theme complexes are very artfully developed. The fourth part (mm. 173-206), moreover, offers a spectacular example of Bruckner's art of heightening, put into effect by the Wagnerian sequence-cum-transposition technique that Schönberg would later censure, by means of which Bruckner, however, achieves veritably dramatic effects. What is developed and heightened is the *Miserere* cry, which now also appears in augmentation and inversion. At the culmination of the movement (mm. 1990296), the trombones, the contrabass tuba and the low strings intone, in triple *forte*, variants of the head motif from the main subject. The harmonic foundation of the passage, a fluctuating, sharply dissonant and unresolved thirteenth chord (g sharp-c sharp-b sharp–d sharp–f sharp–a–e) has the effect of a tone cluster of overwhelming force.

With these sounds Bruckner attained a non plus ultra of modernity in 1894, advancing into regions that already anticipate Expressionism. From here it is not far to, say, Schönberg's early Expressionist works, such as the symphonic poem *Pelleas and Melisande* of 1903. In view of that, it is a total mystery why Schönberg did not see the progressivity of Bruckner's music.

There can be no question that both the "modernity" and the "tone" of that music strongly impressed Mahler. A comparison of the latter's music with that of Bruckner quickly reveals both relationship and difference. Images of nearness and distance appear, as it were, automatically.

Mahler comes closest to Bruckner in certain types of movement, certain beginnings and ends of movements, as well as in characters like the march, the funeral march, the chorale, the hymn and the landler.[30] He differs most radically from him where he indulges in his fondness for shrill sound effects and for the seemingly trivial, as well as where he enters the region of satire, irony, the grotesque, even sarcasm – areas wholly alien to Bruckner. Bruckner strove for, and attained, an ideal of purity and homogeneity of style – an ideal Mahler turned away from.

Afterword

In a letter of 1902 to August Göllerich, Gustav Mahler professed that Bruckner's life and aspirations had not been without an impact on his own development as both artist and man.[1] To Bruno Walter, too, he often referred to Bruckner as his "predecessor" and voiced his conviction that his work was continuing in the direction Bruckner had taken. At the same time, Walter was precise in defining the specific differences between the two composers. "If Bruckner's musical message," he observes, "derives from the sphere of the sacred, the passion of the prophet speaks from Mahler, always seeking, again and again in battle, ending in mild resignation, whereas an unshakable consoling *affirmation* emanates from Bruckner's tone world."[2]

Twenty years later, Theodor W. Adorno, in his now famous Mahler "physiognomy," depicted the relation between the two somewhat differently. According to him, fracturedness is the "experiential core" of the reflective Mahler, "the feeling of the alienation of the musical subject." The tone of the "traumatic" in his music, too, is nothing other than a subjective factor of this fracturedness. By contrast, Adorno spoke of Bruckner's "unspoiled forest darkness" ("walddunkle Unberührtheit"), and from it traced Bruckner's supposed "unbroken use" of the language of forms. The difference between the two was one of tone of voice and intention. Bruckner's intention was affirmative, that of Mahler, on the other hand, took its tone from unreserved sadness or mourning.[3]

That Bruckner's intention was "affirmative" seems immediately convincing when one thinks of the radiant, positive, apotheosizing conclusions of his outer movements, the emphatic trumpet signals and fanfares. Even so, the experience of fractruredness was by no means unknown to him. The experienced listener registers its earmarks in funeral march-like and numerous anxiety-provoking passages in his symphonies – specifically also in the coda of the opening movement of the Eighth Symphony (second version of 1890), the ending that gives poetic expression to the idea of the "death clock."

Throughout his life, Bruckner sought consolation for the adversities of existence in art. The quoted sentence from a letter to Rudolf Weinwurm, "The whole world vexes me – only art is left to me,"[4] could stand as a motto over his biography. "My only joys are my symphonies," Bruckner, harassed by his duties, said to Robert Fuchs, a colleague at the Vienna Conservatory.[5] When he began to sketch the Adagio of the Fifth, he was in a deep depression. "My life has lost all joy and pleasure – in vain and for nothing," he wrote on January 12, 1875, to Moritz von Mayfeld.[6] It therefore seems only logical that the Adagio should begin in a tone of lamentation and sadness. Taken as a whole, however, the "Faith Symphony" is a vigorous work. Bruckner – the originator of the monumental symphony – was dedicated to an idea of sublimity, strength and power. One year after the great economic depression of 1874, he remarked: "As the present world situation, seen spiritually, is one of feebleness, I seek refuge in strength and write vigorous music."[7]

Ever since the '60s, international interest in Bruckner's music has continued to grow. One could speak of a "Bruckner Renaissance." Decisive impulses for this came from the recording of all the symphonies and major sacred works under Eugen Jochum. After him, numerous prominent conductors have attended to Bruckner's monumental symphonic oeuvre: Herbert von Karajan, Karl Böhm, George Solti, Bernhard Haitink, Carlo Maria Giulini, Daniel Barenboim, Eliahu Inbal and, above all, Sergiu Celibidache and Günter Wand. Today, there are about a dozen complete recordings available on CD. Not infrequently, concert series take place in which the entire cycle is performed.

There are numerous reasons for this interest. In Austria, Bruckner was advanced to the role of "national composer." In 1974, the Bruckner House was erected in Linz on the right bank of the Danube, an imposing circular edifice housing one of Europe's most beautiful concert halls. In the 'eighties, the Linz "sound cloud" became noted and notorious – an unconventional experiment of electronically transmitting Bruckner music from the Bruckner House over gigantic loudspeaker towers to both banks of the Danube. And in 1878, the Anton Bruckner Institute, Linz (ABIL), was established, whose achievements have been immense. It put Bruckner research on a scientific basis for the first time, and all the way round has unfolded an admirable, virtually unparalleled activity. Relevant documents have been collected and largely published, important aspects of the great artist's biography been brought to light, his oeuvre has been analyzed in diverse directions, and the history of Bruckner reception been illuminated in numerous ways. At the now renowned, initially annual, Bruckner symposia, international research has focused on specific themes. From the start, the angle of vision was a wide one, taking Bruckner's cultural and social surroundings and the work of his most important contemporaries into close contextual consideration. The volume of publications is astonishing.

No less important is how great Bruckner conductors succeeded in showing off the unique qualities of his music to advantage, often for the first time. Countless listeners are now familiar with Bruckner's highly expressive tonal language, which had shocked so many of his contemporaries, and are moved by the magnificence and ecstatic fervor of his symphonies. I myself had repeatedly occasion to observe how absorbedly the regularly sold-out houses listened to the performances of Bruckner's symphonies under Günter Wand. I had similar experiences in Linz's Bruckner House, in the Great Hall of Vienna's Music Society, in Munich under Sergiu Celibidache and in St. Florian under Christoph Eschenbach.

By "aura" one usually means the emanation, the effectiveness, the enveloping atmosphere, the unique expression of a work of art. The term may explain to a certain extent why some art works remain alive and continue to affect people for decades, even centuries after their origination, while the majority sinks into Hades. The rank of a musical work of art is not due merely to the compositional logic and mastery of compositional technique, but also depends on such factors as what one might call "tone," "gesture," "character," "idiom," "expression" and, well, "aura," No one will deny that the symphonies and the great sacred works of Bruckner are to an exceptional degree surrounded by an aura.

During a lively discussion evening at the assembly hall of the University of Tübingen, the eminent theologian Hans Küng asked me, whether Bruckner's new relevance might have something to do with the religious grounding of his symphonies. I answered in the affirmative at the time, and still do. Bruckner is timely because like no other contemporary – excepting only his great model Richard Wagner – he hurled his spear so far into the future, because, today more than ever, many listeners appreciate the modernity and originality of his musical language, because in an age of disorientation, the question as to the meaning of existence – the arch-question of all religions – is raised again with a new urgency, and, finally, because especially today uncounted human beings have developed a sense for spirituality and for the spiritual in his stirring music.

Appendix

Notes

Part One: A Character Portrait

Who Was Bruckner?

[1] Ferdinand Pfohl, *Gustav Mahler. Eindrücke und Erinnerungen aus den Hamburger Jahren*, ed. Knud Martner (Hamburg, 1973), 15. Max Auer (246) ascribes this aperçu to Hans von Bülow, who, in a letter to Wilhelm Zinne of 1887, spoke of the "anti-musical nonsense of the oddball Bruckner" (Briefe, 27).

[2] Erich Wolfgang Partsch, "Der 'Musikant Gottes' – Zur Analyse eines Stereotyps," in Bruckner – skiziert, 235-259.

[3] Manfred Wagner in Bruckner in Wien, 66-71.

[4] The prevailing personality research is cognitively oriented. In Bruckner's case, however, one must seek to do justice to the emotional side of his complex personality as well.

[5] To Andrea Harrandt we owe a first-rate annotated edition of all of Bruckner's letters.

[6] Elisabeth Maier, Verborgene Persönlichkeit, 1:xi-xxxix.

[7] Manfred Wagner, "Gefahr der Anekdote," in Bruckner Symposion 1977, 27-33.

[8] Erwin Ringel, "Psychogramm für Anton Bruckner," in Bruckner Symposion 1977, 19-26.

[9] C. George Boeree, *Personality Theories* (Shippenburg University Pr, 2006).

[10] Sigmund Freud, "Eine Kindheitserinnerung des Leonardo da Vinci" (1910), in Studienausgabe X: *Bildende Kunst und Literatur*, 4th ed. (Frankfurt am Main, 1969) 87-159; p. 156.

[11] Bruckner – skizziert.

[12] G – A. 4/2: 130, 133.

[13] Schalk, 92.

[14] Theodor W. Adorno, *Berg: Der Meister des kleinsten Übergangs.* Österreichische Komponisten des xx. Jahrhunderts, vol. 15 (Vienna, 1968), 41.

[15] Schalk, 76, 87f.

[16] Bruckner in Wien, 75-160.

[17] Louis, xiiif.

[18] Hruby, 38f.

[19] Friedrich Eckstein, "Die erste und die letzte Begegnung zwischen Hugo Wolf und Anto Bruckner," in *In Memoriam Anton Bruckner. Festschrift zum 100. Geburtstag Anton Bruckners.*, ed. Karl Kobald (Zurich, Vienna, Leipzig, 1924), 44-59; p.57.

[20] Klose, 97f.

[21] G. – A. 4/2: 14-24; Bruckner – skizziert, 30ff.

[22] Theodor W. Adorno, *Mahler. Eine musikalische Physiognomik* (Frankfurt am Main, 1960), 92f.

[23] Ibid., 180f.

[24] G. – A. 1:197.

[25] Commenda, 17.

[26] Leopold Kretzenbacher, "Meisterdieb-Motive," in *Wunder über Wunder. Gesammelte Studien zur Volkserzählung* (Vienna, 1974), 137-161.

Authoritarianism and Self-Assurance

[1] Josef Kluger, "Anton Bruckner und das Stift Klosterneuburg,: in *In memoriam Anton Bruckner*, 121f.

[2] G. – A. 2/1:188.

[3] Briefe 2:119f.

[4] Auer, 247.

[5] Herbert Killian, ed., *Gustav Mahler in den Erinnerungen von Natalie Bauer-Lechner*, (Hamburg 1984), 43.

The World as "Bad Lot"

Source of motto: Briefe, 1:42.

[1] Schalk, 92.

[2] Briefe, 1:1.

[3] Briefe, 1:2f.

[4] Briefe, 1:41.

[5] Briefe, 1:42.

[6] Briefe, 1:44.

[7] Briefe, 1:46.

[8] Briefe, 1:51.

[9] Ibid.

[10] Briefe, 1:66.

[11] Ibid.

[12] Briefe, 1:90.

[13] Briefe, 1:92.

[14] Auer, Briefe, 178; Briefe, 1:242.

[15] G. – A. 4/3:435

Neurosis

[1] Briefe, 1:69.

[2] Louis, 177.

[3] Briefe, 1:99, 130.

[4] Briefe, 1:134.

[5] See my *Gustav Mahler: Visionär und Despot. Porträt einer Persönlichkeit* (Zurich, Hamburg, 1998), 80f.

[6] Otto Kitzler to August Göllerich, 1897; quoted from Bruckner-Brevier, 148.

[7] Verborgene Persönlichkeit, 1:392; see Briefe, 2:80.

[8] Auer, 127.

[9] Bruckner-Handbuch, 80f.

[10] Letter to Cathedral Dean Schiedermayr, January 23, 1870; Briefe, 1:116.

[11] Briefe, 1:94.

[12] Gerhardt Nissen, ed., *Zwangserkrankungen. Prävention und Therapie* (Berne, Göttingen, Toronto, Seattle, 1996), 7.

[13] Auer, Briefe, 395; Briefe, 2:21f.

[14] Josef Schalk to Hermann Levi, October 18, 1887; Briefe, 2:25

[15] Bruckner-Brevier, 133.

[16] Eduard Hanslick, *Fünf Jahre Musik* [1891-1895] (Berlin, 1896), 190-193.

Libido

Source of motto: G. – A.4/3:162.

[1] G. – A. 4/3:253f.

[2] G. – A. 4/1:121-124.

[3] Bruckner – skizziert, 87.

[4] G. – A. 3/1:217f.

[5] Briefe, 1:14.

[6] Briefe, 1:58.

[7] G. – A 2/1:353-357.

[8] Briefe, 1:59.

[9] Kitzler, 31.

[10] Briefe, 1:278.

[11] "'Anton Bruckners letzter Flirt'. Aus den Erinnerungen eines Philharmonikers," in *Neues Wiener Journal,* May, 19, 1929. Quoted from G. – A. 4/3:243-246.

[12] G. – A. 4/3:251f.

[13] Louis, 167.

[14] Verborgene Persönlichkeit, 1:xxxiiiff.. – Briefe, 2:74f.

[15] Bruckner-Handbuch, 247.

Emotionality

Source of motto: Briefe, 1:82, of March 16, 1868.

[1] See Othmar Wessely, "Anton Bruckner als Briefschreiber," in Bruckner-Symposion 1983, 89-93.

[2] Briefe, 1:19.

[3] Briefe, 1:115.

[4] Briefe, 1:116.

[5] Hruby, 35.

[6] Stradal, 858, 971.

[7] Briefe, 1:18.

[8] Briefe, 1:15.

[9] Briefe, 1:68.

[10] Briefe, 1:77.

[11] Andrea Harrandt, "'...den ich als einzigen wahren Freund erkenne...': Anton Bruckner und Rudolf Weinwurm," in Bruckner-Symposion 1994, 37-48.

[12] Thomas Leibnitz, *Die Brüder Schalk und Anton Bruckner* (Tutzing, 1988).

[13] Briefe, 1:202.

[14] Schalk, 71; Briefe, 2:1.

[15] Briefe, 1:58.

[16] See G.– A 4/2:323ff.

[17] Briefe, 1:260.

[18] August Humer, ed., *Die Brucknerorgel im Alten Dom zu Linz* (Linz, 1996), fig. 10.

The "Passionate Urge to Compose"

[1] Text of the application in Louis, 282.

[2] For basics, see Elisabeth Maier, Franz Zamazal, *Anton Bruckner und Leopold von Zenetti* (Graz, 1980).

[3] G. – A. 4/1:70ff.

[4] Briefe, 1:29.

[5] Briefe, 1:32. Correction in Briefe, 2:356.

[6] Briefe, 1:75.

[7] Briefe, 1:136f.

[8] Briefe, 1:143.

[9] Briefe, 1:147.

Securing an Income

Source of motto: Briefe, 1:154, of February 13, 1875.

[1] G. – A. 4/3:576.

[2] Rolf Keller, "Die letztwilligen Verfügungen Anton Bruckners," in Bruckner-Jahrbuch 1982/83, 95-115; p. 102.

[3] Verborgene Persönlichkeit, 1:351.

[4] Eckstein, 22.

[5] Göll, 1:154.

[6] Briefe, 1:31f.

[7] Briefe, 1:93f.

[8] Letter to Wilhelm, Baron Schwarz von Senborn, June 22, 1874., Briefe 1:149.

[9] Briefe, 1:148.

[10] Briefe, 1:153.

[11] Briefe, 1:154.

[12] Elisabeth Maier in Bruckner in Wien, 207.

[13] Bruckner-Brevier, 58.

[14] Briefe, 1:274.

[15] Commenda, 135f.; Bruckner – skizziert, 130.

[16] Bruckner-Brevier, 60.

[17] See Louis, 279ff; Bruckner-Handbuch, 500ff.

[18] See Alfred Orel, *Ein Harmonielehrekolleg bei Anton Bruckner* (Berlin, Vienna, Zurich, 1940), 79-82; Rudolf Flotzinger, "Zur Bedeutung des Selbststudiums in Bruckners musikalischer Ausbildung," in Bruckner-Symposion 1988, 51-59.

Persecution Mania

Source of Motto I: Briefe 1:130, of November 2, 1871
Source of Motto II: Auer, Briefe, 252f.; Briefe, 2:162, of December 5, 1891.

[1] G. – A. 4/2:501f.

[2] Hruby, 26. Verborgene Persönlichkeit 1:xii.

[3] Briefe, 1:52.

[4] Ibid. On the choral circle *Frohsinn*, see the article in Bruckner-Handbuch, 255f.

[5] Bruckner-Handbuch, 376f.

[6] Briefe, 1:129.

[7] Briefe, 1:128.

[8] Briefe, I:129.

[9] Ibid.

[10] Briefe, 1:130.

[11] Briefe, 1:153f.

[12] Commenda, 74f.; Bruckner – skizziert, 145f.

[13] Briefe, 1:213.

[14] Briefe, 1:281.

[15] Louis, 304f.; Bruckner-Brevier, 130.

[16] Bruckner-Brevier, 130f.

[17] Schwanzara, 43.

[18] Ibid., 44.
[19] Briefe, 1:163.
[20] E. Maier in Bruckner in Wien, 192, n.188
[21] Briefe, 1:153.
[22] G. – A. 4/1:302.
[23] Briefe, 1:213.
[24] Briefe, 1:293.
[25] Max Kalbeck, *Johannes Brahms*, vol. 3 (Berlin 1912), 404.
[26] Klose, 244.
[27] Ibid. 241.
[28] Briefe, 1:273.
[29] Briefe, 1:275.
[30] Briefe, 1:294.
[31] Bruckner-Brevier, 133.
[32] See Johannes-Leopold Mayer in Bruckner in Wien, 135f.
[33] Briefe, 1:304
[34] Briefe, 1:313.
[35] Renate Grasberger, *Bruckner-Ikonographie*, Part 1: Ca. 1854-1924. Anton Bruckner Dokumente und Studien 7 (Graz 1990), 1:167, no. 78/79; also in Bruckner-Handbuch, 29.

Worries about the Success of the Work

Source of motto: Briefe, 1:252, of April 17, 1885.

[1] Gräflinger, Briefe. 147.

[2] Bruckner-Handbuch, 309f.

[3] Ibid., 252f.

[4] Bruckner to his copyist, Leopold Hofmeyer, November 11, 1889; Briefe, 2:59.

[5] Bruckner-Handbuch, 290ff.

[6] Letter of September 7, 1885; Briefe, 1:273.

[7] Ingrid Fuchs, "'Künstlerische Väter' und 'Vormünder'. Bruckner und die zeitgenössischen Dirigenten seiner Symphonien," in Bruckner-Symposion 1994, 65-85.

[8] Briefe, 1:271.

[9] Bruckner-Handbuch, 453; Rolf Keller in Bruckner-Jahrbuch 1984/85/86, 95f.

[10] Briefe, 1:234.

[11] Letter to Eduard Rappoldi, May 11, 1885; Briefe, 1:262.

[12] Elisabeth Th. Hilscher, "Genie versus Markt. Anton Bruckner und seine Verleger," in Bruckner-Symposion 1994, 139-150.

[13] Briefe, 1:224.

[14] Bruckner-Handbuch, 143f.

[15] Klose, 113.

[16] Rolf Keller, "Das 'amerikanische Ehrendoktorat' für Anon Bruckner," in Bruckner-Symposion, 1992, 73-92.

[17] Facsimile of the acceptance speech in Bruckner-Handbuch, 142.

Interest in the Extraordinary

Source of motto: *Neue Freie Presse* of February 26, 1885; quoted from Bruckner-Brevier, 132.

[1] Klose, 97f.

[2] Verborgene Persönlichkeit, 1:152.

[3] Ibid., 155-160.

[4] G. – A. 4/2:14-24.

[5] G. – A.4/1:70ff.

[6] Bruckner-Brevier, 99.

[7] Schwanzara, 61.

"Sympathy with Death"

Source of motto: Oskar Loerke, *Anton Bruckner: Ein Charakterbild* (Berlin, Frankfurt am Main, 1938), 171f.

[1] Thomas Mann, *Ausgewählte Essays in drei Bänden* (Frankfurt am Main, 1978), 56.

[2] Briefe, 1:44, 47.

[3] Briefe, 1:78.

[4] G. – A. 2/1:66f.

[5] Bruckner – skizziert, 158,160f.

[6] Hruby, 19f.

[7] G. – A. 4/2:567-570.

[8] Ibid.

[9] Commenda, 85; Bruckner – skizziert, 53.

[10] Bruckner Jahrbuch 1982/83, 98ff.

[11] Julius Bistron, "Das Notizbuch Anton Bruckners. Ein musikhistorischer Fund"; quoted in Verborgene Persönlichkeit, 1:465-471.

Religiosity

Source of motto: Schalk, 92.

[1] Klose, 97.

[2] Briefe, 1:86.

[3] Friedrich Blume, article on Bruckner in *Musik in Geschichte und Gegenwart*, 1st ed. (Kassel, 1952), Column 359.

[4] Letter to the Prince Archbishop of Vienna of February 23, 1876; Briefe, 1:159.

[5] Leopold Nowak, *Te deum laudamus. Gedanken zur Musik Anton Bruckners* (Vienna, 1947), 29.

[6] Franz Kosch, "'Der Beter Anton Bruckner'. Nach seinen persönlichen Aufzeichnungen," in Bruckner-Studien 1964, 67-73.

[7] E. Maier, Verborgene Persönlichkeit 1, xxxv.

[8] Joachim F. Angerer, "Bruckner und die klösterlichen Lebensformen seiner Zeit," in Bruckner-Symposion 1985, 41-51; p. 49.

[9] G. – A. 3/1:276.

[10] Eckstein, 23.

[11] Leopold Nowak, "Der Name 'Jesus Christus' in den Kompositionen von Anton Bruckner," in *Über Anton Bruckner. Gesammelte Aufsätze* (Vienna, 1985), 77-87; p. 83.

[12] Arthur Nikisch, "Bruckner-Erinnerungen," in *Neues Wiener Journal* of October 11, 1911; quoted from Decsey, 142f.

[13] G. – A. 4/3:218.

[14] Ludwig van Beethoven, *Konversationshefte* (Leipzig 1972), 1:235.

[15] G. – A. 4/3:220f.

[16] G. – A. 4/2:92.

[17] Commenda, 54; Bruckner – skizziert, 67.

[18] G. – A. 4/2:135.

[19] Hruby, 38f.

[20] Commenda, 51; Bruckner – skizziert, 68.

Part Two: Sacred Music

Personality and Oeuvre

> Source of motto: Karl Amadeus Hartmann – Waldemar Wahren, letters about Bruckner, in *Neue Zeitschrift für Musik*, vol. 126 (1965), 272-276, 334-338, 380-387; p. 274

[1] Oskar Lang, *Anton Bruckner. Wesen und Bedeutung*, 2nd ed. (Munich, 1943), 21; 1st ed. 1924.

[2] Louis, xiiif.

[3] Erich Schwebsch, *Anton Bruckner. Ein Beitrag zur Erkenntnis von Entwicklungen in der Musik*, 2nd ed. Augsburg, n.d.), 82 (1st ed. Stuttgart, 1921).

Music as Religious Confession

> Source of motto: Richard Wagner, "Über Franz Liszts symphonische Dichtungen," in *Sämtliche Schriften und Dichtungen* (popular edition), 16 vols. 6th ed. (Leipzig, n.d.), 5:191.

[1] Albert Camus, *Der Myhus von Sisyphus. Ein Versuch über das Absurde* (Hamburg, 1959).

[2] Sigmund Freud, *Abriß der Psychoanalyse. Das Unbehagen in der Kultur* (Frankfurt am Main, 1965), 65.

[3] Gerhard Fricke, *Wackenroders Religion der Kunst* (Iserlohn, 1948).

[4] In Wilhelm Heirich Wackenroder, *Phantasien über die Kunst für Freunde der Kunst* (1799), second section no. IX: Die Symphonien. Quoted from the collected edtion of Wackenroder's works and correspondence (Heidelberg: Lambert Schneider, 1967), 251.

[5] E. T. A. Hoffmann, *Schriften zur Musik. Nachlese* (Munich, n.d.), 212.

[6] *Franz Liszt's Briefe*, ed. La Mara, vol. 8 (Leipzig, 1905), 171: "On peut dire que la Musique est religieuse par essence et comme l'âme humaine 'naturellement chrétienne'."

[7] de la Motte-Haber, ed., *Musik und Religion* (Laaber, 1995).

[8] See Constantin Floros, *Gustav Mahler*, vol. 3: Die Symphonien (Wiesbaden 1985), 47-74.

[9] Schwanzara, 78.

[10] Josef Kluger, "Schlichte Erinnerungen an Anton Bruckner," in *Jahrbuch des Stiftes Klosterneuburg* (Klosterneuburg, 1910), 120.

[11] Briefe I, p. 259

[12] Thus on the voices of the choral mass for Maundy Thursday WAB 9 (1844), and in two compositions of the Year 1885, the antiphon *Ecce sacerdos* and the gradual *Virga Jesse.*

[13] See his letters to Anton Imhof Ritter von Geißlinghof and to Johann Herbeck, both of December 30, 1867, Briefe I, p.75f.

[14] For specifics, see pp. 112-114 below.

[15] Johan Wolfgang von Goethe, *Dichtung und Wahrheit*, 2:7.

A New, Dramatic Conception of the Mass

Source of motto: Louis, 204.

[1] Franz Grasberger, ed., *Anton Bruckner zum 150. Geburtstag. Eine Ausstellung im Prunksaal der Österreichischen Nationalbibliothek, May 29 to October 12, 1974* (Vienna, 1974), 64.

[2] G. – A. 3/1:246.

[3] *Anton Bruckner zum 150. Geburtstag*, 64.

[4] Floros, *Brahms und Bruckner*, 43ff., 158ff., 167-70.

[5] Franz Liszt, *Gesammelte Schriften*, ed. Lina Ramann (Leipzig, 1881), 2:55ff.

[6] Eva Diettrich, "Die Neudeutschen im Spiegel der Wiener katholischen Presse," in Bruckner-Symposion 1984, 67-70.

[7] Stradal, 974.

[8] Theodor Müller-Reuter, *Lexikon der deutschen Konzertliteratur* (Leipzig, 1909), 357-361.

[9] Letter of Liszt to Carl Haslinger, 1857. *Franz Liszt's Briefe*, ed. La Mara (Leipzig, 1905), 8:129-132.

[10] Rudolph Stephan, "Bruckner und Liszt. Hat der Komponist Franz Liszt Bruckner beeinflußt?" in Bruckner-Symposion 1986, 169-80. See my rebuttal in discussion on the topic of Bruckner and Liszt, ibid., 181-188.

[11] Quoted from Manfred Wagner, *Bruckner* (Mainz, 1983), 77.

[12] Quoted from Franz Gräflinger, *Anton Bruckner. Leben und Schaffen (Umgearbeitete Bausteine)* (Berlin, 1927), 77-80; p. 78.

[13] Manfred Wagner, *Bruckner*, 79.

The Credo Settings

[1] Gerold Wolfgang Gruber, "Die Credo-Kompositionen Anton Bruckners," in Bruckner-Symposion 1985, 129-143.

[2] See Othmar Wessely, "Historische Schichten in Bruckners Missa solemnis in b-Moll," in *Bruckner-Vorträge. Anton Bruckner et la musica sacra* (Rome, 1986), 15-19.

[3] F. W. in *Neue Zeitschrift für Musik* of September 27, 1893; quoted in Louis, 337.

[4] Constantin Floros, *Gustav Mahler*, vol 2: *Mahler und die Symphonik des 19. Jahrhunderts in neuer Deutung*, 2nd ed. (Wiesbaden 1987), 256-259; (1st ed., 1977).

[5] A sort of trial version of these funeral chorales can be observed in the two equales (WAB 114 and 149) for three trombones, which Bruckner composed late in January of 1847 in St. Florian on the occasion of the death of his great-aunt and godmother Rosalia Mayrhofer (1770-1847). See Bruckner Handbuch, 44f.; also Othmar Wes-

sely, "Zur Geschichte des Equals," in *Beethoven-Studien*, ed. Erich Schenk (Vienna, 1970), 341-360

[6] Gräflinger, *Anton Bruckner* (1927), 77-80.

[7] Cf. Dieter Michael Backes, "Die Instrumentation in den Messen von Anton Bruckner – eine Studie zum Phänomen des Symphonischen in Bruckners Kirchenmusik," in Friedrich Wilhelm Riedel, ed., *Anton Bruckner. Tradition und Fortscritt in der Kirchenmusik des 19. Jahrhunderts* (Sinzing, 2001), 253-305; p. 255.

Religious Tone Symbolism

[1] Haas, 63, 67-70.

[2] See Constantin Floros, *Der Mensch, die Liebe und die* Musik (Zurich, Hamburg, 2000), 34f.

[3] Manfred Wagner, "Der Quint-Oktavschritt als 'Majestas'-Symbol bei Anton Bruckner," in *Kirchenmusikalisches Jahrbuch,* 56 (1972): 97ff. ; also Wagner, *Bruckner* (1983), 378-382

[4] See the article by Imogen Fellinger in Bruckner-Symposion 1985, 145-153.

[5] Nowak, *Gesammelte Aufsätze*, 77-87.

[6] Haas, 67.

[7] These particulars in the *Kyrie* of the F minor Mass and the *Te Deum* are here noticed for the first time.

[8] Schwanzara, 273.

[9] Hartmut Krones, "Musiksprachliche Elemente aus Renaissance und Barock bei Anton Bruckner," in Bruckner-Symposion 1997, 53-72.

[10] G. – A. 4/2:691f.

[11] Elisabeth Maier, "Der Choral in den Kirchenwerken Anton Bruckners," in Bruckner-Symposion 1985, 111-122.

[12] Otto Biba, "Der Cäcilianismus," in Bruckner-Symposion 1985, 123-128; Hartmut Krones, "Bruckners Kirchenmusik im Spiegel des Cäcilianismus," in Riedel, ed., *Anton Bruckner* (2001), 91-104.

[13] See Floros, *Brahms und Bruckner*, 52ff.

Jubilant and Devout Music

[1] Winfried Kirsch adduces the concepts of (contemplative) "immersion" or absorption (*Versenkung*) and "ecstasies" (*Ekstase*) to demarcate the expressive diapason of much of Bruckner's church music. See his article in Riedel, ed., *Anton Bruckner* (2001), 339-358.

"Let Me Not Be Confounded in Eternity" – The *Te Deum*

[1] On the genesis of the work, see Haas, 93f, and Leopold Nowak's preface to the edition of the *Te Deum* in the Complete Critical Edition (Anton Bruckner, *Sämtliche Werke*, vol 19 [Vienna, 1962/1998]).

[2] Commenda, 88; G. – A.4/2:142; Bruckner – skizziert, 62.

[3] Briefe, 1:259.

[4] See Ernst Kähler, "Studien zum Te Deum und zur Geschichte des 24. Psalms in der Alten Kirche," in *Veröffentlichungen der evangelischen Gesellschaft für Liturgieforschung*, 10 (Göttingen, 1958).

[5] Peter Griesbacher: *Bruckners Te Deum. Studie*, Regensburg 1919, 2.

[6] Franz Liszt, *Gesamtausgabe*, vol. 5/2; republished from *Franz Liszt's musikalische Werke* (ed. Franz Liszt-Stiftung [Leipzig]) (Farnborough, Hants.: Gregg Press Ltd., 1966).

[7] Ernst Decsey (64f.) reports that in his lecture courses in Vienna Bruckner loved to cite the sentence "Mi contra fa – diabolus in musica."

[8] Mozart's Requiem KV 626 virtually served as a model for Bruckner's own requiem WAB 39 of 1848/49. As entries in his pocket calendar indicate, Bruckner immersed himself in the study of Mozart's way of leading the voices in the Requiem as late as 1876 and 1877. See Verborgene Persönlichkeit, 1:51f., 55f.

[9] Quoted from Louis, 319f.

[10] Briefe, 1:283.

[11] Briefe, 1:285.

[12] Alma Mahler, *Gustav Mahler. Erinnerungen und Briefe*, 2nd ed. (Amsterdam, 1949), 138.

[13] *Gustav Mahler Briefe*, new, enlarged and revised ed. by Herta Blaukopf (Vienna, Hamburg, 1982), 98.

[14] Andrea Harrandt, "'Gustav Mahler. O! mögen Sie nur der Meinige bleiben ...' Unbekannte Briefe zu zwei Aufführungen von Bruckners Te Deum in Hamburg," in Erich Wolfgang Partsch, ed., *Gustav Mahler. Werk und Wirken* (Vienna, 1996), 50-63; p. 52.

[15] Auer, Briefe, 388; Briefe, 2:173.

[16] For details, see my essay "Von Mahlers Affinität zu Bruckner," in Bruckner-Symposion 1986, 109-117.

[17] Louis, 209.

[18] See Friedrich W. Riedel, "Kirchenmusik als politische Repräsentation. Zur Vertonung des *Te Deum laudamus* im 18. und 19. Jahrhundert," in Peter Ackermann, Ulrike Kienzle and Adolf Nowak, eds., *Festschrift für Winfried Kirsch zum 65. Geburtstag* (Tutzing, 1996), 117-129.

[19] Theodor Müller-Reuter, *Lexikon der deutschen Konzertliteratur* (Leipzig, 1909), 245-250; p. 247.

[20] G. – A. 4/2:141f.

[21] Briefe, 1:217.

Music as Song of Praise – Psalm 150.

Source of motto: Paul Celan, *Gedichte in zwei Bänden* (Frankfurt am Main, 1975), 2:26.

[1] G. – A. 4/3:230ff.

[2] Letter to Emil Fink, July 1, 1893. See Auer, Briefe, 274; Briefe, 2:225.

[3] Kurth, 1278.

[4] Siegfried Ochs, *Geschehenes, Gesehenes* (Leipzig, Zurich, 1922), 316. See also my *Brahms und Bruckner*, 201f.

[5] Auer, Briefe, 272; Briefe, 2:218.

[6] *Wiener Abendpost* of November 18, 1892; quoted from Louis, 329f.

[7] *Wiener Presse* of November 19, 1892; quoted from Louis, 331f.

[8] *Deutsches Volksblatt* of November 25, 1892, in G. – A. 4.3:279ff.

[9] Haas, 87f. On the reception history, see Winfried Kirsch, "Anmerkungen zu einem Spätwerk: Anton Bruckner's 150. Psalm," in Christoph-Hellmut Mahling, ed., *Anton Bruckner. Studien zu Werk und Wirkung* (Tutzing, 1988), 81-99.

Part Three: The Symphonies

The Fiction of "Absolute Music"

Source of motto: Haas, 1.

[1] Julius Bistron, "Anton Bruckner. Ein Kunstproblem im Menschlichen," in *Die Republik*, April 28, 1919.

[2] Karl Grebe, *Anton Bruckner in Selbstzeugnissen und Bilddokumenten* (Reinbek, 1972), 7.

[3] See the exchange at the Linz Bruckner-Symposion 1992, 215f.

[4] Carl Dahlhaus, *Die Idee der absoluten Musik* (Kassel, 1978), 23.

[5] Wilhelm Seidel, article "Absolute Music" in *Die Musik in Geschichte und Gegenwart*, 2nd ed. (Kassel, Stuttgart, 1994), columns 14–23; col. 16.

[6] Floros, *Brahms und Bruckner*, 155-225.

[7] Carl Dahlhaus, "Bruckner und die Programmatik. Zum Finale der Achten Symphonie," in Christoph-Hellmuth Mahling, ed., *Anton Bruckner* (1988), 7-32. See also Gernot Gruber, "Zum Verhältnis von Strukturanalyse, Inhaltsdeutung und musikalischer Rezeption. Exemplifiziert an Bruckners Achten Symphonie," in Bruckner-

Symposion 1992, 129-142; and the critique by John Williamson in *Music & Letters*, 71 (February 1990): 112-115.

[8] See my *Der Mensch, die Liebe und die Musik* (Zurich, Hamburg, 2000).

Originality and Modernity

Source of motto: G. – A. 3/1:167.

[1] Rudolf Louis, *Anton Bruckner*. Moderne Essays, ed. Dr. Hans Landsberg, no. 49 (Berlin, 1904), 12.

[2] Herbert Killian, *Gustav Mahler in den Erinnerungen von Natalie Bauer-Lechner* (Hamburg, 1984), 32.

[3] Auer, Briefe, 395; Briefe, 2:21.

[4] August Halm, *Die Symphonie Anton Bruckners* (Munich, 1923), 102.

[5] Alfred Einstein, *Größe in der Musik*, pocket ed. (Kassel, 1980), 38; orig. Zurich, 1951.

[6] Wilhelm Furtwängler, *Johannes Brahms. Anton Bruckner* (Stuttgart, 1971), 31.

Matters of Style

Source of motto: Ernst Bloch, *Zur Philosophie der Musik* (Frankfurt am Main, 1974), 50f.

[1] Observe, e.g., the modal harmonies at the end of the exposition (mm. 239-256) of the opening movement of the Third Symphony. On Bruckner's relation to Palestrina, see Othmar Wessely, "Beharrung und Fortschritt im Schaffen des jungen Bruckners," in Bruckner-Symposion 1977, 35-42.

[2] See Karl Schütz, "Von der Orgel-Improvisation zur Symphonie. Ein Beitrag zur Klangvorstellung Anton Bruckners," in *Bruckner-Studien* (1975), 271-284.

[3] Floros, *Brahms und Bruckner*, 55-83.

[4] Constantin Floros, "Parallelen zwischen Schubert und Bruckner," in *Festschrift Othmar Wessely zum 60. Geburtstag* (Tutzing, 1982), 133-145.

[5] Floros, *Brahms und Bruckner*, 158-166.

[6] Kurth, 233-251.

[7] Richard Wagner, *Oper und Drama*, Pt. 3: "Dichtkunst und Tonkunst im Drama der Zukunft," in *Sämtliche Schriften und Dichtungen* (Leipzig, n.d.), 4:192.

How Bruckner Came to the Symphony

[1] See Kitzler's certification of Bruckner's studies, dated July 10, 1863 in Grasberger, Ausstellungskatalog, 71: "Instrumentation und Komposition."

[2] Letter to Rudolf Weinwurm, October 8, 1863; Briefe, 1:37.

[3] Otto Kitzler, *Musikalische Erinnerungen mit Briefen von Wagner, Brahms, Bruckner und Rich. Pohl* (Brünn/Brno, 1904), 29.

[4] Ibid., 30.

[5] Briefe, 1:37.

[6] See Othmar Wessely, "Bruckners Mendelssohn-Kenntnis," *Bruckner-Studien* (Vienna, 1975), 81-112.

[7] For details, see my article "Zu Bruckner's frühem symphonischen Schaffen," in Bruckner-Symposion 1988, 173-190.

[8] G. – A. 3/1:165-169

[9] G. – A. 3/1:170

[10] G. – A. 3/1:297-300; p. 300

[11] G. – A. 3/1:225-228.

[12] Auer, 93f.

[13] Auer, Briefe, 167; Briefe, 2:119.

[14] Max Graf, "Anton Bruckner. I. Persönlichkeit. II. Der Entwicklungsgang," in *Die Musik*, 1 (1901/02): 1268.

[15] Letter to Professor Simon Leo Reinisch, October 19, 1891; Briefe, 2:153.

[16] G. – A. 4/2:166.

Autobiographic Elements in the Second and Third Symphony

Source of motto: Schwanzara, 97.

[1] See Floros, *Brahms und Bruckner*, 155ff.

[2] G. – A. 3/1:473.

[3] Auer, Briefe, 167; Briefe, 2:119.

[4] Haas, 112.

[5] Bruckner-Brevier, 286.

[6] Floros, *Brahms und Bruckner*, 161.

[7] Mm. 258-265 in the version of 1873, mm. 229-236 in the 1878 version, mm. 227-234 in the 1889 version.

[8] The note is absent from the corresponding (variant) passage in the first version.

[9] G. – A. 4/1:260. Bruckner's following communication to Leopold Hofmeyer is also relevant in this context: "The day of the festival of St. Theresia," he wrote on October 13, 1882, "has always been important to me: I always had to celebrate the cherished name day of my blessed mother." Briefe, 1:199.

[10] This mass was first published by August Göllerich in vol. 1 of his great biography (173-189).

[11] It first occurs in the *Ave Maria* motet for four voices of 1856 (WAB 5). Robert Haas (45, 80, 121) called it "Marienkadenz" ("St. Mary's cadence").

[12] According to Haas (120), it owed its genesis to a "Christmas carol." Unfortunately, Haas does not specify it.

[13] Bruckner's undated letter of condolence to Cosima Wagner on the death of Richard Wagner closes with the sentence, "Er ruhe sanft!" ("May he rest in peace!"); Briefe, 1:201.

[14] Kurt Singer, *Bruckners Chormusik* (Stuttgart, Berlin, 1924), 29.

[15] Hans Heinrich Eggebrecht, *Musik im Abendland* (Munich, 1991).

The Allegiance to Richard Wagner

[1] Kitzler, 30.

[2] Briefe, 1:90f.

[3] Auer, Briefe, 166ff; Briefe, 2:119f.

[4] Verborgene Persönlichkeit, vol. 2, fig. 2.

[5] Briefe, 1:145f., – See the reproduction of the dedicatory page in the edition of the first version of the Third Symphony (*Sämtliche Werke*, 3/1 (Vienna, 1977).

[6] My article "Die Zitate in Bruckners Symphonik" (Bruckner-Jahrbuch 1982/83, 7-18) provoked a lively discussion among the experts. My approach was continued by Wolfgang Kühnen (Bruckner-Jahrbuch 1991/92, 31-43) and by Elisabeth Reiter (Bruckner-Jahrbuch 1994/95, 79-89. Of the "critical" responses I have to say that they argue solely philologically and simply ignore the evident musical connections. See EgonVoss (*Die Musikforschung*, 49 [1996]: 403-406, and Hans-Joachim Hinrichsen (in *Bruckner-Probleme* [Stuttgart, 1999], 115-133.

[7] Briefe, 1:139.

[8] G. – A. 4/1:288, 299ff.

[9] Briefe, 1:150.

[10] Briefe, 1:249.

[11] P. Marsop in *Berliner Tageblatt* of August 10, 1885; quoted from Bruckner-Brevier, 159ff.

[12] Auer, Briefe, 168; Briefe, 1:239, 257, 274.

[13] Erwin Horn in Bruckner-Handbuch, 339ff.

[14] For the following citations, see G. – A. 4/2:671; Schwanzara, 138; Bruckner-Brevier, 317; and my article, "Bruckners Symphonik und die Musik Wagners," in Bruckner-Symposion 1984, 177-83; p. 178.

The Triad of the Middle Symphonies

[1] G. – A. 4/3:107-110, 255.

[2] Kurth, 509f.

[3] Letter to Arthur Nikisch, November 5, 1884; Briefe, 1:225.

[4] Note in this respect, e.g., the main subject of the opening movement with its minor chord in the fourth degree, or the "song period" in the Finale, at C in the score.

[5] For a detailed analysis of the *Romantic*, see my *Brahms und Bruckner*, 171-181.

[6] See my *Gustav Mahler*, 2:76-79.

[7] Kurth, 931.

[8] Auer, Briefe, 366f.; Briefe, 2:253.

[9] Quoted from Andrea Harrandt, "Gustav Schönaich – ein 'Herold der Bruckner'schen Kunst'," in Bruckner-Symposion 1991, 63-71; p. 66.

[10] Haas, 137.

[11] Kurth, 932.

[12] Quoted from Louis, 311.

[13] Ibid., 312.

The Seventh – a Second "Wagner Symphony"

Source of motto: According to Franz Gräflinger, *Anton Bruckner. Leben und Schaffen* (1927), 202.

[1] Bruckner to Arthur Nikisch, August 6, 1884; Briefe, 1:218.

[2] *Der Merker*, 9 (1918), 202.

[3] Letter to Felix Mottl, May 9, 1885; Briefe, 1:259.

[4] Cf. the harmonic analysis of the Adagio in August Halm, *Die Symphonien Anton Bruckners* (Munich, 1923), 188-198.

[5] See my *Gustav Mahler*, 2:142.

[6] Siegfried Ochs, *Geschehenes, Gesehenes*, 316.

[7] See Wolfgang Doebel, *Bruckners Symphonien in Bearbeitungen* (Tutzing, 2001), 391-398.

[8] G. – A. 4/2:83.

[9] G. – A. 4/3:19.

[10] *Briefe*, 1:245.

[11] This review was also reprinted in Vienna's *Deutsche Zeitung* of March 15, 1885.

[12] *Briefe*, 1:245.

[13] *Briefe*, 1:254.

[14] *Briefe*, 1:257f.

[15] *Bruckner-Brevier*, 133.

Secular and Religious

[1] Ernst Bloch, *Zur Philosophie der Musik* (Frankfurt am Main, 1974), 54.

[2] Robert Schumann, article "Character," in *Damenkonversationslexikon*, ed. Herloßsohn und Lühe. Quoted from Schumann, *Gesammelte Schriften über Musik und Musiker*, ed. Martin Kreisig, 2nd ed. (Leipzig, 1914), 207.

[3] See my article, "Bruckner und Mahler. Gemeinsamkeiten und Unterschiede," in Bruckner-Symposion 1981, 21-29.

[4] According to Robert Haas, *Vorlagenbericht* for the edition of the Fourth Symphony in the *Kritische Gesamtausgabe* (Vienna 1936), xiv; see also Haas, 127.

[5] Compare the Recordare of Mozart's Requiem.

[6] Leopold Nowak, "Symphonischer und kirchlicher Stil bei Anton Bruckner," in *Über Anton Bruckner*, 47-54.

[7] *Franz Liszt's Briefe*, ed. La Mara (Leipzig, 1893-1905), 2:284.

[8] Theodor Helm, "Anton Bruckner als Tondichter," in *Österreichische Musik- und Theaterzeitung* of November 1-15, 1896; quoted from Louis 340-345.

[9] Werner Korte, *Robert Schumann* (Potsdam, 1937), fig. 17.

[10] For details, see my *Brahms und Bruckner*, 203-210.

[11] G. – A. 4/2:663.

Imaginations – Bruckner's Associations in the Eighth

[1] Bruckner – skizziert, 11, 65ff; Louis, 179.

[2] Richard Specht, in *Tagespost*, June 14, 1914.

[3] Bruckner – skizziert, 149f., 100f.

[4] Klose, 94f.

[5] Floros, *Brahms und Bruckner*, 181.

[6] C. G. Jung, *Archetyp und Unbewußtes* (Augsburg, 2000), 121.

[7] Leopold Nowak, "Anton Bruckner, der Romantiker," in *Über Anton Bruckner*, 167.

[8] Bruckner to Felix Weingartner, January 27, 1891; Auer, Briefe, 237f. – See also Floros, *Brahms und Bruckner*, 182-186, and the facsimile of two pages of the letter, ibid., 227f.

[9] Floros, *Gustav Mahler*, vol. 3: *Die Symphonien* (Wiesbaden, 1985), 304ff.

[10] Jörg Rothkamm, *Gustav Mahlers Zehnte Symphonie. Entstehung. Analyse, Rezeption* (Frankfurt am Main, 2003), 153-162.

[11] Hartmut Schäfer, "Die Musikautographen von Gustav Mahler," in Bayerische Staatsbibliothek, ed., *Gustav Mahler. Briefe und Musikautographen aus den Moldenbauer-Archiven in der Bayerischen Staatsbibliothek* (Munich, 2003), 214-218.

[12] Bruckner to Theodor Helm, March 26, 1892; Briefe, 2171.

[13] Carl Rademacher, *Wodan – St. Michael – Der Deutsche Michel*, Volk und Kunst III (Cologne, 1934), 100.

[14] Österreichische Nationalbibliothek, Music Collection MusHs 6051, fol. 4 recto, last accolade.

[15] Heinz Schöny, *Bruckner-Ikonographie* (Vienna, 1968), 78; Renate Grasberger, *Bruckner-Ikonographie*, Pt. 1: ca. 1854 to 1924 (Graz, 1990), 53.

[16] Stradal, 859.

The Ninth: Bruckner's "Farewell to life"

[1] Alma Mahler, *Gustav Mahler. Erinnerungen und Briefe*, 2nd ed. (Amsterdam, 1949), 145f.

[2] G. – A. 4/3:457.

[3] John A. Phillips, "Neue Erkenntnisse zum Finale der Neunten Symphonie Anton Bruckners," in Bruckner-Jahrbuch 1989/90, 115-203; p. 129.

[4] G. – A. 4/3:248.

[5] Auer, Briefe, 281; Briefe, 2:256.

[6] Stradal, 1073f.

[7] For basics, see my article, "Zur Deutung der Symphonik Bruckners. Das Adagio der Neunten Symphonie," in Bruckner-Jahrbuch 1981, 86-96.

[8] G. – A. 4/3:457.526f.

[9] Anton Bruckner, *IX. Symphonie. Entwürfe und Skizzen*, presented by Alfred Orel (Vienna, 1934).

[10] Bruckner-Handbuch, 434.

[11] See Hans Hubert Schönzeler, *Zu Bruckners IX. Symphonie. Die Krakauer Skizzen. Eine Bestandsaufnahme* (Vienna, 1987); Mariana E. Sonntag, "A New Perspective of Anton Bruckner's Composition of the Ninth Symphony," in Bruckner-Jahrbuch

1989/90, 77-114; Gunnar Cohrs, "Der Mikrofilm der Krakauer Bruckner-Skizzen in der Österreichischen Nationalbibliothek," in Bruckner-Jahrbuch 1994/95/96, 191ff.

[12] Anton Bruckner, *IX. Symphonie d-Moll Finale* (unvollendet). Facsimile edition of all the autograph music pages. Presented and annotated by John A. Phillips (Vienna, 1996). Hereafter cited as Facsimile Edition.

[13] Verborgene Persönlichkeit, 2:400.

[14] Bruckner-Jahrbuch 1989/90, 116.

[15] Anton Bruckner, *IX. Symphonie d-Moll. Finale.* Reconstruction of the autograph score from the extant Sources. Performance version by Nicola Samale, John A. Phillips and Giuseppe Mazzuca, with assistance from Cunnar Cohrs (Adelaide, 1992). The bar numbers in the following music examples refer throughout to this edition.

[16] Facsimile edition, 24f., 33.

[17] Ibid., 24.

[18] Bruckner-Jahrbuch 1989/90, 120f.

[19] I refer to the recording of the Ninth (including the Finale) by the Neue Philharmonie Westfalen under Johannes Wildner. SonArte SP 13 (1998).

[20] Cf. article *Psalmen* in Bruckner-Handbuch, 343ff.

[21] Thus on pp. 3f., 6, 12ff., 16, 19f. of the Facsimile Edition.

[22] Ibid., 37.

[23] Österreichische Nationalbibliothek, Music Collection 3194 fol. 3 recto; Facsimile Edition, 6.

[24] Orel, "Entwürfe und Skizzen," 27*.

[25] According to Decsey, 216.

[26] G. – A. 4/3:15.

[27] Schwanzara, 97f.

[28] Facsimile Edition, 202.

[29] Haas, 3f.

[30] See my *Gustav Mahler*, 2:123.

[31] Facsimile Edition, 8, 10.

[32] Orel, "Entwürfe und Skizzen," 139*.

[33] Cf. Haas, 61.

[34] For basics, see Rainer Boss, "Die Fuge bei Anton Bruckner. Ein bedeutendes Kriterium seines Personalstils," in Bruckner-Jahrbuch 1994/95/96, 135-56.

[35] Facsimile Edition, 21ff., 27, 261ff.

[36] G. – A. 4/3:615.

[37] Orel, "Entwürfe und Skizzen," 138*; Facsimile Edition, 308.

[38] Verborgene Peersönlichkeit, 1:xxxvi.

[39] Ibid., 1:461f., 2:385f., figs. 77-80.

[40] Schalk, 65; Briefe, 2:334.

[41] Kurth, 730-737.

Reflections on the Bruckner Interpretion – Günter Wand, Eugen Jochum, Sergiu Celibidache

Source of motto: Quoted from Richard Specht, *Gustav Mahler* (Berlin, Leipzig, 1913), 87.

[1] Wolfgang Seifert, *Günter Wand: So und nicht anders. Gedanken und Erinnerungen*, 3rd ed. (Hamburg, 1999), 362.

[2] Ibid., 91.

[3] Ibid., 391.

[4] Ibid., 463.

[5] Schalk, 85.

[6] For details, see my article, "Historische Phasen der Bruckner-Interpretation," in Bruckner-Symposion 1980, 93-102.

[7] Seifert, 462.

[8] See my article, "Die Fassungen der Achten Symphonie von Anton Bruckner," in Bruckner-Symposion 1980, 53-63.

[9] Deutsche Grammophon SKL 929-939.

[10] Karl Schumann, "Der Bruckner-Dirigent Eugen Jochum," in the supplement to the recording of the nine symphonies under the label of the Deutsche Grammophon, p. 21.

[11] Seifert, 463.

[12] Eugen Jochum, "Zur Interpretation der Fünften Symphonie von Anton Bruckner. ein Rechenschaftsbericht," in Bruckner-Studien 1964, 53-59.

[13] Seifert, 370.

[14] RCA LC 0316.

[15] Stradal, 858.

[16] Schalk, 85.

[17] EMI CLASSICS 5 56690 2.

[18] RCA RD 60784.

The Progressive

[1] Ernst Krenek, for example, declares impressively his belief in the idea of progress in art. See Josef Rufer, ed., *Bekenntnisse und Erkenntnisse. Komponisten über ihr Werk* (Munich, 1981), 239f.

[2] Arnold Schönberg, "Brahms, der Fortschrittliche," in *Stil und Gedanke. Aufsätze zur Musik*, ed. Ivan Vojtech (Frankfurt am Main, 1976), 35-71.

[3] Schönberg, "Nationale Musik," ibid., 250-254.

[4] Ibid., 41.

[5] Ibid., 123-133; p. 128.

[6] Ibid., 126.

[7] Karl Amadeus Hartmann, "Lektionen bei Anton Webern," in *Kleine Schriften*, ed. Ernst Thomas (Mainz, 1965), 26-32.

[8] Anton Webern, *Der Weg zur neuen Musik*, ed. Willi Reich (Vienna, 1960), 34-37.

[9] Josef Polnauer, "Paralipomena zu Berg und Webern," in *Österreichische Musikzeitschrift*, 24 (1969), 292-296.

[10] Alban Berg's Viennese library (Trauttmannsdorffgasse 27) contains copies of several of Bruckner's symphonies.

[11] Theodor W. Adorno, *Berg. Der Meister des kleinsten Übergangs* (Vienna, 1968), 36.

[12] G. – A. 3/1:247.

[13] Schwanzara, 238, 190, 125.

[14] Hans Paumgartner in *Wiener Abendpost* of November 18, 1892. Quoted from Louis, 329f.

[15] Ludwig Speidel in *Wiener Fremden-Blatt* of January 17, 1885. Quoted from Louis, 313.

[16] August Wilhelm Ambros in *Wiener Abendpost* of October 28, 1873. Quoted from Louis, 305-308.

[17] Gustav Dömpke in *Wiener Allgemeine Zeitung* of January 17, 1885. Quoted from Louis, 313-317.

[18] Kurth, 561, 565.

[19] Arnold Schönberg, *Harmonielehre* (Leipzig, Vienna, 1911), 430f.

[20] See my article, "Zur Gegensätzlichkeit der Symphonik Brahms' und Bruckners," in Bruckner Symposion 1983, 145-153; pp. 150f.

[21] Ludwig Speidel in *Wiener Fremden-Blatt* of November 18, 1881. Quoted from Bruckner-Brevier, 226.

[22] *Neue Zeitschrift für Musik*, 81 (1885), 244.

[23] Gustav Dömpke in *Wiener Allgemeine Zeitung* of January 17, 1885. Quoted from Louis, 316.

[24] Eduard Hanslick in *Neue Freie Presse* of February 26, 1885. Quoted from Louis, 317.

[25] Österreichische Nationanbibliothek, Music Collection S.m. 28.234 fol. 15 recto.

[26] Arnold Schönberg, "Komposition mit zwölf Tönen," in *Stil und Gedanke*, 72-98; pp. 73f.

[27] Floros, *Gustav Mahler*, 2:303ff.

[28] Schwanzara, 125.

[29] Kurth, 563.

[30] See my article, "Bruckner und Mahler. Gemeinsamkeiten und Unterschiede," in Bruckner-Symposion 1981, 21-29.

Afterword

[1] Max Auer, "Bruckner und Mahler," in *Bruckner-Blätter*, 3 (1931): 23-26. See also G. – A. 4/1:448f.

[2] Bruno Walter, "Bruckner und Mahler," in Rudolf Stephan, *Gustav Mahler. Werk und Interpretation* (Cologne, 1979), 15-20; p. 15.

[3] Theodor W. Adorno, *Mahler. Eine musikalische Physiognomik* (Frankfurt am Main, 1960), 49, 38, 92f., 48, 70.

[4] Briefe, 1:51.

[5] G. – A. 4/1:31, n.1.

[6] Briefe, 1:153f.

[7] Hans Sittner, "Anton Bruckner und die Gegenwart," in Bruckner-Studien 1964, 99-104; p. 103.

Biographical Dates

1824	Anton Bruckner is born on September 4 in Ansfelden (Upper Austria).
1835/37	His confirmation godfather Baptist Weiß gives him lessons in organ playing and through-bass in Hörsching.
1837/40	As choir boy at St. Florian. Lessons in organ playing from Anton Kattinger.
1841/43	Teaching assistant in Windhag near Freistadt.
1845	From September, teacher in St. Florian (until 1855).
1849	Completes the Requiem in D minor.
1850	Appointed provisional Chapter organist on February 28.
1854	Missa solemnis premiered at St. Florian on September 14.
1855	Passes examination for rank of seconday school teacher in Linz (January). From July on, study of music theory with Simon Sechter.
1856	Joins choral circle *Frohsinn* in Linz in March. Appointed organist at the Old Cathedral in Linz.
1860	Elected first chorus master of choral circle *Frohsinn* (November 7). On November 11, his mother dies in Ebelsberg near Linz.
1861	Passes the famous examination at the Conservatory of the Society of the Friends of Music in Vienna with distinction (November 19). From December (until 1963), studies theory of form, instrumentation and composition with Otto Kitzler in Linz.
1862	Composes a march in D minor and three orchestral pieces in October / November. Works on the Overture in G minor in December.
1863	The Overture is completed. The "study symphony" in F minor and the Psalm 112 are written. On July 10, he completes his studies with Kitzler but continues to study with Ignaz Dorn until 1865.
1863/64	Works on the *Germanenzug* ("The Germanic Migration").

1864	The Mass in D minor is written (May to late September).
1865	Travels to Munich in May/June for the third performance of *Tristan und Isolde* and meets Richard Wagner.
1865/66	Genesis of the first Symphony.
1866	Composes the Mass in E minor (August to late November).
1867	From May 8 to August 8, he undergoes a health cure at the Coldwater Institute in Bad Kreuzen. On Septembetr 10, his teacher Simon Sechter dies. On September 14, he begins work on the Mass in F minor.
1868	Re-elected chorus master of *Frohsinn* (January 15). On April 4, he conducts the final chorus of Wagner's *Die Meistersinger.* On July 6, he is appointed Professor of Harmony, Counterpoint and Organ at the Conservatory of the Society of the Friends of Music in Vienna, and on September 4, "Prospective Austro-Hungarian Court Organist" in Vienna. Completes the F minor Mass on November 9.
1869	Between January 24 and September 12, the subsequently annulled Symphony in D minor, the so-called "Nilth," is written. In April/May, Bruckner achieves triumphs as organist in Nancy and Paris.
1870	On January 16, his sister Maria Anna dies in Vienna. In October, he is hired as substitute teacher for piano at the Teacher Seminary St. Anna (until 1874).
1871	Highly successful organ concerts in London (July/August).
1872	On July 16, the F minor Mass premieres at the court parish church of St. Augustine, under Bruckner's baton. Second Symphony completed (September 11).
1872/73	Work on the Third Symphony.
1873	Visits Richard Wagner in September in Bayreuth, who accepts the dedication of the Third Symphony.
1874	Genesis of the Fourth Symphony (January to November).
1875	On February 14, Bruckner begins work on the Fifth Symphony. On November 18, he is appointed (unpaid) lecturer for harmony and counterpoint at the University of Vienna.

1876	Completion of the Fifth Symphony (May 16th). Attends the third performance of the *Ring of the Nibelung* in Bayreuth.
1876-78	Work on the second version of the Third Symphony
1877	On December 16, Bruckner conducts the premiere of the Third Symphony (version of 1877) in Vienna.
1878	Bruckner is appointed a regular member of the court orchestra (January 19). The Third Symphony (version of 1876/78) is published by music publisher Theodor Rättig.
1878-80	Work on the second version of the Fourth Symphony.
1879	Bruckner completes the String Quintet in July; in August he begins work on the Sixth Symphony.
1880	Travels to Oberammergau and to Switzerland in August/September.
1881	Completes the draft of the *Te Deum* in May and completes the Sixth Symphony in September. On September 23, he begins work on the Seventh Symphony.
1882	Attends the premiere of *Parsifal* on July 26 in Bayreuth.
1883	Completes the Seventh Symphony. On February 13, Richard Wagner dies in Venice.
1884	On March 7, Bruckner completes the second version of the *Te Deum*. Begins work on the Eighth Symphony in the summer. In August, the "Perg Preludium" (WAB 129) is written. On December 30, Arthur Nikisch performs the Seventh Symphony in Leipzig.
1885	On March 10, Hermann Levi conducts a triumphant performance of the Seventh Symphony in Munich.
1886	On January 10, premiere of the *Te Deum* under Hans Richter in Vienna. On March 21, first performance of the Seventh Symphony in Vienna, likewise under Hans Richter. On July 8, Bruckner is awarded the Knight's Cross of the Francis-Joseph Order. On September 23, he is given an audience by Emperor Francis Joseph I.
1887	Completes the first verson of the Eighth Symphony on August 10. On September 21, he begins work on the Ninth Symphony.

1888	Premiere of the Fourth Symphony (1887/88 version) on January 22 under Hans Richter in Vienna.
1890	Completion of the second version of the Eighth Symphony, March 10. On July 12, Bruckner is given leave from teaching at the Conservatory. On December 21, premiere of the Third Symphony (1889 version) under Hans Richter in Vienna.
1891	Completion of the "Vienna Version" of the First Symphony (April 18). On November 7, Bruckner is awarded an honorary doctorate at the University of Vienna. On December 13, the "Vienna Version" of the First Symphony is premiered in Vienna under Hans Richter.
1892	On June 29, Bruckner completes Psalm 150. On October 28, he retires from his service at the Court Orchestra. On December 18, premiere of he second version of the Eighth Symphony under Hans Richter in Vienna.
1893	From April to August 7, composition of *Helgoland*. On November 10, Bruckner makes his will. On April 9, premiere of the Fifth Symphony under Franz Schalk in Graz. On November 25, premiere of the Second Symphony (printed version) under Hans Richter in Vienna. On November 30, the Adagio of the Ninth Symphony is completed.
1895	On May 24, Bruckner begins work on the Finale of the Ninth Symphony.
1896	Work on the Finale of the Ninth Symphony. On October 11, Bruckner dies in Vienna. The burial takes place on October 15 in the crypt beneath the great church of the collegiate church of St. Florian.

Abbreviations

Auer = Max Auer, *Anton Bruckner. Sein Leben und Werk*, 2nd ed. (Vienna, 1934)

Auer, Briefe = *Anton Bruckner, Gesammelte Briefe. Neue Folge*, ed. Max Auer (Regensburg, 1924)

Briefe = *Anton Bruckner, Sämtliche Werke*, vol 24.1. Briefe 1, 1852-1886, ed. Andrea Harrandt and Otto Schneider (Vienna, 1998); vol. 24.2 Briefe 2, 1887-1896 (Vienna, 2003)

Bruckner-Brevier = Alfred Orel, *Bruckner. Brevier. Briefe – Dokumente – Berichte* (Vienna, 1953)

Bruckner-Handbuch = *Anton Bruckner. Ein Handbuch*, ed. Uwe Harten (Salzburg, Vienna, 1996)

Bruckner-Jahrbuch 1980ff. = *Bruckner-Jahrbuch*, ed. Anton-Bruckner Institute Linz and Linzer Veranstaltungsgesellschaft mbH (Linz 1980, 1981, 1982/83, 1984/85/86, 1987/88, 1989/90, 1991/92/93, 1994/95/96, 1997-2000)

Bruckner in Wien = *Anton Bruckner in Wien. Eine kritische Studie zu seiner Persönlichkeit,* ed. Franz Grasberger (Anton Bruckner. Dokumente und Studien 2) (Graz, 1980)

Bruckner – skizziert = Renate Grasberger and Erich Wofgang Partsch, *Bruckner – skizziert. Ein Portrait ausgewählter Erinnerungen und Anekdoten* (Anton Bruckner. Dokumente und Studien 2) (Vienna, 1991)

Bruckner-Studien 1964 = *Bruckner-Studien. Leopold Nowak zum 60. Geburtstag*, ed. Franz Grasberger (Vienna, 1964)

Bruckner-Symposion 1977 = *Bruckner-Symposion im Rahmen des Internationalen Bruckner-Festes Linz 1977. Bericht*, ed. Franz Grasberger (Linz, 1978)

Bruckner-Symposion 1980ff. = *Bruckner-Symposion im Rahmen des Internationalen Bruckner Festes Linz 1980ff. Bericht*, ed. Anton Bruckner Institut Linz and Linzer Veranstaltungsgesellschaft mbH (Linz, 1980ff.)

1980	*Die Fassungen*
1981	*Die österreichische Symphonie nach Anton Bruckner*
1982	*Bruckner-Interpretation*
1983	*Johannes Brahms und Anton Bruckner*
1984	*Bruckner, Wagner und die Neudeutschen in Österreich*
1985	*Anton Bruckner und die Kirchenmusik*
1986	*Bruckner, Liszt, Mahler und die Moderne*
1987	*Bruckner und die Musik der Romantik*
1988	*Anton Bruckner als Schüler und Lehrer*
1989	*Orchestermusik im 19. Jahrhundert*
1990	*Musikstadt Linz – Musikland Österreich*
1991	*Bruckner-Rezeption*
1992	*Anton Bruckner. Persönlichkeit und Werk*
1993	*Entwicklungen – Parallelen – Kontraste. Zur Frage einer "österreichischen Symphonik"*
1994	*Bruckner-Freunde – Bruckner-Kenner*
1995	*Zum Schaffensprozess in den Künsten*
1996	*Fassungen – Bearbeitungen – Vollendungen*
1997	*Bruckner – Vorbilder und Traditionen*
1998	*Künstler-Bilder*
1999	*Kreativität und Gesellschaft*
2000	*Musik ist eine bildende Kunst*

Commenda = Hans Commenda, *Geschichten um Anton Bruckner* (Linz, n.d.)

Decsey = Ernst Decsey, *Bruckner: Versuch eines Lebens* (Stuttgart, Berlin, 1922)

Eckstein = Friedrich Eckstein, *Erinnerungen an Anton Bruckner* (Vienna, New York, 1923)

Floros, Brahms und Bruckner = Constantin Floros, *Brahms und Bruckner. Studien zur musikalischen Exegetik* (Wiesbaden, 1980)

G. – A. = August Göllerich and Max Auer, *Anton Bruckner. Ein Lebens- und Schaffensbild*, 4 vols. (Regensburg, 1922-1937; reprint 1974). Volumes cited as 1, 2/1, 2/2, 3/1, 3/2, 4/1, 4/2, 4/3, 4/4

Gräflinger, Briefe = Anton Bruckner, *Gesammelte Briefe*, ed. Franz Gräflinger (Regensburg, 1934)

Haas = Robert Haas, *Anton Bruckner* (Die Großen Meister der Musik) (Potsdam, 1934)

Hruby = Carl Hruby, *Meine Erinnerungen an Anton Bruckner* (Vienna, 1901)

Kitzler = Otto Kitzler, *Musikalische Erinnerungen mit Briefen von Wagner, Brahms, Bruckner und Rich. Pohl* (Brünn/Brno, 1904)

Klose = Friedrich Klose, *Meine Lehrjahre bei Bruckner. Erinnerungen und Betrachtungen* (Deutsche Musikbücherei, vol. 61) (Regensburg, 1927)

Kurth = Ernst Kurth, *Bruckner*, 2 vols. (Berlin, 1925)

Louis = Rudolf Louis, *Anton Bruckner*, 2nd ed. (Munich, 1918) (1st ed. 1905)

Nowak, Über Anton Bruckner = Leopold Nowak, *Über Anton Bruckner. Gesammelte Aufsätze 1932-1984* (Vienna, 1985)

Schalk = Franz Schalk, *Briefe und Betrachtungen. Mit einem Lebensabriß von Victor Junk*, ed. Lili Schalk (Vienna, Leipzig, 1935)

Schwanzara = *Anton Bruckner. Vorlesungen über Harmonielehre und Kontrapunkt an der Universität Wien*, ed. Ernst Schwanzara (Vienna, 1950)

Stradal = August Stradal, "Erinnerungen aus Bruckners letzter Zeit," in *Zeitschrift für Musik*, vol. 99 (1932), 853-860, 971-978, 1071-1075

Verborgene Persönlichkeit = Elisabeth Maier, *Verborgene Persönlichkeit. Anton Bruckner in seinen Aufzeichnungen* (Anton Bruckner. Dokumente und Studien, vol.11) 2 vols. (Vienna, 2001)

WAB = Renate Grasberger, *Werkverzeichnis Anton Bruckner* (WAB) (Tutzing, 1977)

Works by Anton Bruckner

The Anton Bruckner Complete Edition has the merit of presenting the works of the master cleansed of all foreign additions and edited, in a philologially impeccable form, in the sound-shape intended by the composer. But one has to distinguish between the "Old" and the "New" *Gesamtausgabe*. The Old edition, under the direction of Robert Haas, presented Bruckner's larger works between 1930 and 1944. The New, critical Edition, supervised for decades by Leopold Nowak and published in 1951 by the Musikwissenschaftliche Verlag in Vienna, differs from the Old not only by its degree of completeness but also in that the individual versions of the symphonies are edited separately. Today, Bruckner's music is generally played the world over in accordance with the New Complete Edition ("Blue Series").

The first register of the works of Anton Bruckner (WAB), edited by Renate Grasberger and published in Tutzing in 1977, orders and numbers Bruckner's compositions by genre: sacred vocal (choral) music (WAB 1-54), secular vocal music (WAB 55-95), orchestral works (WAB 96-109), chamber music (WAB 220-223), wind ensembles (WAB 114-116) and organ compositions (WAB 125-131). A second, more complete edition of the register is in preparation.

The following lists only those works of Bruckner's that have been discussed in detail here. Unless otherwise noted, references to the *Gesamtausgabe* are always to the New Edition.

Sacred Music

Missa solemnis in B flat minor (WAB 29)
Genesis: April/May to August 8, 1854 in St. Florian
Premiere: September 14, 1854 in St. Florian
Gesamtausgabe: vol XV, 1975; Revision Supplement 1977

Mass in D minor (WAB 26)
Genesis: May/June to September 29, 1864; "revised" summer 1876, "newly revised" 1881/82
Premiere: November 20, 1864, in the Old Cathedral Linz, Bruckner conducting
Gesamtausgabe: vol XVI, 1957

Mass in E minor (WAB 27)
Genesis: 1st version August to November 25, 1866, in Linz;
2nd version reworked 1876, 1882, 1885
Premiere: 1st version September 29, 1869, in Linz under Bruckner,
2nd version October 4, 1885 in the Old Cathedral in Linz under Adalbert Schreyer
Gesamtausgabe: 1st version vol. XVII/1, 1966; 2nd version vol. XVII/2, 1959

Mass in F minor (WAB 28)
Genesis: September 14, 1867, to September 9, 1868, in Linz;
Revisions 1876, 1877, 1881, 1890-93 in Vienna
Premiere: June 16, 1872, in the church of St. Augustine in Vienna under Bruckner
Gesamtausgabe: vol. XVIII, 1960

Te Deum (WAB 45)
Genesis: 1st version May 3 to17, 1881 (unfinished);
2nd version September 28 to March 7, 1884
Premiere: January 10, 1886, in Vienna under Hans Richter
Gesamtausgabe: vol. XIX, 1962

Psalm 150 WAB 38)
Genesis: 1892, completed June 29, 1892
Premiere: November 13, 1892, in Vienna under Wilhem Gericke
Gesamtausgabe: vol. XX/6, 1964

The Symphonies

Symphony in F minor (WAB 99) "study symphony"
Genesis: January 7 to May 26, 1863, in Linz
Premiere: 1st, 2nd & 4th movement on March 18, 1923, in Klosterneuburg under Franz Moißl, 3rd movement on October 12, 1924, in Klosterneuburg
Gesamtausgabe: vol. X, 1973; Revision Supplement 1981

Symphony in D minor, annulled (WAB 100)
Genesis: January 24 to September 12, 1869, in Vienna and Linz
Premiere: October 12, 1924, in Klosterneuburg under Franz Moißl

Gesamtausgabe: vol. XI, 1968; Revision Supplement 1981

First Symphony in C minor (WAB 101)
Genesis: 1st version January, 1865, to April 14, 1866, in Linz
2nd version March 12, 1890, to April 18, 1891, in Vienna
Premiere: Linz version May 9, 1868, in Linz under Bruckner;
Viennese version December 13, 1891, in Vienna under Hans Richter
Gesamtausgabe: Linz version vol. I/1, 1953; Viennese version vol. I/2, 1980

Second Symphony in C minor (WAB 102)
Genesis: 1871 to September 11, 1872; revised version 1877
Premiere: 1872 version October 26, 1873, in Vienna under Bruckner; printed version November 25, 1894, in Vienna under Hans Richter
Gesamtausgabe: 1872 version vol. II/1, 2005; 1877 version vol. II/2, 1965

Third Symphony in D minor (WAB 103)
Genesis: 1st version 1872/73; 2nd version 1876/78; 3rd version 1887/1889
Premiere: 2nd version December 16, 1877, in Vienna under Bruckner;
3rd version December 21, 1890, in Vienna under Hans Richter
Gesamtausgabe: 1st version vol. III/1, 1977; 2nd version vol. III/2, 1981; 3rd version vol. III/3, 1959; supplement 1876 Adagio vol. III/1, 1980

Fourth Symphony in E flat major (WAB 104)
Genesis: 1st version 1874; 2nd version 1878-80; 3rd version 1887-1889
Premiere: 1878/80 version February 20, 1881, in Vienna under Hans Richter;
1874 version September 20, 1975, in Linz under Kurt Wöss; 3rd version in Ferdinand Loewe's re-orchestration January 22, 1888, in Vienna under Hans Richter
Gesamtausgabe: 1874 version vol. IV/1, 1975; 1878/80 version vol. IV/2, 1953.

Fifth Symphony in B flat major (WAB 105)
Genesis: February 14, 1975, to May 16, 1876; revision 1877; completion January 4, 1878
Premiere: October 23, 1935, in Munich under Siegmund von Hausegger; Arrangement by Franz Schalk April 9, 1894, in Graz under Schalk
Gesamtausgabe: vol. V, 1951; Revision Supplement 1985

Sixth Symphony in A major (WAB 106)
Genesis: August/September 1879 to September 3, 1881
Premiere: middle movements on February 11, 1883, in Vienna under Wilhelm Jahn;
Abridged performance Feburary 26, 1899, in Vienna under Gustav Mahler
Gesamtausgabe: vol. VI, 1952; Revision Supplement 1986

Seventh Symphony in E major (WAB 107)
Genesis: 1881-1883
Premiere: December 30, 1884, in Leipzig under Arthur Nikisch
Gesamtausgabe: vol. VII, 1954

Eighth Symphony in C minor (WAB 108)
Genesis: 1887 version probably June/July, 1884, to August 10, 1887;
1890 version mid-October, 1887, to March 10, 1890
Premiere: 1890 version December 18, 1892, in Vienna under Hans Richter
Gesamtausgabe: 1887 version vol. VIII/1, 1972; 1890 version vol. VIII/2, 1955

Ninth Symphony in D minor (WAB 109)
Genesis: 1887-1894 (1st–3rd movement); Finale May 24, 1895 to time of death
Premiere: 1st–3rd movement in Ferdinand Loewe's arrangement February 11, 1903, in Vienna under Loewe; original version on April 2, 1932, in Munich under Siegmund von Hausegger
Old Gesamtausgabe: vol. IX; special printing: Drafts and Sketches of the Ninth Symphony, Vienna, 1934 (Alfred Orel)
New Gesamtausgabe: vol. IX, 1951; Reconstruction of the autograph score from extant sources, John A. Phillips, 1994; Facsimile edition, John A. Phillips, 1994; vol. IX (critical new edition of the first three movements), 2000. Supplement to vol. IX (2nd movement: Scherzo and Trio: Drafts), 1998

Selective Bibliography

Antonicek, Theophil: *Anton Bruckner und die Wiener Hofmusikkapelle* (Anton Bruckner. Dokumente und Studien 1), Graz 1979

Auer, Max: *Anton Bruckner. Sein Leben und Werk,* 2nd ed. Vienna 1934

Backes, Dieter Michael: *Die Instrumentation und ihre Entwicklung in Anton Bruckners Symphonien,* 2 vols., Mainz 1993

Bruckner-Journal (since 1997)

Chord and Discord (1932-1998)

Doebel, Wolfgang: *Bruckners Symphonien in Bearbeitungen. Die Konzepte der Bruckner-Schüler und ihre Rezeption bis zu Robert Haas,* Tutzing 2001

Doernberg, Erwin: *Anton Bruckner. Leben und Werk,* Munich - Vienna 1963

Fischer, Hans Conrad: *Anton Bruckner. Sein Leben,* Salzburg 1974

Göllerich, August/Auer, Max: *Anton Bruckner. Ein Lebens- und Schaffensbild,* 4 (9) vols., Regensburg 1922-1937. Reprint 1974

Gräflinger, Franz: *Anton Bruckner. Leben und Schaffen* (Umgearbeitete Bausteine), Berlin 1927

Grandjean, Wolfgang: *Metrik und Form. Zahlen in den Symphonien von Anton Bruckner,* Tutzing 2001

Grasberger, Franz: *Anton Bruckner zwischen Wagnis und Sicherheit. Ausstellung 4.-29.9.1977.* Musiksammlung der Österreichischen Nationalbibliothek, Linz 1977

—: Schubert und Bruckner, in: Otto Brusatti (Ed.): *Schubert-Kongreß 1978,* Graz 1979, 215-218

—: Selbstkritik, Uberzeugung und Beeinflussung. Zum Problem der Fassungen bei Bruckner, in: *Bruckner-Symposion* 1980, 33-38

Grasberger, Renate: *Bruckner-Bibliographie* (bis 1974) (Anton Bruckner. Dokumente und Studien 4), Graz 1985

—: *Bruckner-Ikonographie.* Teil 1: Um 1854-1924 (Anton Bruckner. Dokumente und Studien 7), Graz 1990

—: *Bruckner-Bibliographie II* (1975-1999) und Nachträge zu Band I (bis 1974) (Anton Bruckner. Dokumente und Studien Band 12), Vienna 2002

Haas, Robert: *Anton Bruckner* (Die großen Meister der Musik), Potsdam 1934

Hawkshaw, Paul: *The Manuscript Sources for Anton Bruckners Linz Works. A study of his working methods from 1856 to 1886,* New York, Columbia University, Phil. Diss. 1984

—: Bruckners Psalmen, in: *Bruckner-Vorträge. Bruckner-Tagung* 1999, Vienna 2000, 21-34

Horn, Erwin: Articles about Bruckner's Motets, in: *Musica sacra* 101 (1981), 102 (1982), 103 (1983), 104 (1984) und 116 (1996)

—: Die Orgelstücke Bruckners, in: *Bruckner-Vorträge. Bruckner-Tagung* 1999, Vienna 2000, 21-34

Horton, Julian: *Bruckner's Symphonies: Analysis, Reception and Cultural Politics,* Cambridge University Press 2004

Howie, Crawford, Hawkshaw, Paul und Timothy Jackson (Hrsg.): *Perspectives on Anton Bruckner,* Ashgate, Aldershot 2001

Jackson, Timothy L.: The Enharmonics of Faith: Enharmonic Symbolism in Bruckners »Christus factus est«, in: *Bruckner-Jahrbuch* 1987/88, 7-20

—: Schubert as »John the Baptist to Wagner-Jesus«: Largescale Enharmonicism in Bruckner and his models, in: *Bruckner-Jahrbuch* 1991/92/93, 61-107

Korstvedt, Benjamin M.: *Anton Bruckner: Symphony No. 8*, Cambridge 2000

Kurth, Ernst: *Bruckner,* 2 vols., Berlin 1925

Leibnitz, Thomas: *Die Brüder Schalk und Anton Bruckner,* Tutzing 1988

Mahling, Christoph-Hellmut (Ed.) *Anton Bruckner. Studien zu Werk und Wirkung. Walter Wiora zum 30. Dezember 1986,* Tutzing 1988

Maier, Elisabeth: *Anton Bruckner. Stationen eines Lebens,* Linz 1996

Metzger, Heinz-Klaus and Rainer Riehn (Ed.): *Anton Bruckner* (Musik-Konzepte 23/24), München 1982

—: *Bruckners Neunte im Fegefeuer der Rezeption* (Musik-Konzepte 120/121/122), Munich 2003

Nowak, Leopold: *Anton Bruckner. Musik und Leben,* Linz 1973

—: *Über Anton Bruckner. Gesammelte Aufsätze 193'2-1984,* Vienna 1985

Orel, Alfred: *Anton Bruckner. Das Werk - Der Künstler - Die Zeit,* Vienna and Leipzig 1925

Phillips, John A.: Die Arbeitsweise Bruckners in seinen letzten Jahren, in: *Bruckner-Symposion* 1992, 153-178

—: Neue Erkentnisse zum Finale der Neunten Symphonie Anton Bruckners, in: *Bruckner-Jahrbuch* 1989/90, 115-203

Riedel, Friedrich Wilhelm (Ed.): *Anton Bruckner. Tradition und Fortschritt in der Kirchenmusik des 19. Jahrhunderts,* Sinzig 2001

Riethmüller, Albrecht (Ed.): *Bruckner-Probleme. Internationales Kolloquium 7.-9. Oktober 1996 in Berlin,* Stuttgart 2000

Röder, Thomas: *Auf dem Weg zur Bruckner-Symphonie. Untersuchungen zu den ersten beiden Fassungen zu Anton Bruckners Dritter Symphonie,* Stuttgart 1987

Scheder, Franz: *Anton Bruckner-Chronologie, 2* vols., Tutzing 1996

Steinbeck, Wolfram: *Anton Bruckner. Neunte Symphonie d-Moll,* Munich 1993

Wagner, Manfred: *Bruckner,* Mainz 1983

—: *Der Wandel des Konzepts. Zu den verschiedenen Fassungen von Bruckners Dritter, Vierter und Achter Symphonie,* Vienna 1980

—: *Anton Bruckner. Sein Werk - Sein Leben,* Vienna 1995

Wessely, Othmar: Bruckners Mendelssohn-Kenntnis, in: *Bruckner-Studien* 1975, 81-112

Williamson, John (Ed.): *The Cambridge Companion to Bruckner*, Cambridge University Press 2004

Author's Papers

Zur Antithese Brahms-Bruckner, in: *Brahms-Studien* Band I, Hamburg 1974, 59-90

Brahms und Bruckner. Studien zur musikalischen Exegetik, Wiesbaden 1980 (with full bibliography)

Die Fassungen der Achten Symphonie von Anton Bruckner, in: *Bruckner-Symposion* 1980, 53-64

Zur Deutung der Symphonik Bruckners. Das Adagio der Neunten Symphonie, in: *Bruckner-Jahrbuch* 1981, 89-96

Thesen über Bruckner, in: *Anton Bruckner* (Musik-Konzepte, Cahier 23/24), ed. by Heinz-Klaus Metzger and Rainer Riehn, Munich 1982, 5-14. Englisch in: *The Bruckner Journal,* March 1997, 4-5; July 1997, 8-9, November 1997, 10-11

Parallelen zwischen Schubert und Bruckner, in: *Festschrift Othmar Wessely zum 60. Geburtstag,* hrsg. von M. Angerer und E. Diettrich, Tutzing 1982, 133-145

Bruckner und Mahler. Gemeinsamkeiten und Unterschiede, in: *Bruckner-Symposion* 1981, 21-29

Historische Phasen der Bruckner-Interpretation, in: *Bruckner-Symposion* 1982, 93-102

Gedanken über Brahms und Bruckner, in: *Österreichische Musikzeitschrift* 38 (1983), 398-402

Die Zitate in Bruckners Symphonik, in: *Bruckner-Jahrbuch* 1982/83, 7-18

Zur Gegensätzlichkeit der Symphonik Brahms' und Bruckners, in: *Bruckner-Symposion* 1983, 145-153

Bruckners Symphonik und die Musik Wagners, in: *Bruckner-Symposion* 1984, 177-184

Von Mahlers Affinität zu Bruckner, in: *Bruckner-Symposion* 1986, 109-118

Diskussionsbeitrag zum Thema Bruckner und Liszt, in: *Bruckner-Symposion* 1986, 181-188

Bruckner - der Progressive, in: *Anton Bruckner. Leben. Werk. Interpretationen. Rezeption. Bericht zum V. Internationalen Gewandhaus-*

Symposium anlässlich der Gewandhaus-Festtage Leipzig 1987, Leipzig 1989, 144-149

Anton Bruckner in neuer Sicht (Japanese), in: *The ongakugeijutsu,* April 1989, 77-81 and May 1989, 80-85

Anton Bruckner, in: *Heritage of Music,* Vol. III: the Nineteenth-Century Legacy, ed. by Michael Raeburn and Alan Kendall, Oxford-New York 1989, 215-225. German in: Michael Reaburrn und Alan Kendall: *Geschichte der Musik,* Vol. III, Munich 1993, 211-223

Zu Bruckners frühem symphonischen Schaffen, in: *Bruckner-Symposion* 1988, 173-190

Weltliches und Religiöses in Bruckners Symphonik, in: *Bruckner-Symposion* 1989, 179-188

Brahms, Bruckner und die Wiener Philharmoniker, in: *Symposion »Klang und Komponist«,* Tutzing 1992, 157-165

Zur Einheit von Persönlichkeit und Werk, in: *Bruckner-Symposion* 1992, 11-18

Bruchstücke einer großen Konfession. Zur Musik Anton Bruckners, in: *Das Orchester* 45, 10 (1997), 2-7

On Unity between Bruckners Personality and Production, in: Crawford Howie, Paul Hawkshaw and Timothy Jackson (ed.): *Perspectives on Anton Bruckner,* Ashgate, Aldershot 2001, 285-298

Zum spirituellen Gehalt des Finales der IX. Symphonie. Eine semantische Analyse, in: *Bruckners Neunte im Fegefeuer der Rezeption* (Musik-Konzepte 120/121/122), Munich 2003, 108-131

„Meine einzige Freude sind meine Symphonien". Anton Bruckner in neuer Sicht, in: Internationale Bruckner-Gesellschaft (Ed.): Studien & Berichte, Mitteilungsblatt 65, November 2005, 6-13

Numerous reviews in the Bruckner-Jahrbücher and in *Österreichische Musikzeitschrift.*

Photo Credits

Anton Bruckner at age 39: Direktion der Museen of Vienna.

Anton Bruckner at the age of 70: Bildarchiv, Österreichische Nationalbibliothek Wien.

The sister Maria Anna: with the kind permission of the Family Gustav Hueber, Vöcklabrück.

The birth house in Ansfelden near Linz: Wikipedia, photo by Greg Kraftschik, GNU license for free documentation.

The brother Ignaz: Bildarchiv, Österreichische Nationalbibliothek Wien.

The sister Rosalia: Hans Conrad Fischer, *Anton Bruckner. Sein Leben*, Residenz Verlag, Salzburg 1974, p.18.

The Bruckner Organ in the Old Cathedral in Linz: Wikipedia, photo by Greg Kraftschik, GNU license for free documentation.

Rudolf Weinwurm: Hans Conrad Fischer, *Anton Bruckner. Sein Leben*, Residenz Verlag, Salzburg 1974, p.96.

Felix Mottl: Bildarchiv, Österreichische Nationalbibliothek Wien.

Eduard Hanslick: Bildarchiv, Österreichische Nationalbibliothek Wien.

The brothers Josef and Franz Schalk: Anton Bruckner Institute, Linz.

Josefine Lang: Anton Bruckner Institute, Linz.

Minna Reischl: Hans Conrad Fischer, *Anton Bruckner. Sein Leben*, Residenz Verlag, Salzburg 1974, p.89.

Index of Names

Adorno, Theodor W...1, 10, 12, 63, 161, 170, 177
Almeroth, Carl 42, 148
Ambros, August Wilhelm.................172
Assmayr, Ignaz 14, 16
Auer, Max..48, 102, 109, 219, 221, 226, 183
Augustine........13, 35, 65, 114, 216, 223
Bach, Johann Sebastian ...66, 73, 85, 89, 118, 120, 167, 168
Bache, Walter 142
Bauer-Lechner, Natalie......................15
Bayer, Franz..............................95, 158
Beethoven, Ludwig van...1, 7, 8, 14, 16, 38, 45, 48, 51, 83, 100, 101, 103, 104, 106, 107, 108, 111, 122, 124, 126, 129, 133, 143, 149, 158, 159, 168, 171
Bératon, Ferry...................................148
Berg, Alban..................10, 63, 168, 170
Berlioz, Hector...28, 29, 67, 68, 92, 100, 101, 103, 104, 125, 133
Bistron, Julius 99
Bloch, Ernst 103, 134
Blume, Friedrich................................50
Böhler, Otto 39
Brahms, Johannes 1, 7, 8, 14, 16, 36, 37, 39, 41, 43, 44, 50, 52, 63, 67, 101, 106, 118, 130, 131, 143, 146, 153, 166, 168, 169, 170, 172, 220, 221, 229, 230
Bruckner, Ignaz 47
Bruckner, Maria Anna (Nani)17, 20, 24, 47, 52, 54, 216
Bruckner, Theresia......................24, 117
Buhz, Ida...23
Bülow, Hans von 119, 183
Camus, Albert....................................65
Celan, Paul...93
Celibidache, Sergiu.. VII, 161, 166, 167, 178, 179
Chopin, Frédéric 100, 167
Cohrs, Gunnar..................................152
Commenda, Hans 12, 220

Dahlhaus, Carl 99, 100
Decsey, Ernst 7, 220
Demar, Marie....................................26
Dessoff, Otto....................................110
Diernhofer, Josef.............................122
Dömpke, Gustav 37, 38, 172, 173
Dorn, Ignaz 16, 20, 29, 67, 145, 171, 215
Dürrnberger, Johann August.............. 27
Dvořák, Antonin 74
Eckstein, Friedrich....... 43, 51, 155, 220
Eggebrecht, Hans Heinrich............. 118
Einstein, Alfred............................... 102
Eschenbach, Christoph 179
Floderer, Wilhelm............................ 40
Fraenkel, Dr. Alexander 11, 45
Francis Joseph I. 14, 32, 144, 217
Freud, Sigmund 9, 65, 183
Fuchs, Ingrid.............................. 41, 177
Furtwängler, Wilhelm..................... 102
Gabrieli, Giovanni 103
Gadamer, Hans-Georg 8
Goethe, Johann Wolfgang von ... 24, 63, 66, 77
Göllerich, August 12, 13, 14, 32, 48, 51, 109, 110, 144, 155, 159, 171, 177, 221, 226
Grebe, Karl 10, 99
Haas, Robert 78, 79, 80, 82, 96, 99, 114, 127, 162, 164, 221, 222, 226, 227
Halm, August.................................. 102
Hanfstaengl, Franz.......................... 133
Hanslick, Eduard... 8, 21, 31, 32, 34, 35, 36, 37, 38, 39, 43, 44, 46, 58, 95, 100, 101, 129, 132, 134, 173
Harrandt, Andrea 2, 26, 219, 183
Hartmann, Karl Amadeus 63, 170
Hausegger, Siegmund von 162, 224, 225
Haydn, Joseph.. 45, 69, 78, 80, 141, 161
Hellmesberger, Joseph..................... 92
Helm, Theodor 38, 43, 112, 131, 143, 147
Herbeck, Johann 18, 27, 34, 41, 50
Heuberger, Richard..................... 39, 93

232

Hirschfeld, Robert 96
Hoffmann, E.T.A. 65
Hruby, Carl 25, 32, 48, 221
Hueber, Rosalie 24, 47
Hyrtl, Josef 49
Jochum, Eugen . VII, 161, 165, 166, 178
Kachelmeyr, Kathi..............................22
Kaiser, Josef Maria..........................120
Kalbeck, Max........................37, 38, 39
Kant, Immanuel 51
Kattinger, Anton........................27, 215
Kaulbach, Hermann..................133, 142
Kierkegaard, Søren 64
Kitzler, Otto.16, 19, 23, 28, 36, 67, 106, 107, 109, 119, 215, 221
Klose, Friedrich 37, 44, 45, 50, 146, 221
Kluger, Josef...........13, 22, 66, 117, 118
Kretzenbacher, Leopold......................12
Krzyzanowski, Rudolf........................37
Küng, Hans 179
Kurth, Ernst .93, 99, 102, 105, 124, 127, 128, 161, 165, 172, 174, 221, 227
Lachner, Franz..................................107
Lang, Josefine................22, 23, 26, 59
Lang, Oskar 64, 99, 165
Laurencin d'Armond, Ferdinand Peter
....173
Levetzow, Ulrike von 24
Levi, Hermann......21, 38, 39, 40, 41, 43, 66, 86, 102, 130, 131, 133, 217
Liszt, Franz 8, 28, 29, 36, 44, 65, 67, 68, 69, 70, 72, 74, 75, 76, 83, 84, 87, 100, 101, 103, 104, 116, 121, 133, 141, 142, 220, 229
Lobe, Johann Christian.....................106
Loerke, Oskar 46
Loidol, Oddo......................................82
Louis, Rudolf.....11, 19, 64, 67, 92, 101, 102, 221
Löwe, Ferdinand 43, 152, 162, 164
Ludwig II. of Bavaria ..14, 41, 119, 133, 161
Mahler, Gustav 1, 7, 8, 11, 12, 15, 19, 44, 63, 66, 74, 91, 100, 102, 127, 129, 145, 147, 149, 161, 162, 168, 170, 175, 177, 220, 225, 229, 183

Maier, Elisabeth 2, 8, 160, 221, 227, 183
Manet, Edouard................................. 47
Mann, Thomas 46, 65
Marcel, Gabriel 64, 65
Marschner, Franz 10, 27, 45, 111
Marx, Adolph Bernhard................... 106
Maslow, Abraham............................... 9
Maximilian, emperor of Mexico........ 47
Mayer, Friedrich 27
Mayer, Johannes-Leopold................. 11
Mayfeld, Betty von 14, 90, 108
Mayfeld, Moritz von. 23, 30, 31, 32, 33, 36, 108, 178
Mayr, Friedrich Theophil................... 67
Mazzuca, Giuseppe......................... 152
Meißner, Anton................................. 51
Mottl, Felix ... 15, 40, 41, 42, 43, 46, 57, 127
Mozart, Wolfgang Amadeus... 8, 45, 69, 89, 91, 118, 122, 141, 158, 161, 168
Nietzsche, Friedrich.................... 11, 12
Nikisch, Arthur ... 15, 19, 40, 42, 51, 92, 130, 133, 217, 225
Nissen, Gerhard 20
Nowak, Leopold ... 50, 67, 82, 141, 162, 219, 221, 222, 228
Oberleithner, Max von....................... 83
Oblat, Ludwig................................. 150
Ochs, Siegfried 132
Orel, Alfred............. 152, 219, 225, 228
Orff, Carl... 89
Palestrina, Giovanni Pierluigi da 46, 84, 103, 117, 141
Pascal, Blaise 64
Paumgartner, Hans................... 95, 171
Perfall, Karl Baron von.................... 133
Pfitzner, Hans 46
Phillips, John A........ 152, 153, 225, 228
Polnauer, Josef................................ 170
Porges, Heinrich 133
Puchstein, Hans................................. 96
Raabe, Peter 112
Rademacher, Carl 147
Rättig, Theodor 43, 217
Reisch, Dr. Theodor.................. 30, 109
Reischl, Minna 59

Reiter, Henriette..................................23
Richter, Ernst Friedrich 106
Richter, Hans.15, 36, 37, 38, 39, 40, 41, 90, 217, 218, 223, 224, 225
Ringel, Erwin....................9, 10, 21, 183
Rolland, Romain................................65
Rousseau, Jean-Jacques 65
Rudigier, Franz Joseph............15, 17, 30
Sailer, Franz.....................................27
Samale, Nicola................................152
Schalk, Franz.......10, 11, 16, 26, 50, 58, 127, 132, 162, 163, 164, 166, 167, 218, 221, 224
Schalk, Joseph ...21, 41, 43, 50, 58, 102, 130, 161
Scheu, Josef.......................................129
Schiedermayr, Johann Baptist............25
Schönaich, Gustav 39, 127
Schönberg, Arnold.....63, 157, 168, 169, 170, 172, 173, 174, 175
Schubert, Franz....10, 16, 17, 48, 72, 73, 75, 90, 101, 103, 104, 124, 139, 141, 143, 168, 226, 227, 229
Schumann, Clara......................108, 118
Schumann, Karl 165
Schumann, Robert 67, 100, 108, 134, 143, 166
Schwanzara, Ernst 46, 221
Schwarzara, Ernst 156
Schwebsch, Erich 64, 99
Sechter, Simon...16, 27, 28, 32, 67, 104, 106, 158, 171, 215, 216
Seiberl, Josef......................................16
Seidel, Wilhelm 99
Singer, Kurt 118
Sittard, Joseph..................................91
Specht, Richard...............................145
Speidel, Ludwig...........39, 90, 171, 172
Spohr, Ludwig..................................145
Stekel, Wilhelm 9
Stockhausen, Karlheinz.....................63
Stradal, August 25, 48, 68, 122, 149, 150, 166, 221

Strauß, David Friedrich 11
Strauss, Richard......... 63, 100, 168, 169
Stremayr, Karl Edler von............. 29, 31
Swarowsky, Hans 1, 161
Tappert, Wilhelm........................ 31, 35
Thaner, Emma.................................... 22
Thiard-Laforest, Josef....................... 23
Tieck, Ludwig................................... 65
Traumihler, Ignaz 84
Uhde, Fritz von................................. 42
Vergeiner, Anton 34, 43
Wackenroder, Wilhelm Heinrich....... 65
Wagner, Cosima 121
Wagner, Eva 121
Wagner, Manfred................... 7, 81, 183
Wagner, Richard.... VII, 8, 9, 14, 15, 19, 28, 36, 38, 40, 41, 44, 46, 63, 64, 66, 67, 74, 101, 103, 104, 105, 112, 115, 118, 119, 120, 121, 122, 124, 125, 129, 130, 131, 132, 133, 134, 135, 136, 144, 147, 150, 161, 168, 169, 170, 172, 179, 216, 217, 220, 229
Waldeck, Karl 23, 33, 122
Walter, Bruno 177
Wand, Günter... VII, 161, 162, 163, 164, 165, 166, 167, 178, 179
Weber, Carl Maria von 108, 124
Webern, Anton von. 168, 170, 171, 172, 173
Weingartner, Felix von.... 139, 144, 146
Weinwurm, Alois.............................. 32
Weinwurm, Rudolf... 17, 18, 19, 22, 23, 25, 26, 28, 32, 33, 34, 36, 47, 57, 90, 159, 177
Weiß, Johann Baptist........... 27, 47, 215
Wesendonck, Mathilde 63
Wesendonck, Otto............................. 63
Witt, Franz Xaver 84
Wolzogen, Hans von........ 110, 119, 130
Zellner, Leopold Alexander............... 34
Zenetti, Leopold von......................... 27
Zimmermann, Bernd Alois............. 166
Zinne, Wilhelm 22, 23, 39, 91, 149, 183